Reason To Be

Gail Elloian

Published by Benoy Publishing
735 H Bragg Drive
Wilmington, North Carolina 28412

ISBN#0-9720809-9-6
LCCN#2002109249

Printed in the United States

*I am the now evolved from yesterday who
will form tomorrow. I exist only in this moment
—for in the blink of an eye, I will become more.*

. . . a woman of the knowing

The knowing philosophy is a gift
of the spirit and is dedicated to
Stephen Yedinak
Who would understand.

and to my husband, Peter Elloian, and my son,
Carlton Yedinak– without their input the knowing would
have remained conversation over the dinner table.

Acknowledgments

A warm thanks to Buzzy Benoy of
Benoy Publishing for giving me a voice.

Ralph Benoy, artist/editor for
understanding the desire for perfection.

To the Charlaps, Allan and Barbara,
who have always believed.

Jim O'Herron for his time, patience, and expertise.

My son, Charly Yedinak, a writer of song who gets his
creativity from his mother!!

. . . and a very special thank you to Sue and Scott Fowler
whose generosity can never be fully repaid.

Cover Design by Carlton Yedinak
Author's Photograph by Carlton Yedinak

Prologue

In the beginning . . .
Tibet, 1088

High in the Tibetan mountains a sect of warrior priests faithful to the old religion of Bon Shamanism feared both for their temple's survival, and for the safety of an order of female mystics who had been entrusted to their care.

Word had reached the temple that an influx of the followers of the Indian monk, Atisa, and his Kadampa sect had settled in the valley. Most troubling was that one of the Kadampa monks had the ear of the ruling Mongol prince. The monk whispered that these women possessed mystical powers beyond comprehension. Powers which could alter nature, command the wind and water, and create fire from out of the air. These powers, the monk insisted, could destroy the prince, bring an end to his rule, even to his very life.

When Nahid, the eldest of the female seers was appraised of the threat, she retreated high into the mountains to meditate, to divine the most feasible of possible futures.

The dark walls of the cave glowed red in the flames of the fire. Nahid sat motionlessly, eyes closed, sinking deeper and deeper into the darkness of all time. Images formed and dissipated, splintering off into as many pathways as there was lives that would be affected by her decision. Flashes of sound brought the distinctive clash of sword against sword, the thunder of horses hooves against stone–a battle enjoined, blood, flowing like a scarlet river.

With a shudder, Nahid opened her eyes. She knew that to stay would bring the Mongol's wrath down on the temple and in their wake death and destruction.

Sadly, Nahid knew that in time, no matter what course of action was taken in the here and now, a confrontation with those who would destroy the women would come. The inevitable battle, though centuries away, would force those survivors among the women to disband, to wander alone without the benefit of community, with no way to understand the force that lived within. With no means of assimilating the power's continuing evolution.

Nahid saw madness and death and the cessation of all she understood the power to be. She wrapped her fur closer around her body seeking warmth from the cold fear that held her in its grip. And out of the wind of future time came a whisper of hope. The mysteries would survive, embodied in three who would be relentless in their efforts to bring the force out of darkness and into the light of a spiritual renaissance.

Even so, it was with a heavy heart that Nahid made her way down the steep mountain trail. For many years the temple had been her home, a haven. Now all that was familiar and safe would be gone. She must speak with the priests and the women of her order. Tell them of her decision.

The temple bells called the female mystics and the warrior priests together in the great hall. Nahid stood in front of the altar and looked down at the faces of those she loved and for whom she was responsible. She spoke forcibly of her belief that once the women were gone, the temple would be left in peace.

Nahid's words of sacrifice fell on deaf ears. Her counterpoint among the priests smiled at her naivete. Even though the temple could not be successfully defended against the Mongol attack, its spiritual essence dwelled within each of their souls. No matter the cost, the women would be guided from this place of danger to a new sanctuary. And so it was, in the darkness of a starless night that their journey began.

Days later, from their vantage point on a cliff above the temple grounds, the Kadampa monks watched the Mongol horde ride into the temple grounds. They were greeted not as expected by the women mystics and the priests, but by the mocking, discordant clang of wind chimes, and the bleat of grazing sheep.

Before the Kadampa monks could intervene and claim the deserted temple as their own, the warlord, in a frenzy of frustration and rage, ordered the temple burned to the ground and its stone altar broken into a thousand pieces.

Miles away, the warrior priests were guiding the women along the treacherous cliffs, climbing higher and higher up into the mountains. It was hoped that before the winter storms blocked the mountain pass, they would have made it through to the western slopes. But freezing rain followed by an early blizzard forced them to take refuge in the caves that ran deep into the mountains. Winter had come early and would stay late.

Drifting snow filled the pass and the mountain stream froze over. Water was obtained by chipping through the ice. Food was sparse, and the occasional rabbit was considered a feast. As winter held its grip, it became necessary for the priests to forage further and further afield for bare subsistence. Surprisingly, spirits remained high and there was no loss of life.

With the coming of spring, the warrior priests and the women trekked west through the mountain pass to find a location which could be easily protected. Where it would be possible to lay the foundation for all that was yet to be.

St. Lawrence River Valley, 1922

On the cliff above the cove, a solitary woman stood motionless, staring out across the river. As she watched, the pale rising sun streaked the silvery waters with shades of rose. Towering pines cast long shadows on the mirror smooth surface of the bay. Out in the channel, sheets of ice still floated, the river not yet free of winter's tenacious grip. She shivered, and wrapped the forest green cloak tighter over her silk nightgown. Her eyes blurred with tears. If only she had listened to Kathleen. Her knowing had warned that he was a villain, a contemptuous man who would bring pain and sorrow. But she had not heeded the warning, and now she was lost, adrift in a dark, emotionless void.

Below her, the water was flat and calm, but she knew that beneath its reflective surface it swirled and twisted, ignoring the stillness of the air above. Its waters would be frigid, a mind numbing cold. A cold to freeze out the memory of his loathsome touch, to cleanse away the fear that had destroyed her very essence.

She closed her eyes and listened but she could no longer hear the world song. Her bare feet moved across the pink granite to the very edge of the cliff. She raised her arms and dove. The cloak spread away from her body like the wings of a bird. Then she was gone, pulled deep under the icy waters. Her tortured spirit and the river's were as one.

Present

St. Lawrence River Valley

Clara Dunn Eaton sat on the edge of the dock. Her bare sun tanned legs dangling above the river. The breeze off the water did little to counter the smothering August heat. She rubbed the glass of iced tea across her forehead and read from the yellowed pages of the handwritten journal. Ethan Hawk's words took on a life of their own. The people he wrote of, her ancestors, were easily visualized.

Her concentration was interrupted by a group of teenagers riding by on wave runners. She glanced up and shielding her eyes against the sun's glare, returned their salute.

Off in the west, she saw that the sky was slowly turning a darker blue, and the wind coming off the river was beginning to pick up. The scent of gathering moisture was in the air and she knew the storm front would quickly move in. She closed the journal and hurried toward the house.

Once inside, Clara curled up in her bedroom window seat and watched the storm come down the river. There was a strange stillness, and the sky became a canvas of grey highlighted by green and yellow with ominous dark clouds. As she watched, the ghostly veil of a line squall crept up the river bringing with it ear shattering claps of thunder. Jagged lightening bolts slashed across the sky. Wind and sheeting rain curtained the river transforming its island and the boats out in the channel into nebulous forms from out of a nightmare.

The air coalesced around her and she stared out into the pounding rain. Little by little Clara felt the world slip away.

Drifting shapes formed, then dissipated. Broad ribbons of

luminous color sliced through the darkness, gradually fading into a pale, shadowy tinge. Out of the formless landscape, the image of a man, tall, and broad shouldered became visible. His face was familiar as out of a dream. Almost imperceptibly, his features changed, slowly becoming a different face, and yet again, and again.

Switzerland

Simon Hawk came out onto the wood deck holding a mug of steaming coffee. His day had begun two hours before with a session of Tai Chi, followed by his morning run. On alternate days his routine would vary with Akikdo, weight training, and laps in the basement pool. He had long ago learned to accept his body as if it were in and of itself a weapon. Through discipline he had come to understand and respect its weaknesses as well as its strengths.

Sipping his coffee, he listened to the commonplace sounds of the neighborhood. From the valley came the distinct chime of cow bells, and off in the distance the sputtering misfires of a laboring tractor. On the path below, the six Hepburn children chattered and giggled their way to the village school. The family's long haired collie playfully circled the group, barking and nipping at their heels. When the mug was drained, he went through the sliding glass door into a large living room where a stained glass skylight cast blue, red, and green patterns across the hardwood floor.

His log chalet was well off the beaten track–not easily accessible. He had selected it for precisely those reasons. No drop in visitors, no surprises. Privacy was important to him. One could even say it was essential.

He rinsed the coffee mug and set it on the drain board. In the bathroom, he showered and dressed in soft, well-worn jeans, cotton turtle neck, and a pair of old moccasins. Time for his work day to begin.

His study was small with a single leaded glass window. Stacks of books haphazardly climbed the walls. A leather chair faced a make shift desk he had created out of a slab of marble resting across two saw horses. On its surface was a lap top computer and laser printer. Off to one side was a stack of yellow legal pads, and a chipped mug filled with pens and sharpened pencils.

Simon knew he would spend the better part of the day in this room where he was presently at work on his fourth novel. His books, two of which had been made into successful films, had afforded him financial independence. The critics had been kind but unable to categorize his style. Ultimately, they opted to describe him as a philosophical Tom Clancy.

Simon sat down in the leather chair and leaned back to read the previous day's pages. The red felt tipped pen scrawled lines between lines, mercilessly slashing out whole paragraphs and repositioning others. By the time his editing was completed, the pages resembled a Chinese puzzle. He turned on the computer and pulled up the section he had been working on and began to enter the rewrite. So deep was his concentration that he failed to hear the first ring of the front door bell. The second ring came strident and unceasing.

Angrily, Simon stalked to the heavy double front door and flung one side open. Illuminated in the bright sunlight was his grandfather.

Adam Hawk looked into his grandson's face and saw a younger version of himself. They shared the same chiseled features and strong jaw line. But where Adam's black hair was streaked with grey, Simon's was the color of a raven's wing. Both had dark, slanted yellow/green eyes which often caused people to wonder of their origins. "Simon."

"Grandfather?"

"Simon, might I come in?"

"Of course, please." Simon stood aside to allow his grandfather to precede him into the great room.

Adam turned to face his grandson. "Simon, it's time you came home."

From the tone of Adam's voice, Simon could tell the request was not being lightly made. Adam Hawk was the singular member of Simon's family who understood his self-imposed exile. It was Adam who understood the many facets of Simon's character knew Simon could be taciturn and unrelenting, but was never judgmental.

During Simon's formative years, his father, David Hawk had rarely been home. The family's transnational investment bank had superseded everything and everyone. His mother was a cherished memory, one more of imagination than substance. She had died of a massive cerebral hemorrhage when Simon was only six, his sister, Judith barely out of diapers.

When Simon looked back on his childhood, he realized his father had not been an intentionally unkind man. He never returned from a trip without a gift for his children. It was just that a far greater gift would have been his presence.

Consequently, it was his grandfather, Adam who taught him to sail and play golf, who attended graduations, and never missed a birthday. Adam who had taught him to challenge both his body and his mind. Between grandfather and grandson was a bond which was as much of the spirit as of blood.

By the time Simon was in his teens, he had ceased to wonder or care what it would have been like to have a father whose dependable presence could be taken for granted. But the true split between father and son came with Simon's refusal to enter the family bank.

Instead, Simon had chosen to work for the government in a covert capacity. A choice which earned him his father's anger and contempt. It had also cost Simon the woman who was to have been his wife. The woman who instead had married his father.

Since that time, Simon had not returned to his family's New Orleans house. His sister, Judith was now the heir apparent. The only family he communicated with was Adam . . . and whatever his grandfather asked of him he would do.

4

New York City, New York

The sky over Manhattan was a smug pot of muted blue dirtied by a haze of pollution. From the air, the city was an endless grey landscape dotted by the green of its parks, small oasis' in the midst of the concrete prison. It had been some time since Simon had found it necessary to endure the claustrophobic life of the city dweller.

He thought of the years he had lived as an exile, first in Paris, then Venice to finally settle in Switzerland. Living in the mountains close to nature prompted internal peace, a freeing of his true self. Only the urgency of his grandfather's summons had brought him back to the world he had left behind. He felt as though he had been gone a lifetime.

Simon passed through Customs and Immigration without incident and picked up his rental car. Surprisingly, the drive into the city was familiar. Its inner geography was still clear in his mind, and he easily found the Central Park address.

Pale sunlight filtered in through the tall, narrow, sheer curtained window where Sylvia Dunn Mitchell waited behind the large partner's desk. It was purposely positioned where the light would be the most flattering. She stared at her hands. Their knuckles were enlarged by arthritis, and under the seemingly translucent skin, she could see blue veins, and the brown spots of age that no cosmetic could quite fade away. She sighed as if unable to believe time's betrayal.

Time had once been a friend, an undefined plateau shimmering with invitation. No longer. Now eternity's darkness encroached, signaling her end–perhaps the end of all that had been or might yet be accomplished.

Still, as a family the Dunns and Mitchells were fortunate. Dunn House was able to remain an independent entity and at the same time maintain its consistently high publishing standards. And her son, Carson Mitchell had been successful in averting a hostile takeover of his media empire. But now with the discovery of Ethan Hawk's journal, the Hawk and Dunn families would be forced to confront the past with its history of madness and murder. The knowing was omnipresent but she could no longer trust her abilities. She felt useless, old and useless.

The study door opened, and Simon Hawk preceded the butler into the large, uncluttered room with its high ceilings, broad moldings, and hardwood floors accented by a single Aubusson carpet. Simon found it luxurious without being pretentious. As he walked toward Sylvia, she smiled. The smile was oddly curious, even mocking. She welcomed him without rising from the throne like chair. A tilt of her head indicated he should be seated in the chair in front of the desk.

The butler offered Simon a cut glass tumbler of Glenfiddich on the rocks. He took a sip and wondered without surprise how much more she knew of him.

"Simon, thank you for agreeing to meet with me here rather than at Dunn House. These days I rarely leave my home."

She did not elaborate, nor did he ask. Her presence held Simon enthralled. A living legend who even now in her late seventies possessed an ageless beauty. Any imperfections in her porcelain white skin were obscured by the depth of beauty in her oblique green eyes. A woman who was still capable of effortlessly spinning a spell.

Sylvia rested her head against the back of her chair. "Your grandfather, Adam, my grandson, Stephen, and my son, Carson all promise me you are to be trusted, that your credentials are impeccable," she told him, not adding that she generally relied solely on her own judgment. "I understand the acquiring of your investigative skills is classified information, but then I have no real need to know. I've decided to ask for your help."

Simon smiled with inward amusement. Six years ago when Dunn House had agreed to publish his first book, he had hoped to meet its renowned head, Sylvia Dunn Mitchell. His timing had been off for by then she no longer came into the office, choosing instead to work out of her Central Park mansion.

It had fallen to Stephen Mitchell, Sylvia's grandson, to guide Simon through the publishing maze. Now he was finally meeting this legendary woman, but was very much afraid the services she desired were from a past he had hoped was just that–past.

After leaving government service, Simon had severed his connection to the covert community. With the success of his books, he had begun to wonder if he was running away from his former life or toward another. One thing was certain. He controlled his own destiny.

Sylvia's voice claimed his attention. "Simon, do we have an agreement?"

"First I must know the nature of this project. Privileged information was once an integral part of my life–my stock in trade if you will. Consider your remarks to me as those spoken in the confessional. As for assisting you, I accepted this appointment out of respect for both you and my grandfather. But I haven't as yet decided if I want to be involved."

The green eyes studied him. "Most people are eager to work for me. I believe you have a three-book contract with Dunn House. Why is this different?"

"No offense intended. It's just that I need to understand the nature of the service required of me."

"Then let's examine your involvement . . . possible involvement from that perspective." Sylvia watched him closely. Easily discernable was the relaxed power in the body of an athlete. She suspected his true self would be much more difficult to perceive. "Most of what I know of you comes from your writing and clearly defined professional credentials. Yet, on a personal level, I know next to nothing."

"I value my privacy. Those close to me know this. If they wish to remain so, they do not discuss my personal life."

"Secrecy always makes one curious," Sylvia said softly, not revealing that she knew he had been agented out with consular cover and within a few years had become disillusioned by the double standard under which he was forced to operate. Rumors in the intelligence community placed him as a renegade whose friends then and now were cut from the same cloth. Simon Hawk was a fascinating man, despite or perhaps because of the menace in him. "But I did persevere," she continued. "Yet again on a personal level, I reached a brick wall. I did manage to ferret out some events of a quasi-professional nature."

A sardonic smile curled Simon's lips, but his eyes held honor and something else both bitter and wary. ""Need I ask what these were?"

The sound of his voice startled her. "Probably not, but I will mention that a close friend tells me he owes you a debt of honor. I understand you rescued his daughter from a very messy situation and managed to do so without publicity."

Simon silently sipped his scotch.

"Remarkable, a modest hero."

"What would you have me do? Shuffle my feet, twist my hat in my hand and say 'ah, shucks, Mam, warn't nothin'?"

Her laughter bubbled. "Check, if not mate."

"I'm sure the queen still has room to maneuver," he parried. "Now what is it that requires my expertise?"

Sylvia's eyes clouded and for a brief moment she looked all of her seventy-eight years. "Tell me, Simon, what do you know of the Hawk family genealogy and its connection with the Dunns?"

"For some time now I've not been involved with family. It would seem it falls to you to make me understand why I should give a damn."

Sylvia leaned forward and pushed a button on the intercom. "Hudson, please bring us," she glanced at Simon. "Coffee, tea, wine, another drink?"

"Coffee is fine."

"Hudson, coffee will do. And please ready a guest room for Mr. Hawk."

"Mrs. Mitchell . . . "

"Sylvia, please."

"Sylvia, please don't put yourself out. I've booked a suite at the Plaza."

"Forgive me. I didn't mean to be precipitous. It's just that there's so much ground to cover, I thought it would be simpler if you stayed here."

Simon heard a hint of fear and unexpressed need in her voice. He inclined his head. "Then I accept your gracious hospitality."

Hudson came into the room carrying a silver serving tray. On it was a large carafe of coffee, fresh fruit, and a plate of a brie with a basket of crackers.

"Thank you, Hudson. As always, you anticipate my needs."

When the door closed behind Hudson, Sylvia picked up the thread of their conversation. "I suppose it would be best to simply begin at the beginning with the Dunns. It is their history which is the root source of my concerns."

"How so?" Simon asked.

Sylvia forced a smile. "Please, Simon, allow me to tell the story in my own way. Without the background . . . even with the background you may find what I have to say difficult to believe."

Simon inclined his head. "I promise to listen."

"The inference being to listen is all you're promising. Point taken." Sylvia said. "I'll begin with the Dunns. They were of the English aristocracy with estates in both England and Ireland. Their Irish holdings were in . . . I'm afraid I can't recall exactly where, but somewhere near the Irish sea. My grandfather used to say he came from English nobility but had an Irish soul. At any rate, Andrew Dunn fell in love with and married Moria Killarney. The Killarneys were tenet farmers. According to family stories, they were feared by some, revered by others."

"English aristocracy marries the daughter of an Irish tenet farmer, feared or revered not withstanding," Simon wryly said. "I can well imagine how, ah, happy, Andrew's parents were."

"I would guess less than elated, but then the Killarneys were no more pleased," Sylvia said with a smile. "Keep in mind, Ireland was dying . . . the great famine of the eighteen-forties. Survival was first and foremost. Irish hatred of English land owners boiled over. The Fenians burned English estates and the violence spread."

"And Andrew and Moria were caught in the cross fire," Simon muttered.

"Precisely, there was certainly no future for them in Ireland and in England, Moria would have had to endure the contempt of Andrew's family. So, just as so many others were doing, they choose America–Boston, where Moria had family."

"Andrew worked for Killarney Printers and waited for the right opportunity to present itself. When the firm was contracted to print leaflets' advertising the sale of large parcels of land in northern New York State along the St. Lawrence River, his interest was peaked."

Simon settled back in his chair. "The St. Lawrence–that's as far north as it gets. I can't imagine the land was in great demand."

"Probably not. At that time Northern New York was still a wilderness–horrendous winters. At any rate, Andrew learned logging was, in today's terminology, its growth industry. He was soon on his way to the St. Lawrence. Moria stayed behind in Boston until he could find them a home.

"Family accounts tell that Andrew traveled down river with the timber rafts, then rowed as oarsman in a bateau back upriver. He must have worked like a man possessed because it wasn't long before Moria joined him. They lived frugally, saving every cent they could to purchase land. It was then that the Dunns and Hawks were first enjoined."

Simon was surprised to find he was becoming caught up in the telling. "How did they meet?"

"An Iroquois, Manson Hawk saved Andrew's life. It was the beginning of a life long friendship that has spanned generations."

"Hawk. I'll be dammed, native Americans."

It was obvious that Simon was surprised to learn of the Hawk genealogy. Sylvia wondered why he had never been told of his roots.

"Fascinating, please go on."

"Hawk and Andrew both had the same goal–land. By pooling their funds, they were able to purchase a large tract on the American side of the river. They made money, first from the lumber through paper mills, then by reselling land at tremendous profit."

Simon was both intrigued and mystified by his family antecedents. "What time frame are we in?"

"Late eighteen hundreds."

The study door suddenly opened. "It's all right Hudson, no need to announce me. Mother knows who I am," Lydia Eaton said with a laugh.

Simon glanced over his shoulder and saw a woman of indeterminate age. She might have been thirty or sixty with the carriage and grace of a dancer. Same oblique green eyes as her mother, and beautiful.

As she reached the desk, Simon rose and waited for an introduction.

"Simon, as you've undoubtedly concluded," Sylvia said with affection. "This rather pushy individual is my daughter, Lydia Eaton. Lydia, Simon Hawk."

Lydia gestured for Simon to sit down. She pulled a matching chair next to his and mischievously smiled. "Ah, we have yet another Hawk. I've met your father, and sister, and grandfather. How is it I've missed knowing you?"

Simon winked at Sylvia and said, "I'm afraid I'm this generation's black sheep. There may have been others, but I wouldn't know. Your mother is presently enlightening me."

"Then you're learning of the Dunn's checkered past as well. They're hopelessly entwined." Lydia poured herself a cup of coffee. "So Mother, where did you leave off?"

"Before we were so rudely interrupted, I was giving Simon a quick summation of the generations preceding Clara Hawk's suicide," Sylvia dryly said.

"I humbly apologize and promise not to overstay my welcome. I really only have a few minutes. I'm meeting John at the Four

11

Seasons for dinner, then we've a gallery opening. And . . ." She pulled a bound manuscript from a leather envelope. "Ethan Hawk's journal, transcribed as requested."

"Did you FedEx Adam a copy," Sylvia asked?

"Per your instructions." Lydia glanced at her watch and frowned. "Oops, got to run." She handed the transcript to Simon. "Your ancestor was quite a good writer, must run in the family." She gave her mother a kiss on the cheek and with concern in her voice said, "Now don't stay up too late, and please give me a call tomorrow. I'd like to hear how things went. Simon, I trust we'll meet again." Then she disappeared as abruptly as she had appeared.

Simon laid the manuscript pages on the desk. "Ethan Hawk's journal?"

"Yes, death and retribution in the nineteen-twenties. Which strangely enough sheds light on a murder some forty years later." Sylvia's voice was a whisper of unassueged pain and grief. "The death of my daughter, Elizabeth . . . my beautiful Libby dead in a sea of blood, slaughtered by some despicable animal."

"Are you sure you want to go on? This can wait," Simon compassionately offered. "Why not rest for a while and pick it up later?"

"No, this has waited far to long as it is. Now I'm afraid I must digress. There are a few names I don't recall, but they're important only in the sense of family genealogy."

"Any more names and I'll be hopelessly confused. It's a bit like who's on first."

"No matter, the Dunns and Hawks to this point are supporting roles. The main characters are about to come on stage."

"Interesting analogy."

"Indeed . . . all the worlds a stage, etcetera, etcetera. Frankly, it's easier to view this as a drama rather than a personal tragedy." Sylvia wanted to explain that her trepidation came from out of what her family called the knowing. A precognitive gift or in some cases a curse that all the Dunn women beginning with Moria Killarney seemed to possess, but it was too soon. Simon must first agree to her request for his assistance. He must first be convinced that past reality was becoming the present, and would surely taint the future.

"I understand," Simon said. "Please go on. I can sort out the details later."

With Simon's unconscious commitment, Sylvia felt a lifting of the oppressive fear she had lived with since the reading of Ethan Hawk's journal. "Clara Hawk and Thomas Dunn marry. The year is nineteen-sixteen, and herein lies the foundation for all that follows. Perhaps at this point you should read Ethan Hawk's journal."

Simon stretched his legs out across the footstool. The maple cannon ball bed looked inviting, but he knew he wouldn't sleep. He reached for the brandy Hudson had placed on the marble topped stand and pensively watched the flickering flames in the tiled fireplace.

Dinner with Sylvia had been most pleasant. As if by mutual consent, they spoke in generalities–art, music, the theater, baseball, the old Yankees: Yogi Bera, Joe Dimaggio, Mickey Mantle. Sylvia was a fan, and a knowledgeable one.

Now it was time to pay the piper. He picked up the transcript and began to read, quickly becoming immersed in the words of his great-grandfather, Ethan Hawk. His handwriting was bold and distinctive.

As I sit here at my desk, I can watch the river–ageless, beautiful. Standing motionless out on the point is a great blue heron, and I can hear the smaller birds singing from out of the marsh.

For all of my years I've been privileged to live here in the North country along the majestic, mysterious, St. Lawrence. My home is Hawk House. A house conceived from out of my imagination, and constructed of oak beams, stone, and glass–a sanctuary for the generations of Hawks still to come.

Now time has become a shadow play with what remains

of my life being played out over a timeless ground. I believe death to be a continuation, another form of life. But before I die, I must set history straight and record the truth, the truth of Clara's death.

These events occurred long ago, but they are as alive in my mind as if they were taking place as I write. Clara was blood of my blood, my sister, my friend—a part of my very soul. You should have seen her, beautiful with fine features, clear, olive complexion, and black hair as black as a cloudless night sky.

Yet Clara was so much more than beautiful. She was softly spoken with a spiritual calm I envied. Although she had been educated in France, she had great pride in her heritage. A shaman once told me she sang the world song, and though she walked with man, she was one with the spirit. A warning? Perhaps, but no matter, she was gone too soon.

When Clara married by best friend, Thomas Dunn, I couldn't have been more pleased. Their's was a true marriage, a kind of reunion of the self with the self. I remember hoping to someday find someone with whom I could share that same intimacy.

Although I believe, I've accomplished life's most difficult task—an understanding of my true self, Clara's death and those events stemming from it remain unresolved.

Simon stopped reading and rubbed his eyes. To know oneself . . . he was still seeking his own truth. Would his destiny be found in the past rather than the future? With a strange reluctance he returned to the manuscript.

In March of nineteen-twenty two Andre Belmont came to The Landing. No one seemed to know where he came from, but it was suspected he was involved in the smuggling of booze from Canada. Since many of our finest citizens were amassing large fortunes from the same, it was an honorable enough endeavor.

Prohibition was in full swing. Never had people wanted to drink more than when the law said they should not.

I met Belmont at a dinner party at Uncle Ben and Aunt Kathleen Dunn's home on Riverwalk. The guests were I, my sister, Clara, and her husband, Thomas Dunn, Thomas' brother, Nicholas and his wife, Eleanor. Belmont and his business partner whose name I no longer recall were the only guests not of the family.

Simon pulled a notebook from his attache case, began a list of questions, and resumed reading.

Andre Belmont was seated next to me and across the table from Clara. Strange how well I remember the details of that evening. Crystal sparkled, and the silk wallpaper glowed rose in the soft gas light. I can still smell the rich aroma of fresh baked bread, taste the crisp brown skin of the Cornish game hens. Like everyone else, Uncle Ben ignored our infamous twenty-first amendment, and fine wine was served with each course.

I noticed Aunt Kathleen looking at a ring that Belmont was wearing. It was of heavy silver with a male figure on one side, a female on the other, the two joined in an embrace. I could tell that for some reason Aunt Kathleen found the ring disturbing. She spoke to Belmont mentioning that it was of unusual design.

Belmont explained that his wife was of Irish descent and that the ring had been handed down through the Devlin family. I recall the name because I felt it better suited to him than his own.

As the evening wore on, Belmont began to show the effects of the wine. His manner grew arrogant boarding on rude. He was the sort of man whose company I would never seek out.

When someone at the table mentioned the authorities were showing an interest in the old tunnels running from

Riverwalk to the river, Belmont was quick to inquire about the purpose of the tunnels. "Perfect for today's bootlegger, nes pa? For what were they intended?"

Clara glanced at me and I saw disgust in her eyes. "They were used to help Southern slaves escape to Canada and freedom," she explained.

"Bah," Belmont snorted in disgust. "Wrong, wrong, wrong. The blacks are lazy, stupid, genetically inferior creatures, one step up from the beast. They are suited only to tend the fields, and serve in the kitchen . . . and the women to warm one's bed."

"Mr. Belmont," Thomas put in. "Please watch your tongue. There are ladies present."

Belmont's eyes narrowed. "Of course, forgive me," he sneered, and rudely turned to his left to carry on a lengthy conversation in French with his business partner.

Clara set her wine glass down with such force the fragile stem snapped. "Never assume because a stranger addresses you in his native tongue that he doesn't understand yours."

Andre Belmont's lips tightened to a thin, cruel line. He angrily tapped the silver ring against the table edge.

Clara's voice was cold with disdain. "This cretin said that to refer to us as ladies was at best a euphemism. But what most offended him was being forced to sit at the table with savages. He'd been told that Ethan and I are half breeds. Even so, I'd make an acceptable bed mate if one could scald away the stink of bear grease. His partner warned him to temper his speech. That they'd been ordered to make the acquaintance of the Dunns and to purchase land the Hawks had for sale. Belmont commented that had it not been for those instructions, he would never have accepted the dinner invitation."

In those days my temper flared quickly and hot. I yanked Belmont from his chair and slammed him against the wall. "You conniving bastard. You'll buy no land here."

Thomas pushed his chair back, but Uncle Benjamin caught his arm. "Leave it. Ethan has it under control."

Nicholas came to me and spoke calmly. "Better let him go. He's turning an interesting shade of purple."

I reluctantly stepped away.

Belmont gasped for breath. When he could speak, he spat, "Peasants, I gladly take my leave."

After Belmont and his partner had gone, Aunt Kathleen, with tears in her eyes, took Clara in her arms. "My dear, you've made a dangerous enemy. Be careful, be very careful."

I knew Aunt Kathleen sensed something the rest of us didn't comprehend. Her sensitivity came from out of the knowing and could be trusted. Later I would remember her words and wish that I had paid more attention. So much tragedy might have been averted.

My fingers grow cramped. I've relived as much of the past as I can for today. I look out of the window and find that it is already twilight. This is the time of day which brings this mysterious quality of light out of which my people believe energy is transformed into a great spiritual current. It is here that nature's secrets are revealed. Past, present, and future merged in a river of time, flowing into a vast sea of knowledge.

Simon paused to write a reminder in his notebook. He found both the knowing and his great grandfather's philosophy intriguing. It was a strange mix. Native American mysticism coupled with some sort of para-normal sensitivity. He wanted to understand both. In anticipation he turned the page.

This morning the river is restless with an ominous stillness in the air. Soon it will storm. There was a storm the day Clara died, as if the very gods cried for her.

During the weeks before Clara's suicide, Aunt Kathleen would awake screaming in the night. She saw death—over and over, she dreamed of death but could not see who would

17

die. We were all concerned for she often sensed the future. I knew of her grandmother who told of a family legend. Wise women who had the knowing, who could foresee the future, perceive what other's could not.

I saw no contradiction. My heritage taught reliance on our true intuitive being. Not in denial of reason, but to overcome the dark, destructive passions inherent in our psyche, to control the irrational savage within. I believed Aunt Kathleen . . . and I was afraid.

Weeks passed. Daily, Clara seemed to change, to retreat from all of us. She grew thin, her pallor grey . . . and I was afraid.

Then on a cold April morning, Clara, clad only in her nightgown and cape, made her way to the ledge above the cove. She drowned in the river she loved.

Death was of her choosing, but none of us who loved her knew why. Tom was a man possessed, grieving one moment, flying into a fury the next. Clara's memory existed in his heart and mind like a living being. Memories which were destroying him. I became concerned for his sanity.

And the Dunn children, they had all loved Clara. Madeleine and Michael were too young to understand and they soon accepted her absence. But Sylvia was older and missed her. She wandered through The Haven like a lost soul.

Clara had been gone almost a year when I received a message from Molly Soames. She ran a local speakeasy appropriately called, Molly's.

Molly's was housed in a Queen Anne brick mansion on the outskirts of The Landing. The first floor had been opened up as a taproom. The second had private dining rooms, enabling gentlemen to entertain ladies who were not their wives. The third floor consisted of bedrooms where ladies of the evening plied their trade. An exclusive club, and expensive–the price one paid for discretion.

I might mention that Molly and I were occasional lovers

but with no ties beyond friendship.

The night I received her message the taproom was full, the bar lined three deep. Ceiling fans did little to disturb the heavy smoke which veiled the dark mahogany walls. A trio hammered out the blues, and in the back room a seemingly unending game of poker was being played.

At the bar, I had a glass of draft with Lyle Coons, the county sheriff, and Mike o'Connor, our local police chief. Prohibition was indeed a success.

Molly gradually made her way over to me. A lovely woman with dark, gleaming, chestnut hair cut in a short cap that framed a pixie face. "Ethan, how good to see you." She glanced around the room and leaned into to me and whispered, "wait a few minutes and join me in the office."

I bought a round for Lyle and Mike and talked with them until I finished my beer. Excusing myself, I slipped down the hall to the office at the back of the house.

Molly was seated on a blue Chippendale sofa. Next to her was a wisp of a girl with curly blonde hair and great blue eyes filled with tears. There was an angry red slash on her cheek.

Molly gestured for me to be seated and said, "Ethan, this is Ellie. She's the reason I asked you here. Ellie, don't be frightened," she reassuringly told the girl. "Just tell Ethan what you've told me."

The girl tried to smile but there were pain and fear in her eyes. "I knew Clara," she said to me. "We'd often take walks together along the river and we'd talk. Last fall she gave me herbs so I could start a window sill garden. She was my friend . . . I truly cared for her. When she died, I couldn't believe it . . ." Her voice trailed off and tears trickled down her cheeks. "I couldn't understand why Clara would want to kill herself. Me maybe . . . not Clara."

I glanced at Molly. Her frown warned me to be patient.

Like a small child, Ellie wiped her eyes with the back of her wrists. "Last night one of my clients was very drunk,

drunk and mean. Sometimes he seemed to forget I was there. He'd pace and drink from a bottle of cognac. The whole time he kept mumbling about . . ." She paused and lowered her eyes. ". . . about fucking a half breed. He called her a stinking squaw, a highfalutin Indian bitch. He said that when she killed herself, she cheated him of a good lay. I knew he meant Clara, but she would never have let the likes of him near her. He raped her."

Ellie clenched her fists until her knuckles were white. "I know he raped her. I wanted to kill him. Oh God, I wanted him dead."

Molly gently gathered the trembling girl into her arms and comforted her as one would have comforted a frightened child. "Tell him the rest."

"He kept mumbling something about knowing and how the Dunns were stupid . . . didn't understand. He spoke of power and force. Sometimes he was speaking in French. I couldn't make any sense of it, just ramblings."

Rage filled my body. My spirit cried out for vengeance. My voice grew harsh with anger. "Who is he?"

Ellie shook her head. "I don't know but I know he hates the Dunns . . . and, oh, God, what he did to Clara." She touched her cheek. "He hit me. His ring cut my face."

"His name is Andre Belmont," Molly softly said. "Ellie, thank you for telling Ethan. If you're packed, I'll have Carl take you to the station."

"Thank you, Ellie," I said. "You've answered so many questions. This means more to me, to the Dunns and the Hawks than I can say. We won't forget you. If you ever need any help, you have only to ask. Thank you." I took out my money clip and pressed all I had into her hand. "To help you make a new start."

When she hesitated, I added, "Take it for Clara. She'd want you to have it."

After she had gone, I asked Molly why the girl was leaving.

20

"If Belmont should remember talking to her, she could be in danger," Molly explained. "I've sent her to a friend in Albany. What now?"

My hands were clenched into fists. If Belmont were standing in stood in front of me, I would have killed him with my bare hands. "I don't know. That bastard raped Clara, it was his hand that pushed her off that cliff." I looked intently at Molly. "Please keep this to yourself."

"Of course." She reached for my hand. "Ethan, I grieve for Clara, for you and Tom, but nothing you do can bring her back."

"I know, but I can give her spirit peace. Do you know where I might find Belmont?"

Molly shook her head. "He comes and he goes. He might be in tonight or I might not see him for a month."

"When he shows up, let me know. No matter where I am, find me."

"Ethan, Belmont is dangerous. He causes pain for fun. He likes to hurt people. Men who have gotten in his way have disappeared. The people he's involved with have their own agenda, and bootlegging is just a small part of it. Keep in mind, Ellie said he ranted about the Dunns. Be careful, please be careful."

When I left Molly's, I immediately went to The Haven to tell Thomas of Belmont and his rape of Clara.

Thomas listened but his manner was distant. "I suppose I should be relieved to finally know why," he said. "But this only serves to make her death even more senseless. Why didn't she tell us? Did she think we'd blame her?"

I could give him no real answer. "Maybe she was afraid of what else he might be capable of doing. We can never know, only accept."

Tom stared out at the St. Lawrence. "Not a day goes by that I'm not reminded of all that was taken from me, from Clara. She'll never watch another sunset over the river, never have the children we both wanted. The guilt I feel at being

21

alive when she isn't is almost more than I can bear."

He turned to face me and although he didn't raise his voice, it had a hard, forceful edge. "I'm going to kill him."

"No, we are going to kill him."

"How?"

Tom had asked a simple enough question. "Belmont must know why," I said. "Knives, a fight to the death." How simply the end of a life can be decided.

"Clara was my wife. It's between me and Belmont."

"She was my sister, and I'm the better fighter. After all, growing up as a half-breed in a white man's world gave me plenty of practice."

Tom permitted himself a smile. "Based on that premise, I have to dispute your claim. Most of my misspent youth was spent bailing you out of one brawl or another."

"I can see this is getting us nowhere. There's only one way to resolve this. We'll flip a coin."

Tom dug a silver dollar out of his pocket. "Call it."

"Heads." Heads it was. I'd won.

Tom flicked the coin to me. "Must be your good luck charm."

We had appointed ourselves Belmont's judge, jury, and executioners. Belmont would simply disappear–the execution of a monster.

Tom and I realized that actively trying to find Belmont would attract unwanted attention. It would be wiser to wait for Molly's summons. Week's passed. We heard he'd taken a shipment of hooch south but would be back before the river froze over.

Finally, one October night there was a knock on my door. Carl, Molly's bouncer handed me a note. Belmont was at Molly's and he was alone. His skiff was docked at her wharf.

That night the sky was dark with grey clouds sliding across the face of a haunting moon. Heavy fog floated above the black water. I rowed in close to Molly's wharf and drifted the final yards to the jetty.

Once ashore, Tom and I positioned ourselves behind an outcropping of granite where the only path from Molly's to the river made a sharp downward turn. Belmont would come to us.

Hours passed. The cold cramped our muscles with a light drizzle adding to our discomfort. It was nearing dawn when we heard the scrape of footsteps. An indistinct shape moved toward us through the shadows cast by the tall pines overhanging the footpath.

When Belmont was parallel to our hiding place, Tom and I stepped out in front of him. The rain was heavier now and with the wafting fog it was difficult to see.

Belmont slid to a halt. "Hawk? Dunn?" His tone was puzzled but held no fear.

I moved behind Belmont to prevent him from retreating. Tom blocked him from moving forward. "You raped my wife," he rasped. "Rather than live with the degradation she killed herself. Now . . ."

Belmont laughed aloud. "Now you would take your revenge." He held his arms wide. "What will it be–swords, guns at twenty paces or cold-blooded murder?"

The bastard hadn't even bothered pretending innocence. I pulled a bone handled, Bowie knife from its sheath. "Knives–loser dies."

Tom tossed its twin into the ground in front of Belmont. "Pick it up."

Fear briefly flickered across Belmont's face. He slowly squatted and keeping his eyes fixed on me, reached for the knife. He came to his feet in a crouch. Circling sideways, he slapped the knife from his right hand to his left and lunged. I was barely able to sidestep. His next thrust came toward my stomach. I struck his arm upwards with my wrist, and for a moment our bodies were locked together. With my free hand, I clawed at his eyes, and he scrabbled back. I slashed out and felt the blade bite through the flesh of his cheek to nick the bone.

Blood streamed down Belmont's face, and he panted with fury. "Stinking savage, I'll kill you." His blade surged forward. "Kill . . . you."

Instead of retreating as he expected me to do, I moved in toward his body, turning his knife outward with my forearm. His blade sliced flesh but missed the muscle doing little damage. I stabbed upwards and felt the blade enter his body.

The knife fell from his hand, and he slowly slumped to his knees and collapsed to his side. His voice graveled from his throat. "Stinking breed, kill . . . kill you."

Tom picked up the knife and tossed it far out into the river. "Let's get him to his skiff. I'll row him out into the channel. He'll sink like a stone."

"I'll pick you up," I said. "Likely he won't be found until the spring thaw–maybe never."

So it was done. Clara's restless spirit was at peace. But in the writing of this, I realize I had hoped Belmont's death would put an end to it, but this wasn't to be. Our lives had been irrevocably changed and there could be no going back.

Time passed. Spring came, but Belmont's body wasn't recovered, nor did anyone investigate his disappearance. Apparently no one felt his loss, or if they did it was with a sense of relief. I later learned Belmont smuggled not only booze but guns as well. The bastard sold death. His own hadn't come soon enough.

That summer, I married Clarissa Founteau, a woman I met while on an extended business trip to New Orleans. Life became all I hoped it might be. We had one son, Adam who completed our lives. Tom had only his work.

In the mid-thirties, an English friend of the Dunns summered at The Haven. His company did business with Germany. He told of Hitler, of how the Jewish population's property was being confiscated, and that they were being forced into ghettos. He'd even heard rumors of death camps.

Tom found the plight of the German Jew horrendous and was determined to help. His friend put him in touch with an

24

organization who smuggled Jews out of Germany to safety. Tom was killed during the London Blitz, but I believe it was only his body that ceased to exist. His spirit, his soul, had died with Clara. If the Gods are kind, they are together. I will always miss him, just as I still miss Clara.

Through the years, I've tried to learn more of Belmont and his partners. The bits and pieces gleaned convinced me that those men were no more than pawns in a chess game whose end was yet to be revealed. Who are these faceless men? Why had Belmont been told to integrate himself with the Dunns?

Aunt Kathleen felt Belmont was somehow connected to those who had gone before, that what he wanted from the Dunns was not of this time. Her concern was that in some way the Dunns and Hawks were or are intended to play a major role in a plan whose premise we cannot comprehend.

Unanswered questions. Yet this is the truth as I know it to be, but only mine. Each man's truth is his alone. The voice of the universe speaks through the wind and the thunder. It flows in the streams, rivers, and seas, and swells the ocean. We are its ears, its eyes, its mind, its voice. In this the here and now, we search for the human spirits greatest knowledge outside of nature–a revelation of our own inward mystery. We are ever and eternally seekers.

This journal will be secreted within the walls of Hawk House to be found long after I am gone, and my spirit rests upon the winds of eternity.

Simon's sleep was deep, uninterrupted by dreams of the past. When he awoke, he quickly showered and dressed in grey slacks and black silk turtleneck.

When he reached the bottom of the open staircase, he was greeted by the butler. "Mr. Hawk, Madame is in the study. She asks that you join her. May I have breakfast prepared for you?"

"Please. Fresh fruit, any kind. Bagel, coffee."

"Very good, Sir. It will only take a moment."

"Thanks, Hudson," Simon said with a grin. He knew Hudson considered him an interloper, not yet to be trusted. Old family retainers were often more snobbish than their employers. He went on into the study.

Sylvia was again seated behind her desk. She greeted him with a smile. "Did you sleep well?"

"Very well. That is once I got through Ethan's manuscript. I do have a few questions."

"I was sure you would."

Hudson came into the room, set a tray in front of Simon, and poured the coffee. "Your breakfast, Sir."

Simon picked up the coffee cup. "Thanks." He took a sip of the rich, dark coffee and glanced at Sylvia. "Riverwalk is where?"

"Northern New York. In a village on the banks of the St. Lawrence River–The Landing. It was founded by the Dunns and the Hawks."

"I don't recall ever hearing of it," Simon commented.

"Not surprising, your grandfather and father long ago cut their ties to The Landing."

"What sort of a place is it?"

"A small river village, but not at all like the more well known Alexandria Bay. Alex Bay is a typical resort town. The Landing is very upscale, catering to the affluent."

"The Haven?"

"A resort hotel. When the rich and famous discovered the Thousand Islands, my grandfather realized the area's potential. He was convinced the tourist would become a major source of revenue. So convinced that in eighteen eighty-seven The Haven came into existence. It's been run by the Dunns ever since."

"Sounds like quite a place."

"Indeed, it is–large, luxurious. At The Haven you'll find quiet elegance, privacy . . . it's hard to explain. It's the best of the best."

"I see." Simon reflectively paused, then said, "Obviously our families were close, apparently in most ways, they still are. I can't help but wonder why I've never known of the Dunns."

Sylvia's eyes misted and she looked away. "That is a question for your grandfather."

"Fair enough. Now, Clara Dunn's suicide, Belmont's death–how do they have bearing on your daughter's murder some forty years after the fact?"

"Bear with me for a moment. It may seem I'm going far afield but I assure you there is a point."

Simon nodded and picked up an orange and began to peel its skin.

"Back in the early sixties Uncle Ethan, my husband, and I were at a regatta in the Sea Islands just off the Georgia coast. One afternoon we were having a late lunch on the yacht club terrace. All during lunch, Uncle Ethan seemed distracted. He was watching two men who were seated at a window table.

"As these men were leaving the terrace, the older man caught a glimpse of Uncle Ethan. He stopped so suddenly the young man behind him nearly ran him down. It was then that I got a glimpse of the older man's face. It has always stuck in my mind." Sylvia drew an invisible line down her cheek with a fingertip. "There was a scar running down one side of his face."

Simon finished his orange and wiped his hands on a napkin. "I see where you're headed. You think Ethan recognized Andre Belmont and vice versa."

"Uncle Ethan looked like he'd seen a ghost. I know hindsight is always twenty-twenty, but I'd wager Uncle Ethan thought the man was Belmont." Sylvia sighed. "But unfortunately, he never had the chance to find out for certain. The next day Uncle Ethan had a massive heart attack. He recovered sufficiently to go home, but a few days later a second and final attack followed. It wasn't until I read the journal that I remembered the incident, but that man might well have been Andre Belmont."

Simon hid his impatience. "How do you perceive this as tying into your daughter's death?"

"After you hear the rest, you'll see what I mean."

Simon was beginning to believe Sylvia was grasping at straws, but he listened without further comment.

"My daughter, Libby was an artist, one the art world had

begun to notice. She'd had several successful shows and was beginning to sell internationally. Her studio was in an old barn on the border of Hawk and Dunn land. She died there, stabbed to death, her face slashed until she was unrecognizable. The fingers of one hand were broken as if she had desperately tried to hold on to something.

"After Libby's death the studio was unoccupied. Years later, my brother, Michael decided to tear it down." Sylvia opened her desk drawer, took out a small box, and handed it to Simon. "This was found under the floor boards, no more than a few feet from where Libby was attacked."

Simon opened the box and took out the silver ring with the entwined figures of a man and woman. "A similar ring was described in the journal."

"Exactly, but at the time the ring was found, it had no significance. Libby gave parties there, tourists came to buy her paintings, people were in and out all the time. It might have belonged to anyone." Sylvia hesitated, staring at Simon as if deciding whether or not he should be trusted. "Simon, can you believe there are truths beyond logic? That there are intrepid individuals who have the ability to free their consciousness from the mundane, to cross the normal limits into an expanded concept of reality . . . a transformed consciousness?"

An edge of impatience crept into Simon's tone. "I believe there is true mystical experience. Does this have to be with the knowing mentioned in Ethan's journal?"

"It does. In varying degrees, the Dunn women all seem to have this extra sensory perception, to see what others cannot. My Aunt Kathleen had a mental breakdown because of it. My sister, Madeleine foresaw her own death. Libby's seemed to translate into her art. Some of her paintings were of things she had seen only in dreams. Among family it's called the knowing."

A dark, foggy night in London crept to the forefront of Simon's mind. As he approached his Soho flat, he had the feeling that something was wrong. Something or someone was inside. He had climbed to the roof, came down the fire escape, and entered the flat through his bedroom window. Two men waited in the living room. Had he not followed his instincts, he would have been killed the moment he walked through the front door. "I know something of the feeling," he said.

"My own knowing has faded through the years, but I can still sense certain events forming. Simon, I know there's a common thread tying Belmont to Libby . . . and to my granddaughter, Clara. I feel the darkness all around me and the knowing is at its heart."

Sylvia's pallor concerned Simon. "I'll do all I can," he promised.

"So many I've loved gone. First Clara, then Maddy, and my husband, Martin . . . so young, only forty-eight, and Libby . . ." Her voice was choked with tears. "I can't seem to save those I love."

Simon could see that Sylvia's grief was bringing her to the point of collapse. "Could Grandfather tell me the rest?"

Sylvia clasped her trembling hands together. Simon still needed to be told of his uncle, Duncan Hawk's involvement. Perhaps it would be best if he heard it from Adam. "He can but it will be no easier for him."

"Perhaps not, but he is the one who brought me into this. Maybe it's time I reconnect with my family. Time we talk." Simon reached for the telephone. "May I?"

Sylvia nodded and listened while Simon booked himself on the next available flight to New Orleans.

St. Lawrence River Valley

The wind whispered of ancient truths and warned of things best left unseen. Leaves rustled to the ground, baring the tree branches for winter's gown of snow. Soon the river would ice over.

Its silver mirror keeping the secretes that were hidden beneath the dark, restless waters.

Clara Dunn Eaton restlessly tossed and turned, asleep, yet not, lost somewhere in the knowing.

Lightening flashed, torrential rain beat against the stone wall of the manor house. A man cloaked in black, and wearing a floppy brimmed hat pulled low, rode into the courtyard. His horse pranced on the cobblestones as if reluctant to have their journey end. As the man dismounted, a groom hurried from the stables and took the reins. "Do they come," the groom asked?

"Aye, best be gone," the man warned. He hurried through the rain to the front entrance and brought the door knocker down hard again and again until the door was flung open.

A woman in a dressing gown stood captured in the candlelight. Her hauntingly beautiful face was framed by red hair curling long down her back. "Why are you here?"

The man came into the entrance hall and barred the door. He moved with powerful grace, wearing his sword like it was part of him, an extension of his body. "I've come to warn you. The villagers blame you for the rotting crops. They're afraid of you, of your strangeness, the things you see and know that they do not. They would take your life."

Fear stood in the woman's eyes. He took her arm and pushed her toward the stairs. "Dress. There's not much time."

Before the woman reached the stairway, there was a pounding against the door. It trembled beneath the thudding fury. The man took off his cloak and tossed it to the woman. "Wear this, go the back way to the sea. Liam has a boat waiting." He drew his saber.

"I can't leave you alone . . ."

"You must live, go."

Clara, entrapped by the controlling force of the knowing, thrashed against the bed covers. She saw flames, heard screams and the clash of steel on steel. The man, a sword in hand, fighting against overwhelming odds. The woman fleeing into the fog.

Abruptly, she awoke. Her body was chilled, cold and clammy. Remnants of the knowing clung to her like a shroud. The knowing . . . this time of the past.

But whose past? She knew the man had died, his blood pooling on the stone floor. But what of the woman, had she survived? There was no way to be certain until the knowing came again.

In frustration, she punched the pillows into a more comfortable pile and tried to go back to sleep.

New Orleans, Louisiana

Simon's flight to New Orleans had been uneventful. Upon arrival, he found his rental car ready and waiting. His grandfather had wanted to pick him up but he had opted to drive himself. He wanted the time to renew his acquaintance with the city he had once thought of as home. Through the open car windows, he breathed the warm, humid air.

The dark barked oak trees with their foliage so green as to look black in the ashen twilight brought the past into focus. And the crepe myrtle trees, he'd forgotten their beauty.

Once in the city, he turned onto First Street and into the Garden District. Surrounding him were massive mansions veiled by tall boxwood, others encircled by wrought iron fences which were in and of themselves works of art. Soon the double iron lace gates of Hawk House came into view.

Smiling, he drove through the gates and past the towering oak. The same oak tree where he had long ago left his mark. A hawk with its wings out spread was carved into its trunk.

In moments, the huge sprawling antebellum mansion came into view. Above the roof line the sky was purple grey, casting an eerie glaze of violet over the rooftop and blackening the tall chimneys. Bougainvillea vines climbed the columns of the high second gallery and cascaded over the railings. He could smell the sweet, sensual scent of the flowers.

Simon got out of the rental car and stared at the house–home. No . . . no. This place wasn't home. Home was a concept, a place he'd longed for all his life but hadn't as yet found. Listening to Sylvia speak of the bonds of family, of friendship, to read in Ethan's journal of a heritage of which he was completely unaware had served to underscore his own solitariness. He wanted more. It was time to bridge the gap between himself and his family.

The front door opened and Adam Hawk waited in welcome. He must have just come from his law offices because he was still wearing an impeccable, black pinstriped suit. Simon felt Adam looked frail, a pallor under his tan. To see his grandfather looking unwell was like a blow to the heart.

Adam's throat was tight with emotion. "Simon, come in."

Simon stepped past his grandfather and into the foyer. The vast house was quiet but somehow changed. The tall, narrow windows were free of the heavy draperies that Simon remembered. Now flowing sheer curtains let in the sun, and there were vases of fresh-cut flowers on the recessed shelves.

Adam went on into the family living room. Simon followed and saw that here, too, change was evident. An oriental rug in shades of rose glowed against the polished marble floor. The furniture was the same but had been upholstered in warm, jewel tones.

Judith Hawk, Simon's sister stood in the alcove of the bay window. It had been more than eight years since Simon had seen her–a girl then, a woman now. As she turned to face Simon, her sleek dark hair moved with the motion of her head. "I see the prodigal son has returned. Do we kill the proverbial fatted calf?"

Simon smiled without rancor at his sister. He remembered Judith as a little girl. A tom boy really, who had wanted to do everything he did. She had tagged at his heels like an anxious puppy. Me too, me too, had been her childhood mantra.

Surprisingly, there was a hint of tears in her topaz eyes.

Hawk eyes–his eyes, the eyes of his father and grandfather. "Save the hostility, Judith, it's a waste of energy. The bank is all yours. I'm here solely for Grandfather."

Judith blinked back the tears. "Simon, I'm sorry. I've waited for hours to tell you how glad I am you're home, then it came out all wrong. I've missed you."

Suddenly, she was in Simon's arms, her warm tears wetting his collar. He put his arms around her. "Shush now, don't go girl on me," he told her. Just as he had when as a child she'd cry if she couldn't keep up.

Judith pulled away. "Don't tease. I need you to be my friend. Can't we make things right between us?"

Before Simon could answer, she continued in a rush. "I was never mad at you. It was you and Dad who were at odds."

"Sorry, Sis, but I couldn't be what he wanted."

"I know," Judith said. "The bank wasn't for you, but it was what I always wanted. Dad made me feel I'd always be second choice. You–oh shit! Damn it, Simon, you just walked away. You left and never even told me goodbye."

Simon gave her a gentle shake. "Judy, Judy, Judy," he said in his best Cary Grant impersonation. "Let's give each other a second chance. I promise to stay out of the bank. You promise not to write books. Friends?"

Judith smiled, a broad smile which softened her angular Hawk features and made her beautiful. "Can we go sailing before you have to leave?"

"I'd like that."

"One more thing. Call me Judy again and I'll deck you."

"Drinks?" Adam asked.

"Glenfiddich on the rocks," Simon answered. "Judith?"

"A glass of wine will be fine. Oh, Simon, dinner tonight is truly the fatted calf. I asked cook to prepare all your favorites–fresh oysters on the half shell, leg of lamb with mint sauce, and peach melba."

"Sounds incredible." Simon didn't have the heart to tell her that he hadn't eaten red meat in years.

Adam went to the teak wood bar and poured their drinks. "Is it safe to take off my bullet proof vest," he joked?

Judith kissed her grandfather's cheek. "I believe you'd better wait until Dad and Nicole put in an appearance."

As if summoned, a couple came through the French doors from the garden. Nicole Rolliard Hawk hesitantly stepped into the room. Just behind her, Simon could see the tall, powerful figure of his father.

Nicole came forward. "Simon, welcome home. You're looking well."

Simon took a sip of his drink to give himself a moment to regain his composure. Nicole was pregnant. Even to his untutored eyes, he could see she was very pregnant–the continuation of family.

With an unexpected stab of delight, Simon smilingly asked, "My sister or my brother?"

David Hawk protectively put his arm around his wife's shoulders. "We've opted for surprise. When the time is right, nature will let us know. Simon, welcome home."

Adam handed Nicole a tall glass of ice water and David a Stolichnaya martini. He held his own glass high. "To the Hawks–those present, those missing, those returned," and with a salute to Nicole, added, "and those to come."

David in his turn lifted his glass. ""To the Hawks–lawyers, bankers . . . and writers."

"And Native Americans?" Simon asked.

"Yes," his father solemnly answered. "I'm afraid your grandfather and I were remiss in not telling you of our heritage. I apologize. You shouldn't have had to learn our history from a journal."

Before the theme could be expanded upon, Adam broke in. "Please, for tonight, let's just enjoy being together. The past can wait a little longer."

Simon heard the plea in his grandfather's voice and thought that there must be much not covered in the journal. But it had waited this long, it could indeed wait a little longer. "The house looks wonderful. I can't put my finger on what has changed, but

I like it."

Judith linked arms with Nicole. "We are decorators extraordinary . . . truth be told, it was mostly Nicole."

"Nonsense," Nicole put in. "We did it together."

Simon raised his glass. "Ladies, your efforts are to be commended."

David joined Adam and Simon and put his hand on Simon's arm. "I've read every one of your books–incisive, intelligent. Fine writing. I've even seen the films. Some of the philosophical impact is lost, but all in all your work translates well from one medium to the other."

In spite of himself, Simon had to admit his father's praise meant a great deal. He wished he had heard it more in his teens. Wished his father had been there to see his tennis matches, watch his swim meets. Perhaps if he had, the government's offer might not have seemed so attractive.

Dinner was a true purging of the past–no recriminations, no apologies, just simple acceptance. Simon relaxed in a way he hadn't in a long time. He smiled in amusement as Judith mimicked David's personal assistant at the bank.

"The director of City Corp. is standing in front of her desk," Judith said. "He referred to her as Ms. And she broke in with, 'I am Miss, not Ms. thank you very much, Piedmont'."

"A remarkable woman," David wryly said. "She's been with the bank longer than I have. I inherited her from my former father-in-law. I suspect she'll be around after I'm gone."

They lingered over dessert and coffee, reluctant to have the evening end. Nicole sighed and put a hand on the mound of her stomach. "I hate to be a party pooper, but Ms. or Mister here has tired me out. I'm for bed."

"I second the motion," Judith put in. "I've an early day tomorrow. We'll leave you men to your brandy."

David rose from the table and helped Nicole to her feet. "Simon, I'm going to beg off for tonight. I think Father wants to speak with you alone."

"Good night, you three. I'll see you all tomorrow. Sleep well."

David paused at the door. "It's good to have you home, son. We'll talk in the morning."

Simon and Adam went on into the library. Adam poured two brandies and handed a snifter to Simon. As Simon seated himself in a comfortable overstuffed chair, he asked, "Grandfather, how is it I was never told of our Iroquois background or for that matter of the Dunns and The Landing?"

Adam's eyes were shadowed. "To mention one meant speaking of all of it . . . too painful, just too damn painful." He fixed Simon with a cold stare. "To be honest, was it not for the journal, I probably would never have spoken of The Landing or anything connected to it."

Simon could see that Sylvia had been correct in her assumption that speaking of the past would be no easier for his grandfather than it was for her. "I'm sure after I hear the whole story, your reasoning will be clear. Sylvia filled me in on the years preceding the time Ethan wrote of, but we only touched on her daughter's death."

"Libby's death wasn't the only tragedy. We lost Duncan."

"Dad's brother? Somehow I had the impression that he'd died in Nam?"

"Duncan did do two tours in Viet Nam–army ranger. He'd just finished his degree in architecture when his number came up. Strings could easily have been pulled to keep him out, but it wasn't Duncan's style to let someone else pay his dues."

"Than he did survive Nam?"

Adam nodded. "When his military obligation was over, he came home. Viet Nam had changed him. He slept little and when he did he had horrendous nightmares, wasn't eating. Finally, he said he had to get away. He wanted to go to The Landing. It didn't make any sense to move up there in January, the middle of the north country winter. Nothing but the cold, snow, and long, grey days."

Simon held the brandy snifter between his palms to warm the brandy. "How long has it been since you've been back there?"

"Not since Libby's funeral. Her murder . . . slaughter changed everything." Adam sighed and rubbed his temple. "God, she was a lovely creature, but then the Dunn women have always been beautiful. The Dunns and the Hawks–in most ways we're as close now as we were then. I handle their legal affairs, David their investments. It's simply that I cannot bear going back to The Landing, nor can your father."

"I've always thought the Hawks were from right here in New Orleans."

"No, my mother was from here. Consequently, my parents often brought me to New Orleans. I loved the city and when it was time for college, I decided on Tulane. I met your grandmother at a fraternity mixer and the rest is history. As you know, this was once your great grandparent's house. It came to your grand-mother when they died. Helene always called it Hawk House south."

"How was it that you ended up here in New Orleans rather than The Landing?"

"Helene's father offered me a position in his law firm. I worked my butt off to prove it wasn't nepotism. I'm proud to say the firm is still one of the most prestigious in international law. New Orleans was our home for nine months of the year. Summers were spent in The Landing. The Dunn family business justified my time there."

"Grandfather, how did Ethan's journal come to light?"

"For many years, Ethan's Hawk house had been empty–a tar-get for vandals. Clara Dunn Eaton, Lydia's daughter loved the house and acted as unofficial caretaker. Then, two years or so ago, Clara telephoned me. She wanted to buy the house along with five acres of river frontage."

"You sold Hawk house?"

"I did. Your father wanted nothing to do with it, and Judith didn't care. You were gone and certainly had no interest. The house was intended to be lived in and none of us ever would. Clara loved the house just as the Hawks had"

"She discovered the journal, where?"

"In Hawk House, I don't believe she mentioned where."

"I see. Grandfather, I can see that speaking of Elizabeth's death is difficult but you've mentioned Duncan going to The Landing. Is there a connection?"

"Yes. Duncan and Libby . . ." Adam's hand trembled as he reached for his brandy. "The two had known each other since they were children. When college intervened, their paths no longer crossed. In the winter of sixty-three, when Duncan went to The Landing, they became reacquainted. Libby had just broken her engagement to Marcus Pillard."

"What happened there?"

"Apparently Pillard wanted a full time wife to showcase his rising political career. Libby was an artist with her own career. I suppose the fact that Duncan didn't want to own her as Pillard had was part of the attraction."

"Interesting woman."

"She was. I think you'd have liked Libby. She had this wonderful sense of being alive, of living every minute of every day. If it hadn't been for Libby I'm not sure Duncan would ever have gotten back his peace of mind. She helped him to forgive himself for the horrors of Viet Nam. When they married it was quite a celebration."

"Did Sylvia approve of the marriage? I know she hasn't gotten over Libby's death."

"No, and she never will, but she thought Libby and Duncan were the perfect match. For two years it seemed that way. But in the weeks prior to Libby's death, she and Duncan were having very public disagreements. The night before she was killed, they had a loud fight in the dining room at The Haven."

"Was Duncan a suspect?"

"The police never really looked anywhere else."

"How so?"

"The arguments came to light. One of the waiters at The Haven remembered Duncan shouting at Libby that she couldn't do it."

"It?" Simon wondered aloud.

Adam shook his head. "I've no idea. Libby angrily answered

that Duncan couldn't stop her. The *coup de grace* was Duncan shouting what amounted to, you do and you just might die."

"I wouldn't call that evidence."

Adam snorted in disgust. "Nor would I but there's more. When the authorities went to Hawk houses to tell Duncan of Libby's death, they found the house a shambles. Lamps broken, furniture overturned, drawers dumped out onto the floor, paintings torn from the walls. The conclusion was that their battle began there and ended in the studio."

"Duncan?"

"Gone, disappeared."

"Did the police look for him?"

"For months–month after endless months. I've always believed it killed your grandmother. Your father was destroyed. He and Duncan had always been very close. David spent years searching for Duncan, but he never found him."

Adam's eyes lost focus and he stared into space. "The hardest part of all this has been not knowing wether or not Duncan is alive. One thing is certain–he didn't kill Libby. None of us have ever believed he did. Now with the discovery of the journal, we've got a shot at proving it."

Simon swirled the brandy in the snifter. "A long shot, an extremely long shot. Thirty some years . . ."

"Just as supposition," Adam put in. "Let's say Libby was the first to find Ethan's journal and made a connection from the past to what was happening in the present."

"So what? A rape which couldn't be proven. Ethan, Belmont, Tom Dunn–by Libby's time, all the players are dead. Why this late in the game would anyone give a damn?"

Adam's hand slapped the table top with a loud crack. "I give a damn. Sylvia and your father do. All the Dunns and the Hawks do."

"Grandfather, I meant why would anyone on the Belmont side give a damn?"

"If he survived?"

"Same premise," Simon said in dismissal. "Wait forty years to take revenge. I think not. It would make no sense. Is there anything going on in the present that would constitute a threat?"

"Carson Mitchell's media conglomerate just survived a hostile takeover. Harmon Pillard was the force behind the defunct attempt."

"Harmon Pillard," Simon contemptuously repeated.

"You know him?"

"Of him. Pillard picked up on a CIA leak that a cell of agents under deep cover in China had been penetrated and agents doubled. Pillard published without confirmation. People died because Pillard wanted to scoop the competition. I'm not a fan. On the flip side, I don't see him as a hands on killer."

"Did Sylvia tell you she believes the journal ties to Libby's death?"

"She did. Do you concur?"

Adam shrugged. "Who am I to argue. I realize it's little to go on but the Dunn women are generally right in matters of . . ."

"Knowing," Simon finished the sentence for him. "I'd like to get a better fix on what this knowing is but let's move on and get back to it later. Sylvia showed me the silver ring that was found in Libby's studio. It does fit the description of the ring Belmont wore."

Adam thoughtfully sipped his brandy. "True. If the ring was Belmont's, I suppose it's possible that he passed the ring onto a relative. Maybe to someone who lived in The Landing. Another of the proverbial long shots."

"Not if they're still around and have heard about the journal. This knowing, intriguing concept . . . could it have any bearing?"

Adam raised his eyebrows. "Your guess is as good as mine. The Dunns really didn't talk about it. I think they felt it was more an affliction than a gift."

"So if I want more info on the knowing, I'd better ask one of the Dunns."

Adam nodded. "Better you than me. Frankly, I've seen it in action and it makes me very nervous."

"In the journal, Ethan mentioned the name Devlin in conjunction with Belmont. Mean anything to you?"

Adam thought for a moment and said, "No, no it doesn't. So what do we have–the journal, Belmont, this silver ring? Not much, but it's more than we've ever had before." Adam caught Simon's eye. "To change the subject–you and your father . . . ?"

"Maybe now that there's mutual respect, we can have a closer relationship. I'm willing if he is. He and Nicole seem very happy about the baby, and I'm happy for them. I wish them well."

"I take it Nicole is a nonissue?"

"Actually, she always has been. My pride was hurt but I wasn't about to give her the life she wanted. Dad could. They're well matched."

"In the final analogy, it's family that counts." Adam tiredly sighed. "If I may get back to Ethan's journal–what do you make of the final page?"

"Reminded me of cave paintings. Frankly, I can't even venture a worthwhile guess. Maybe the answer is in The Landing."

"You'll go there?"

"Grandfather," Simon mildly censored. "You knew I wouldn't refuse you."

Simon put the four wheel drive jeep Cherokee on cruise control. He was on the final leg of his journey from New Orleans to The Landing. His stay at home had lengthened from a week to two, then it was Christmas and New Year's. It had been a pleasurable time. He had sailed with his sister and grandfather, and golfed with his father. Nicole and he had managed a quiet lunch with no lingering residue of emotion.

He glanced at the map. From his computations, he still had about two hundred miles to go. His thoughts drifted to the knowing. What was it Sylvia had said? A freeing of ones consciousness, to reach an expanded concept of reality. Interesting, he knew scientific research had brought parapsychology out of the realm of soothsayers and psychics and into respectability. The power intelligence organizations–CIA, the old KGB had extensively researched the field. For all he knew, they were still.

His fingers thoughtfully tapped the steering wheel. Extrasensory perception, a sixth sense. Personally, he'd never liked the terminology. The implication was that the sense was outside the norm, extra, unusual. He was more inclined to believe that humankind had through the centuries managed to deplete their intuitive powers, just as humankind had nearly destroyed the environment.

Simon chuckled aloud. His opinion, and opinions were like assholes–everybody had one.

Just as he crossed the border from Pennsylvania into New York, he saw the first snow flakes. Once he reached the Route 481 bypass around Syracuse, the snow became heavy with strong gusts of wind making visibility at times near zero. Traffic had slowed to a cautious forty miles an hour.

By the time Simon reached The Haven's gate house, he was convinced the four wheel drive vehicle was the best investment he'd ever made. He down shifted and crawled along the curving drive to finally reach the parking area.

He brushed the snow off the back of the Jeep and lifted out a single bag. The bitter cold wind made his face ache and he was anxious to get inside. He hurried up the brick steps, through the gleaming brass doors, and into The Haven's lobby. He immediately felt a sense of opulence and tradition. Enchanting hand-painted wall murals, and gracious furnishings contributed to its stately old world charm.

Simon thought that he'd never seen such massive oak pillars. His attention was drawn to the huge fireplace that was large enough for a man to walk into. Its blazing fire warmed the room. He glanced up at the high ceiling with its glittering, crystal chandeliers. From a nearby dining room came the soft, floating strains of a string quartet.

A wonderful kind of welcome seemed to surround him. He felt as though he had come home to a place he'd never been before. He walked over to the reception counter. A young man wearing a navy blazer with staff embroidered in script on the pocket, looked up from the computer monitor.

"Simon Hawk. I've a suite reserved."

"Mr. Hawk, welcome to The Haven. Your suite is ready and waiting."

A bell hop materialized at Simon's side. He wore a waist length version of the staff jacket. The clerk handed the bell hop a key card. "Please take Mr. Hawk's luggage to the East wing. The A Suite. Mr. Hawk, if you'll give Robert the keys to your vehicle, he'll see that it's unloaded."

Simon handed the bell hop his keys and a folded bill. "It's the Jeep. Thanks."

"Oh, Mr. Hawk," the clerk added. "Mr. Dunn is waiting for you in the taproom. Just go straight back behind the staircase. It's clearly marked."

As Simon stepped into the oak-paneled taproom, Lucas Dunn turned from the bar to see who had entered. He realized the man who walked toward him with an easy stride that combined alertness and strength had to be Simon Hawk. He held out his hand. "You must be Simon Hawk. You look just like pictures of seen of your father and uncle. I'm Lucas Dunn, The Haven's present overseer. Please call me, Luke. Lucas is my father."

Simon shook the proffered hand. "Luke."

"Simon, how about a drink? Name your poison."

"Cold draft. Killians if you have it."

"We do." Luke called to the bartender. "John, Killians, two. Let's grab a table," he said and led Simon to a round corner booth.

When they were seated, Luke warily glanced at Simon. He wasn't certain of just how much he should say. "Aunt Sylvia told me why you're here. Thanks for coming. I've been so damn worried."

Simon took a long pull of his beer. "Worried, how so?"

"Clara . . . that's Sylvia's granddaughter, Lydia's daughter–anyway, she hasn't been herself since she found that damn journal. Been having nightmares, premonitions, more than the usual. She's like Aunt Sylvia. She's got the knowing. I swear Clara can read my mind."

Simon couldn't help but smile. "Read your mind?"

"Yep. Take it seriously. I've lived with it all my life. Let me warn you, don't bother lying to them, they'll know."

"Believe me, I'm not amused," Simon answered. "Sometimes you have to take a leap beyond logic."

"With Clara, it's more like jumping off a cliff."

A group of women came into the bar. A petite woman with a mass of brown, curly hair saw the two men and came over to their table. "Luke, we're here for drinks and dinner, Molly's later. Care to join us? Of course, your friend is invited," she added with a smile at Simon.

'Simon, this flirtatious bit of fluff is Lucinda Melrose. Luci, Simon Hawk."

Simon held out his hand. "Lucinda."

She took his hand and held it a beat to long. "Luci, all my friends call me Luci."

"Ah, but we're not yet friends."

"But we will be, after all . . ." She leaned down, and exposing generous cleavage, whispered, "My mother and your uncle used to get it on."

"How interesting?" Simon purposely let his eyes rove the length of her body. "Are you suggesting we make it a family tradition?"

Luke choked on his beer. It wasn't often anyone put Lucinda in her place. He decided to intervene before blood was drawn. "Thanks for the offer, Luci, but I'm still working. Another time."

Lucinda's cheeks were pink, but she was determined to have the last word. "Jazz at Molly's, be a real shame to miss it. Stop by if you finish early enough."

"I'll try," Luke said. "But don't count on it."

Lucinda retreated to the bar and joined the other two women. Luke caught the bartender's eye and with a gesture, indicated he was to get the ladies a drink on him.

Simon raised an eyebrow. "Quite a trio."

"To say the very least," Luke said. "From right to left–Lucinda Melrose, whom you just met, Susan Fowler, and Holly Lawrence. Landing born and bred. You're certain to run into them from time to time."

"Care to fill me in.?"

"Sure. Lucinda is embroiled in a messy divorce. Susan and Holly are career types. All are beginning to worry about the 'ol biological clock."

Simon smiled. "Sounds like a warning."

"It is. I call them the predators. I damn near married Holly, bailed when I figured out her interest was The Haven, not me."

Simon glanced at the women. "Good-looking though."

"Forewarned is forearmed," Luke said only half joking.

"Surly is." Simon saw that the taproom was quickly filling. Waiters were briskly serving trays of drinks and bar snacks. He leaned back and relaxed. "Luke, you've got a good place here."

"Yep," Luke agreed with a smile. "But I'm just filling in to give my folks a few months in Arizona. Dad's dream is that someday I'll take over for him."

"Do I hear a but?"

Luke nodded. "I'm not sure I want it. I'm taking this year to find out. Say Simon. I can shake free in an hour. If you'd like, we can have dinner."

Simon couldn't help but wonder what it was Luke wanted instead of The Haven. "Dinner sounds good. A hot shower even better. Point me to my digs."

"Up the stairs or take the elevator. East wing is clearly marked. You're in A Suite. Tell you what, I'll have dinner sent up. That way we'll have some privacy."

"Works for me. Oh, make that fish, poultry, vegetables. Skip the red meat. I'm not much of a fan."

"Leave it to me. I promise you'll enjoy."

Simon unlocked the door of A Suite and entered a small ivory marble floored alcove. He looked through a pair of open French doors into a large sitting room. A fire in the marble fireplace warmed the pale walls. Deep cushioned couches and chairs pulled the room together in the perfect balance between luxury and comfort.

He glanced into what would be his office. Lap top computer

and laser printer were already set up on a large library table. Ready to go, he thought, right down to the surge protector. In the bedroom with its huge king-sized bed, he found his luggage had been unpacked and put away. Through a sliding glass door, he saw a glassed in balcony equipped with a hot tub. He pulled off his clothes and went into the bathroom.

The marble was warm on his bare feet. The huge bath sheets on the rack were warm to the touch. He discovered both a sunken spa and a Jacuzzi shower. The toilet and bidet were tucked into private alcoves. Decadent fantasies all the way. Certainly an adequate home away from home.

By the time he was out of the shower and dressed in comfortable sweats, Luke was ushering a waiter through the door with a service cart. "Sea food chowder and garden salad with our famous house dressing. Hot out of the oven sourdough bread. For dessert, our very own cheese cake with raspberry sauce. All accompanied by a bottle of white burgundy of no particular vintage. But it's one of my favorites."

The two men ate dinner and talked in generalities. Simon found the food delicious. He rarely had dessert but after a taste of the cheese cake. He finished the slice. He made an a-okay circle with his thumb and forefinger. "Chowder, delicious–a meal all by itself. Cheese cake was perfect. Great dinner."

"Thanks, we're proud of our kitchen," Luke said. "I could use a brandy. You in?"

"Sure. Do I have any?"

"The built in cabinet against the further wall, right end."

Simon opened the double doors to discover a wet bar with a refrigerator.

"Pull down the boxed in stainless steel. You've got a countertop range. Above it is a small microwave. Left end is your multimedia center–television, VCR, fax machine."

Simon found a bottle of Remy Martin and poured the brandy into snifters. He put the bottle on the table between them. "I may never leave."

"I'll take that as a compliment."

"So it is."

Luke stared morosely into his drink. "You think we've got a shot at clearing up this mess?"

"Truthfully, I haven't got a clue."

"What's the first step?"

"Local police. I'll see if I can get the file on Elizabeth Hawk's death."

"Then what, work forward from the info in the journal?"

Simon nodded. "It's a starting point. Do you know of anything in the now that bears looking into?"

"Harmon Pillard recently tried to finesse Uncle Carson out of Mitchell Media."

"My grandfather mentioned it, but putting him in the big picture is a reach."

Luke shrugged. "Marcus Pillard, the senator was engaged to Aunt Libby. She dumped him."

"All this for a wounded ego." Simon shook his head. "I don't think so. What's between Harmon Pillard and your uncle?"

"They've been competitors since they were kids here in The Landing. Pillard's island is just off the point. I guess the two of them competed at everything. Golf, tennis, women, you name it. I'd guess the takeover was more of the same."

"A good thing your uncle came out on top. Carson Mitchell's group reports the news, hard news."

"That is true–no idiots' back fence analysis."

"As opposed to Pillard," Simon tersely said. "Pillards stuff skates right on the edge of the tabloids. But then it's what you'd expect from a greedy, power seeking asshole who believes he has the god given right to influence the public's view of information."

"Whooee! And I thought Uncle Carson didn't like him," Luke said with a grin. "Pillard's sister, Corrine, who by the way is Luci Melrose's mother, lives here in The Landing. We still see quite a lot of Harmon and the Senator."

"Was the sister around at the time of Libby's death?"

"Can't say. It would be in the police file. Listen, if there's any way I can help, let me know. You might want to talk to Clara.

She's got a theory. Problem is she's away."

"Vacation?"

"Nope. She's out in LA setting up one of the Lindquist/Dunn schools."

"They are?"

"Schools for the kids' society have abandoned. The program is philosophically based in the martial arts–physical, spiritual, the whole shebang."

"This Clara, she's involved with the martial arts?"

"Her interest stemmed from a need to control the knowing. She's been at it since she was a kid–black belt in a couple of disciplines. Tai Chi's an interest."

"All that and the knowing too. Interesting woman."

"You don't know the half of it." Luke set his snifter down. "I'd better beat feet. I've got an early breakfast meeting."

"Luke, thanks for dinner . . . and for my temporary digs."

"Thank you for agreeing to help. I know Aunt Sylvia is damn glad you're here."

"Luke, one more thing–Sylvia seemed concerned that the knowing is somehow knitted into this whole scenario. In fact, I felt she was afraid of how it might affect her granddaughter."

Luke's face lost its affable expression. "Simon, all I can tell you is that the knowing makes the hairs on the back of my neck stand up. There's been times when it scared the piss out of me." He shrugged. "If you want to know more, I suggest you ask Clara. But don't be surprised if she doesn't say much. It's not her favorite subject."

"Fair enough."

Luke got up and walked to the door. "Say, once my early meeting is out of the way, I'll be pretty much free until afternoon. If you like, I'll take you into town and introduce you to the police chief."

"Thanks, I'll take you up on it."

The Landing's police station was a small, generic, brick ranch–functional but without the charm of the older buildings found throughout the rest of the village.

A blue uniformed officer showed Simon and Luke into the office of the Chief of Police. "Please have a seat. The chief will be with you in a sec. Oh, Luke, practice tonight at the gym. Be there."

"Right, Rotary's volley ball tournament. Thanks for the reminder," Luke said as he and Simon sat down in front of the desk.

Simon observed that the white walled office was clean, bright, and had the latest in high tech equipment. Through the open door he caught a glimpse of the communication center. Top of the line, he thought. Nothing but the best for The Landing's finest. "You've got a very upscale little town here."

"True," Luke agreed. "All in all a good place to be."

"At the risk of being intrusive. Why the reticence in taking over The Haven?"

Luke rocked back in the chair and stared at the ceiling. "Think Sorbourne, think a degree in philosophy. Options—teach, write, become an ivory tower philosopher, take over the top gun position at Clara's schools . . . or The Haven."

Simon thought that there was much more to the man than met the eye. "Hard choices. The schools, you've mentioned them before."

"When we're finished here, I'll give you a guided tour of our training facility."

"Sounds good."

Chief Michael O'Connor came into his office, nodded a greeting to both men, and sat down behind the desk.

"Chief," Luke said. "I'd like you to meet Simon Hawk. Simon, Chief O'Connor."

"Chief."

"Mr. Hawk."

"Simon, please," Simon requested as he made a quick appraisal of the man. Fifty-five, give or take. Six feet and a couple of inches, good physical shape. A nose that looked as if it had taken a few punches. Cool, grey eyes that seemed to take Simon's measure.

The chief leaned back in his chair. "Okay, let's cut to the

chase—Libby Hawk's murder."

Simon had to smile. "That's about it."

"You've come to the right place. I was the first officer on the scene."

"Who reported the body?"

"I was the one who found her. Libby's studio was right at the village limits. A good spot to make my turn around."

"That morning, what was different?"

"Studio door was partially open, maybe six inches. Went through my mind that when Libby had closed up, she'd forgotten to latch the door. On the other hand, might have been a break-in." The chief's eyes were shadowed. "Wish it had been one or the other."

"What then?" Simon said.

"Called it in, secured the scene. Libby was near the door, kind of lying on her side. Two fingers on the outstretched hand were broken." The chief's face greyed with memory. "Her face was slashed open and she'd been repeatedly stabbed. There was a trail of blood from where her easel was tipped over. She must have tried to crawl for help . . ."

"What type of weapon was used?"

"Wide, deep, cuts. Likely a blade from a hunting knife or something similar. Weapon was never found. Whoever it was used the same knife to slash Libby's paintings to ribbons, left traces of her blood on the canvas. Anything glass was smashed, telephone pulled from the wall."

Simon quickly perceived that for Michael O'Connor the case was still active. It hadn't been shuffled into the never, never land of the unsolved. "Chief, is there any chance, I could see . . . ?"

"Yeah, you can see the file," the Chief said.

Luke smiled. "Aunt Sylvia give you a call?"

"She did, so did Adam. Keep in mind, if I didn't want Simon to see it, he wouldn't have a snow balls chance in hell of getting his hands on it. Libby's murder has always been personal. An objective eye might see something that was overlooked. To everyone here in The Landing, Libby's death was a tragedy. It was hard to get past people's feelings. Neither of you knew her, but she was special. Beautiful, not just outside, inside, too." The chief leaned forward and rested his forearms of the desk top. "I'll tell you something else. Duncan Hawk never killed her."

Simon barked a laugh. "Strange you should say that. I thought he was the only suspect?"

"He was. Duncan disappeared, wasn't around to defend himself. Popular theory was that he killed her in a jealous rage. Bullshit! The chief–"

"Who happened to be this chief's father," Luke put in. "You see, Simon, there's been a Michael O'Connor as Chief of Police for three generations. Kind of the town joke that if the line died out, there'd be no law and order."

The Chief grinned. "Be a fourth when I retire. My son, Mike is the one who showed you in."

"Uh huh." Simon figured he had a lot to learn about The Landing. "Hawk House?"

"As I started to say. My father sent me to Hawk House to break the news to Duncan. He thought a friend should be the one to tell him about Libby, but he wasn't there. I never saw him again."

"Was Duncan different after Nam?"

"Not in the way you mean. Naturally he'd changed, seemed like all the life had gone out of him. He told me how much he hated the war . . . the killing. If it hadn't been for Libby, I don't know if he'd have gotten it back together. No, no way Duncan could have killed her."

"Who else had motive?" Simon insistently probed.

"Motive? Never was any we could find. Maybe your journal points in that direction. If you don't mind, I'd appreciate reading it."

"You got it."

The Chief smiled. "You and I are going to get along just fine. Anyway, when I got to Hawk House, I knocked, rang the bell, no response. I went around back and tried the door, it was unlocked. In those days, nobody locked their back doors. Do now."

"I know the interior had been tossed," Simon put in. "Any

blood?"

"Nope, nowhere."

"Why do you think the house was trashed?"

"I'd say somebody was looking for something."

Simon wondered if someone might have been looking for the journal. "How about the studio?"

"Maybe . . . but more than that, violent rage. You could feel it in the air. Whoever killed Libby hated her, wanted her dead. Which file you want—computer disk or the real deal?"

"Real deal. Chief, the broken fingers, could she have been trying to hold on to something? Say the ring that was found years later?"

"Possible, the broken fingers didn't seem to be a defensive wound." The chief unlocked the bottom desk drawer and took out a thick folder. He saw the surprise on Simon's face. "My Dad's notes and mine are in the margins. I told you this one is person-al. Take your time, but don't let it out of your hands."

"Do you think Duncan Hawk is still alive?"

"I'd like to think he is but it doesn't seem likely."

"Chief, the name Andre Belmont mean anything to you?" Simon tossed the name out, not expecting any real information.

"Belmont. Can't say it does. Why do you ask?"

"Smuggling booze, gun running in the twenties."

"That would be Bureau of Alcohol, Tobacco, and Firearms. Tell you what, I'll see if I can find out anything. But the twenties . . . iffy, real iffy. Research for a book?"

Simon found that he liked the man. There was a finely honed intelligence behind the Chief's small town affability. "It might tie into Libby's murder. You'll understand when you've read the journal."

"Got anything to do with the ring Michael Dunn found in Libby's studio eight, ten years after the murder, the one you men-tioned?"

Simon nodded. Apparently, the chief didn't miss a thing. "Ever find out anything about it?"

"Nothing that amounted to anything. Nobody around here

remembered ever seeing it. Had a metallurgist check it out. Sterling silver, European grade, something about the silver content. I even checked with . . . shit, what do you call them. Yeah, one of them heraldry places. No cigar."

"I think that about covers it for now. I'll probably have more questions after I read the file. Chief, I'd rather our conversation stay confidential."

"If anyone asks and they will, you stopped by to see about a drivers license. Yours international?"

"Yes, it is."

"If you stay, you've got to have New York's."

"Will do, thanks, Chief." Simon reached across the desk and shook the chief's hand. "Thanks for your cooperation."

When they reached the Jeep, Simon locked the file into the storage compartment. "Where to?" He asked as he started the engine.

Luke climbed into the passenger seat. "Head back the way we came. I'll let you know where to turn."

Sun sparkled off the white snow and Simon put on sunglasses. "The schools, how did they come about?"

"Clara, the one with the knowing–she was in Manhattan. When she came out of an antique shop just off Washington Square, a couple of teenagers wearing gang colors tried to mug her. She didn't let them."

"The schools?"

"I'm getting there. That night Clara, me, and my doctoral advisor, Gunnar Lindquist had dinner together. We were talking about the mugging. Gunnar mentioned that society was letting the kids down. No moral leadership. So the kids were making their own rules."

'Sure, gangs as a substitute for family."

"Yeah. In that context, Clara mentioned the martial arts and how it incorporated the values that these kids lack. Gunnar's ears perked up and he asked Clara to explain. Clara told him the martial arts helps to develop confidence, instill personal discipline. Might conceivably raise their consciousness above gang mentality."

"And you three were off and running."

Luke did a drum roll on the dash. "Yes, indeedy. In time the concept reached fruition. Simon, next left toward the river."

Simon followed Luke's directions and pulled into a small gravel parking lot at the side of a barn.

"This is the place," Luke said as he released his seat belt. "It houses seminars for applicants seeking a teaching position at Lindquist/Dunn."

Inside was huge open space. Simon glanced to the right and saw a Kung Fu class in progress. At the far left was an open sided lecture hall where a man was speaking from a podium.

Luke touched Simon's arm. "Let's catch Gunnar's lecture. It'll give you a clearer picture." As they walked, Luke explained, "The group with Gunnar are teachers who have little or no martial arts training. They'll be required to learn or rather begin to learn the martial arts, and rethink their approach to education."

"I take it they have to become adept in one of the disciplines?"

"Yep, it's a must."

Simon turned his attention to the commanding presence of Gunnar Lindquist. A man of snow white hair, penetrating blue eyes, and the hard, carved features of a Viking warrior. He addressed the group with cultured authority.

"To learn one needs inaction at the appropriate time. This gives rise to silence, attentiveness, respect, self-control."

A hand was raised.

"Mr. Seber."

"I know I'm a novice in the martial arts, so maybe I'm missing something. Why is the inclusion of the physical discipline so important?"

Lindquist looked out over the class. "Anyone care to enlighten Mr. Seber?"

A young woman with long, braided hair raised a hand. "It's empowerment. These kids feel they live in an out of control world. The discipline teaches them how to survive–takes away their feeling of helplessness."

"Yes," Lindquist affirmed. "That is why learning the physical discipline is the first requirement.""

Seber's hand was again raised.

Linquist's eyes narrowed. "Yes."

"Why the insistence on the bow?"

"Students, teachers as well bow–the universal body language for respect. The teacher for his pupil; the pupil for his teacher, the lesson, for themselves. All activity has ceased–nothing moves. The mind is ready to focus, to learn."

"All well and good," Seber argued. "But we're talking street kids, gang bangers. You've got to earn their respect. I've been teaching for five years. In my experience, it doesn't happen. Getting them to bow–impossible."

"Respect comes from living example, by having them function within a continuously growing, life affirming philosophy."

"It won't happen with rhetoric," Seber insisted.

Luke walked to the platform. Linquist greeted Luke with a bow and turned over the podium. Luke surveyed the class and smiled. "Our Mr. Seber seems to have overlooked one basic fact. The kids who participate in the school have chosen to do so. The opportunity is offered, they either accept or decline. No one is ever forced. Living examples isn't rhetoric," Luke pointedly said. "The kids come to understand that they're intelligent. That a by prod-uct of this intelligence is responsibility–a step toward self esteem. They're beginning to take action, to take control of their lives. They make things happen rather than allowing life to roll over them. A focus of self–the ability to control what one does through conscious choice, to decide."

Seber stood. "You're telling me because some kid can kick ass, he's in control of his life?"

Luke's expression was cold. "Mr. Seber, the Lindquist/Dunn Schools is a journey in consciousness. A journey it would seem you're reluctant to make."

Gunnar Lindquist caught Luke's eye and pointed at the clock. Luke nodded. "I believe it's time for a change of venues. Your next class awaits. Mr. Seber, may I have a word," he asked?

Gunnar Lindquist walked over to Simon and held out his

hand. "Gunnar Lindquist."

Simon took his hand. "Simon Hawk."

"Ah, yes. Luke mentioned you'd be arriving. I take it you're getting the tour." Lindquist glanced at Luke and Seber. Seber's face was red and his lips thin with anger. Lindquist sighed. "I fear our Mr. Seber is in a spot of trouble."

"I've only known Luke for a short time, but from the expression on his face, I'd say Seber has a problem. These schools are quite a project. Keeping them running must cost a buck or two. Government grants?"

Lindquist raised his hands as if defending against evil. "God no, private sector. In fact, Clara Dunn Eaton is our main fund raiser. Have you met her?"

"Not as yet."

"Were I not an old geezer no other man would get near. She is a gem." With a twinkle in his eyes, he added, "When Clara walks into a room it's very subtle, like a blind being raised to let in the sunlight."

Luke joined them, his face tight with disgust. He glanced at Lindquist. "Mr. Seber will no long be considered for employment."

"I concur," Linquist said. "He simply doesn't grasp the concept."

Luke grimly nodded. "Say, Simon, what do you think?"

"As the old adage goes, the proof is in the pudding."

Luke glanced toward the martial arts class . "Several of those candidates are graduates of our Bronx school. They already have their teaching degrees. We lose some but not as many as you might think."

"Impressive," Simon admitted.

"Gunnar," Luke said. "Will I see you before you leave?"

"I'm afraid not. As soon as I wind up today's session, I'm headed back to the city. I'll give you a call in a few days and tell you who made the cut."

Lindquist turned to Simon. "A pleasure to meet you."

"And I you."

As they made their way to the door, Simon saw Seber angrily

waving his arms and blustering for his peers. Most simply kept on walking.

Luke slumped into the passenger seat and stared out the window. "The work we're doing with the schools is important."

"You don't have to convince me. You've got a tough call to make–the schools or The Haven."

"Yeah." Luke glanced at his watch. "Better head back to The Haven. I've got to meet with my liquor distributor."

Simon nodded and pulled out onto the highway.

"You took your own path," Luke questioned?

"That I did."

"Considering that your grandfather counsels presidents, and your father sits on the World Bank . . . must have been a pressure situation."

"Not really."

"You walked away from one hell of a lot–power, big bucks."

"My choice. One I can live with. The money I have is what I've earned and invested. I'm comfortable, but in terms of real wealth–I'm not rich, nor do I have any desire to be. As for power," he shrugged. "Only over my own life, and that suits me just fine."

"No regrets?"

"Nope." Simon drove to The Haven's rear entrance and parked.

Luke got out and waited while Simon unlocked the compartment that held the Hawk murder file. The two went in the rear entrance. Luke headed toward the kitchen. "Catch you later."

"I'll be around. Thanks for the tour."

Simon was anxious to read the police file and went directly to his suite. He sat down at his desk and leafed through the photographs of the crime scene–a brutal, vicious slaughter. The chief was right, whoever killed Elizabeth Hawk hated her. He put the photos aside and began to read the interrogations.

Interviews with virtually everyone who had known Libby and Duncan Hawk. No favoritism had been shown. The rich and famous were questioned just as thoroughly as the locals. But anything that could be considered evidence was virtually non existent. The only blood found had been Lily's. Finger prints went nowhere. Given the number of people who had access to the studio, even clear prints were virtually worthless. Even so, as many as possible were identified and cross-referenced with those people who had reason to have been there. All alibis were checked.

Simon thoughtfully leaned back in his chair. No one could fault the police. They'd done their job and then some.

In his analysis, Libby had known her killer. The person could conceivably still be living in The Landing or at least was a summer resident. Someone out there knew something–perhaps unwittingly. Shake a few bushes and see what falls out. He locked the file in a drawer. A workout would clear the cobwebs.

When Simon reached the gym it was almost empty. One man was working with the free weights, another on a treadmill, a third on the stair master. The Universal gym was free. He reset the weights and slowly worked through the reps. He finished with extra work on the abdominals, but strength training wasn't enough to stay in peak condition. He stepped onto a treadmill and punched in speed and time.

Through the glass petition, he amused himself by watching an aerobic dance class in progress. No sweat pants for these women. All wore expensive workout gear with highly visible designer logos. When the beat of the music gradually slowed to a cool down tempo. Lucinda Melrose glanced toward the glass petition. She saw Simon and waved.

Simon nodded an acknowledgment. He'd bet money Lucinda would stop by and say hello. He no more than finished the thought when Lucinda came into the room and sauntered over to the treadmill. "Hi, Simon, how's it going?"

"Just fine."

"I've been hearing about you. Everyone's excited that there's a Hawk among us again, especially those of my parents' generation. They all remember your family very well. The whole town is keeping track of your activities."

"What might they be?"

"Let's see. A few days ago, you were at the police station.

Something about a drivers license. Yesterday you were spied at Markham, Melrose, and Fowler–speculation is that you want to build on land the Hawks own along the river. But no one knows for sure why you're really here. And you and Luke have become thick as thieves."

Simon laughed out loud. "Any reports on how many times I've showered?"

"I believe at last count it was five," Lucinda jokingly told him.

Simon thought that since Lucinda seemed to know everyone, she might serve as the catalyst in the shake-up plan. "How about I shower once more, and we'll meet for a drink in the bar?"

"Give me an hour, I want to run home and change." She looked at her watch. "Say we meet at six-thirty in the taproom."

"Taproom, six-thirty." Simon watched her as she walked away. Lucinda was gorgeous, but Simon had the feeling he'd better make certain she understood the ground rules. Tonight didn't mean forever.

Back in his suite, Simon quickly showered and dressed. He had enough time to run a copy of the journal over to the chief's office and be back in plenty of time to meet Lucinda.

Lucinda sat at the end of the bar where she could watch for Simon's approach. She felt like a school girl with her first crush. Simon Hawk was definitely one of a kind. Strength, self assurance, self awareness–he seemed to have created himself. Her mother was right. The Hawk men were something else.

Simon came up behind Lucinda and tapped her on the shoulder. Lucinda looked up and felt butterflies in her stomach. Damn, but he was handsome, exotic. There was something mysterious about him. Certainly unlike anyone she had ever met. His black silk suit was baggy, fashionable, and likely Italian. A white silk turtleneck kept the look casual.

"Lucinda, I hope I haven't kept you waiting."

"Not at all, I've just sat down."

"Glenfiddich and water, tall glass," Simon told the bartender. "Lucinda?"

"Not yet, I just got one. So Simon, what do you think of our little community?"

"The Haven is luxury personified."

"And The Landing?"

"Haven't really seen it. I've only been here a couple of days, and the answer is three."

"Three?"

"Showers, in case anyone should ask."

She playfully punched his arm. "Where do you call home?"

"My formative years were spent in New Orleans. Since college I've lived abroad. I've only recently returned to the states."

"What brought you back?"

"An old journal of my great grandfather's. There might possibly be a connection from his writings to the death of Libby Hawk and Duncan Hawk's disappearance. I said I'd look into it."

"Fascinating. Of course, I've heard of the murder. Very tragic for both families," she commented and quickly changed the subject. "But after living abroad, I'd think living here would be something of a culture shock."

Simon grinned. "Nowadays culture shock is experiencing shock over finding someone with a bit of culture. What about you? "

"Landing born and bred. I went to Smith College, but didn't finish. Instead, I came home and married Clyde Meridian. A real disaster." Lucinda's face lost its social smile. "Not anyone's fault really, probably mine more than his. I guess I knew only that I needed something, but not what . . . or who." She had spoken the truth, and immediately regretted having allowed Simon to see behind the facade.

Two women stood in the doorway obviously looking for someone. Simon recognized them as having been with Lucinda his first night in town. "Lucinda, I think your friends are looking for you."

"Darn, I was supposed to meet them at Molly's. I forgot. See what you do to me." Her coquettish smile was back in place.

The two women came to the bar. The tall blonde laughed. "Ah, ha, now we see why you stood us up. Aren't you going to introduce us?"

Lucinda reluctantly made the introductions. "Susan, Holly: Simon Hawk. Simon; Susan Fowler, Holly Lawrence."

"Susan, Holly, it's a pleasure to meet you," Simon said. He motioned to the bartender. "John, please get us all a drink."

Susan leaned closer to Lucinda. "Luci, Clyde's at Molly's drinking up a storm."

"It's Friday, what else would he be doing?"

Simon handed the women their Chardonnay. "A tables available, shall we all sit down."

A flicker of annoyance crossed Lucinda's face. "Yes, please join us."

Once they were seated, Holly and Susan wasted no time before beginning to flirt with Simon. Their first round of drinks quickly disappeared and Susan called to a waiter for a second. When Simon tossed a fifty on the tray, Holly took his money and handed it back. "Rule one. We take turns paying. Rule two. There is only rule one."

Simon raised his hands. "I bow to tradition."

Holly spoke to the table in general. "Anyone heard when Clara is getting back?"

"Oh, has she been gone?" Lucinda snapped.

Simon decided to push Lucinda's buttons. "Do I sense a little tension?"

Lucinda shrugged and forced a smile. "Let's say Clara and I are like oil and water."

Holly looked at Simon and winked. "Luci doesn't like it that Clara sees right through her."

Lucinda's expression became pinched. She took Simon's hand. "Tell them about your grandfather's journal."

Bingo, Simon thought, right on schedule. "Clara Dunn Eaton, I'll guess the same Clara you just mentioned, found an old journal of my great-grandfather Ethan's in Hawk House."

"Really. How fascinating," Susan said. "I love reading about the area's history. Let's see . . . Ethan. That would probably be the prohibition era. Bootleggers smuggling across the river. It

61

must have been an exciting time."

"Have any of you ever heard of Andre Belmont?" Simon asked. "Ethan refers to him in the journal as a bootlegger."

Susan sipped her wine. "Never heard the name, and I don't recall seeing it in print."

"Might not be his real name," Holly put in. "Smuggling wasn't exactly a legal activity."

"There's another possibility," Susan added. "Many French came to the islands to escape from the French revolution. Take for instance, Count Jacques Donatien Le Ray de Chaumont."

"Point," Simon asked?

"He could have become Jacques Donatien, Jacques Le Ray, Donatien Chaumont."

"Or any combination there of," Simon said thoughtfully.

"I have quite a collection of books on the history of the area. I'll see what I can ferret out," Susan volunteered.

"When did you become so interested in history?" Lucinda sarcastically commented.

Susan smiled knowingly. Luci was already possessive, already thought Simon Hawk belonged to her. Something told her Luci was going to be sadly mistaken. "Always. If you recall, when my grandmother died, I took over her position as town historian."

Holly tapped a glass to get their attention. "Enough sniping. This is Friday and thank God it is. I'm for food, fun, and frolic."

Luke came to their table and pulled up a chair. "Me too. My work day has ended. Ladies, I'm all yours. What say we order up some ribs and wings. Later we'll dazzle Simon with The Landing's night life-a walk on the wild side."

Holly broke in, "Sounds like a plan. First, Molly's, then the *piece de resistance*," she said with a gleam in her eye. "Surfing at Sailors."

After a finger food feast of Buffalo wings, and barbecued ribs washed down with several rounds of drinks, the group decided to move on to Molly's. Lucinda firmly attached herself to Simon.

At Molly's, they all piled into a circular banquette. Simon thought it was still much as Ethan had described: dark wood, dim lighting, overhead fans, and in the corner a trio playing the blues. He leaned back in the shadows and watched.

This was the time of evening when everyone tried too hard to have a good time. Voices grew louder, gestures broader. Jokes were greeted with shrill shrieks of laughter. His drink sat untouched in front of him. It was moments like this when he felt most alone. He wondered what it would be like to share his life with someone he loved. The women in his life came and went. Encounters lasting weeks, a few months, a few days, some only a night. None held his interest, nor had he ever professed to love any of them.

Lucinda slid closer to Simon and leaned against his shoulder. Under the table, her hand stroked his thigh. "Take me home, please," she huskily whispered.

Lucinda's head lay back on the sofa. Her lips were open and smiling. Her pantyhose lay in a tangled heap on the Rya rug. Simon ran his hand slowly up the underside of her calf. At her knee joint, he stroked the soft skin with a light, feathery touch. Her body relaxed and she gasped with pleasure. Using both hands, he stroked upward then firmly and slowly stroked down her thigh, her calf, and across her foot. Slowly, he repeated the touching on the other leg.

Lucinda groaned. "God, I feel it everywhere. Good, oh . . . so good."

Simon used his fingernails instead of his palms. He felt her skin warm as his nails stroked its surface. He slid his hands all the way to the top of her inner thighs. His fingers played lower.

Lucinda stopped him with a touch. "Let's go upstairs."

Simon allowed her to take his hand and lead him up the open staircase and into her bedroom. In the center of the carpeted room, she turned to kiss him. His arms pulled her close, connecting their bodies from face to foot. His lips languidly explored hers. He held the back of her head, the kisses becoming hard, fierce, bringing her to a point of demanding need.

Lucinda felt herself becoming lost in sensation, a long, slow, heady tumble into sensuality. She leaned away and quickly slipped out of her dress.

Simon lowered his head and kissed the tops of her breasts and unclasped the front closure of her bra, leaving her naked before him. Lucinda eagerly unbuttoned Simon's pants and pulled his turtleneck free at the waist. She wanted to feel his naked flesh, the taut muscled body pressed against hers. In response to her unspoken need, he stepped away and removed his clothes. On the bed, his touch remained exquisitely slow, drawing her further and further along the path of sensual pleasure.

Lucinda sensed that she was over matched. Simon seemed capable of giving her more pleasure, more excitement than she could stand. He was a marvelous lover, lingering, stroking, touching, arousing to a point where restraint was no longer possible. She felt the hard length of his penis tantalizingly poised at the lips of her vagina. His strokes were prolonged, a silken penetration reaching deep inside her body. She stopped thinking, wanting only to enjoy this magnificent lovemaking.

Sometime later they lay breathless, their skin glowing with a sweated sheen. Lucinda turned to her side and looked into Simon's face. "Simon, that was wonderful. I mean, it was so good. How can you possible hold back the way you do?"

"Just enjoy. Good sex shouldn't be analyzed."

Lucinda's beauty had always gotten her any man she wanted for as long as she wanted him. And she wanted Simon Hawk. "Simon, when will I see you again?"

"I don't know. Don't look beyond the moment."

"Why? If we get to know each other perhaps. . . ."

"Luci, I don't make long range plans. My life suits me just as it is."

Long after Simon had left, Lucinda lay awake. Some way, there must be a way.

The following morning, Simon jump started his day with an early workout. He ended his strenuous two hour session by swimming laps in the pool, then returned to his suite. He brewed a fresh pot of coffee and went into his study.

Hours later he was still at it. The writing was going well and he hated to quit. The bleating ring of the telephone broke his concentration. He waited for the answering machine to kick in. As soon as he recognized Chief O'Connor's voice, he picked up. "Chief, I'm here."

"Hey, Simon, got something for you. Good news and bad news."

"Give me the bad first."

"Nothing on Belmont. But after reading the journal a couple of times, I mentioned the dinner party to my wife. I told her that it might be helpful to know the name of Belmont's partner. She gave me an idea."

"How so?"

"Rachel said hostesses of Kathleen's caliber kept records of those kind of things: date, menu, guest list. That way no guest was ever served the same thing twice. Kathleen and Benjamin's dinner parties were legend around here. I'd guess she kept one."

"Where might Kathleen's records be? Would they have been saved?"

"I called Luke's mother, Gabriele, out in Scottsdale. She told me their attic is full of old trunks. Some of them belonged to Kathleen and Benjamin. She said you're welcome to take a look. You can pick up the house key from Luke."

"Will do. It's a starting point."

"Heard the sun was coming up when you left Lucinda Melrose's house." The chief chuckled. "You sure don't let any grass grow under your feet."

Even though Simon disliked the intrusive scrutiny of his personal life, he treated it as a joke. "Is nothing sacred in this town?"

"Shit! Of course not. Good hunting."

Simon and Luke surveyed the huge attic. Luke sighed. "We Dunns save everything. You take the right side. I'll start on the left."

The first two trunks Simon opened contained clothes, the

third hats. "Nothing so far, how are you doing?"

Luke leafed through a folder. "This one had bills of lading, bills for furniture. All pertaining to when The Haven was constructed."

Simon opened three more trunks before he found any containing papers. In a lift-out tray were stacks of letters neatly tied with ribbon and postmarked London, England–Thomas Dunn. Simon thought that someday he'd like to read them.

In the next level was several cloth bound ledgers with precise columns of figures–household accounts. Several shoe boxes were at the very bottom of the trunk. Simon opened one and found what appeared to be recipe cards. He pulled one from the back. On one side was the date of the dinner and its menu. On the reverse was the guest list with seating plan. "Luke, I think I've got the right boxes."

They each took a box and flipped through the cards. The guest lists included Cornelis Vanderbilt, President Grant, George Pullman, George and Louise Boldt, many of the era's luminaries. Midway through the file, Luke came across the card they sought. He read aloud. "January fifteenth, nineteen twenty- two. Guest list: Thomas and Clara Dunn. Nicholas and Eleanor Dunn. Jacques Toussaint. Andre Belmont. Ethan Hawk. Right party but limited info. Jacques Toussaint. Name doesn't tell us much."

"Toussaint," Simon repeated. "Fairly common in the south. I can think of several families in New Orleans alone."

Luke stared down at the card. "I've either heard or saw the name. All the old Haven records are on computer disks. Let me search, who knows . . ."

"Let's put things back the way we found them. Your office is the next stop," Simon said as he replaced Thomas Dunn's letters, and Kathleen's records into the trunk.

"Any chance we can take time out for dinner?"

"Where's your work ethic?"

"All work and no play . . . and speaking of play. You missed surfing. Do we consider you and Lucinda an item?"

Simon's eyes grew cold. "Since I've been here, I've treated

people's abnormal interest in my personal life as a joke. Frankly, I'm damn sick of it. If we are to be friends, my private life is just that. What I want you to know I'll tell you and assume it will remain confidential. I'll extend the same courtesy to you. Clear?"

"As a bell," Luke said. "I'll even take a blood oath."

The fierceness left Simon's expressions. "A hand shake will suffice."

Luke stuck out his hand. "If you insist, but I gotta tell you, I'm a little disappointed."

"Why?"

"I've always wanted to do that blood oath thing."

"You're a piece of work," Simon answered. "And to address your question–Lucinda and I are not an item."

"Gottcha, not."

Late evening and Luke was still at his Louis XVI desk staring at the computer monitor. Simon was at work on a second computer that Luke's personal assistant usually used. The high tech equipment seemed out of place in the elegant ambiance of the oak paneled room.

Except for the occasional click of keys, the room was silent. Luke leaned back in his chair and watched the screen. He groaned and shifted position in his chair. "Wish I'd thought to cross reference the old files. This is taking forever." Toussaint scrolled onto the screen. "Hey, Simon, here's one. Henri and Lillian Toussaint: Baton Rouge, Louisiana. Their stay was back in seventy-five, August eighteenth to the twenty-fifth."

Simon exited his computer and rolled the tension from his shoulders. "The Jacques Toussaint you found was from back in the twenties–also Baton Rouge. We've made some progress. Remind me to send the chief's wife some flowers." He glanced at his watch. "Little late to call tonight. I'll try in the morning."

Luke breathed a sigh of relief. "You mean we can call it a day?"

"I do believe we've done our bit for God and country. Say, Luke, do you know anyone with an expertise in Indian lore? I'd like to get an opinion on the drawings in the journal."

"Joseph Cloud. He's our local expert and a writer. Published several books on the Native American. Joe lives about three miles down the road on the river, but he's a touch antisocial. Show up alone and you're likely to be met with the business end of a shot gun. He and my cousin have a special relationship. Wait until Clara gets back. Let her make the intro."

"Always willing to skip looking down the wrong end of a gun. I'll wait."

Luke scrawled the Toussaint information on a sheet of note paper and handed it to Simon. "Here you go." He rubbed his hands together. "Now for a well-deserved drink. I'll have the kitchen make us a prime rib sandwich. Whoops. Me a prime rib sandwich. You?"

"How about grilled chicken breast, horseradish on the side, no mustard or mayo. Bowl of soup, any kind."

"Easy enough." Luke locked the office door behind him. "Meet you in the bar."

Simon walked into the taproom. It was still packed with people waiting for a table in the dining room. A combo was playing a rendition of John Coltrane's, Blue Train. The jazz reminded him of his youth and the smoke-filled bars of Bourbon Street.

Susan Fowler was seated at a side table with her brother, Charles. She saw Simon and waved. "Simon, join us."

Simon reluctantly strolled over to their table. "Thanks, Susan, another time. Luke just ordered us some food."

A couple Simon didn't know came to the table. He quickly retreated to the bar before having to suffer yet another introduction. The Landing may be a small town but it sure seemed to have a large population. He gratefully settled into a corner where there was an extra stool for Luke.

John placed a Glenfiddich and water in front of Simon. "You look like a man who could use a drink. Oh, Lucinda Melrose was looking for you. Hour, hour and a half ago."

"Thanks, John." Simon took a deep swallow of his drink. Something told him he was going to regret last night. "Busy night?"

"Loaded. Capacity reservations, and a ton of walk-in's. Kinda surprising considering there's a real blizzard kicking in."

Luke slid onto the stool next to Simon. "Food's on the way."

"John tells me there's a blizzard out there."

"Yep, it's a-comin'." Luke seemed distracted. He quickly finished the bourbon and water John had placed in front of him and gestured for a second. "Simon?"

"Nope, still on my first. Problem?"

"Nah. Not really. When I was in the kitchen, I was thinking about my folks. Storm like the one that's coming usually meant an early night. Dad would set a table for two in the family dining room and light a fire. Mom would cook his favorite Cajun. Candlelight and good wine. A romantic evening between two people who, after more than thirty years were still lovers, best friends." Luke took a swallow of his drink. "I'm ready for that. I want someone who'll share my life. I want the kind of intimacy my parents have. Bed hopping is beginning to be a real bore. Trouble is, I'm afraid I'll never find the one woman who'll be forever. You know, the whole 'til death do us part scenario."

Simon nodded. "I guess the two of us are more alike than one might think. Last night at Molly's, I wondered the same thing. There's never been anyone I wanted for very long. Christ, women come and they leave. When they're gone there's only relief at their absence. It's so ridiculous that it borders on the comedic."

"Or tragic," Luke added with a wry smile.

"It isn't every man's fantasy."

John came to their end of the bar. "Gentlemen, your food is ready. If you like, I can set you up here at the bar."

Simon thought that Luke was lucky to have John. He was the perfect bartender–never intrusive, never forgot a customer's name or their drink of choice. "Right here's fine."

"Works for me," Luke affirmed.

Both men fell into silence as they hungrily attacked their food. Simon tossed his napkin on the empty place. "Good food, as always. John, can I have my check?"

"Not necessary," Luke said.

"Yes, it is. I pay my own way." He laid the money on the bar. "I'm headed upstairs. I need to edit this morning's pages."

"Let me know how you make out with Toussaint."

"Will do."

Simon had no more than left the taproom when Lucinda Melrose came up to the bar. "Luke, where's your friend? I've been looking for him."

"Which friend? Surprisingly, I have more than one."

"But only one I'm interested in. Simon."

"I believe he's upstairs in his suite–working. Work being the operative word."

"Which suite would that be?"

"Luci, if Simon wanted you to know, he'd have told you."

"Come on, be a friend."

"I am. Now if you'll excuse me. I have to speak with the chef."

In his make shift study, Simon stacked the day's rewrite next to the computer and restlessly wandered into the living room. He poured a brandy and went out onto the glassed in balcony. The raging storm beat against the windows leaving a pattern of white lace. Wind driven snow curtained the outside world. There was a wildness in the air, an elemental violence.

Ethan's journal persisted in Simon's thoughts. Could Libby have been the first to find it? Had it played a role in her murder and Duncan's disappearance? He thought of the knowing and recalled Luke's reaction–fear and trepidation in equal measure. The knowing. Was this power, force–whatever it was, was it part of the equation?

Back in the living room, Simon checked the time. Almost three a.m. He knew he wouldn't sleep. Storms energized him seeming to race in his blood. He recalled Susan Fowler's observation of the French aristocracy and the possible variations one might make of a single name. Andre Belmont might well be a red herring.

In Paris it would be nine Sunday morning. Not too early to

call. Jean-Claude and Elise should be at home with their children. He picked up the telephone.

"*Allo.*"

"Jean-Claude. This is Simon."

"Simon, *mes ami*, where are you? I called your Swiss
exchange, poof no longer there."

"You could have e-mailed."

"Bah, I wish to speak and hear a voice speaking back. Give
me your telephone number and where you are–and why you are
gone from us?"

"I'm in the United States, a small town in Northern New York
State." Simon quickly rattled off his telephone number and
address. "Jean-Claude. I need to pick your brains. I'm looking
for information on a man named Andre Belmont. He and/or his
family left France anywhere from mid to late eighteen hundreds to
early nineteen hundreds."

"Belmont. B E L M O N T. Spelling correct?"

"Yes. It was pointed out that this might be only a portion of
his name. As in count so forth and so on."

"This has to do with why you are in this Landing?"

"In a manner of speaking. Once I get a handle on the problem, I'll fill you in."

"Ha. The old need to know. I comprehend. This Belmont . . .
I'll take a quick electronic stroll through the records of the French
aristocracy. I will do as your yellow pages advise. Let my fingers
do the walking."

"I owe you one."

"Ah, but no, did you not save my life?"

Lingering sadness and regret came through in Simon's tone.
"Perhaps, but so many others died."

"Do not be so hard on yourself. The blame was not yours.
Simon, hold for one moment. Elise just came in from church."

"Simon could hear Jean-Claude explaining who was on the
telephone. A lilting feminine voice sang through the wires.
"Hawk. We miss you. How is your life?"

"My life is fine. Still writing."

"Writing is your work, and that is well and good. But to make the whole life, you need a wife and babies."

"Elise, you're obsessed."

"Do not joke. This is a serious matter. Soon you will be too old, too set in your ways for babies."

"Ah, but Elise, you've always been the woman of my dreams. If only Jean-Claude hadn't found you first."

Elise giggled. "Hawk, you are running from advice because you know I'm right. *Adieu* for now, my friend."

"*Adieu*, Elise."

After a few hours of restless sleep, Simon awoke to a world gone white. He switched on the television to the weather channel. There was a declared state of emergency in St. Lawrence, Lewis, and Jefferson counties. Roads were closed, power lines downed. Many homes and communities were without electricity. The North Country winter was living up to its reputation.

A knock on the suite door disturbed his viewing. He opened it. "Luke?"

"Simon, I could use a little help. Clara called on her cell phone. She's at the rest stop out on the main highway. Can't get down the side road. She said she'd ski in, but she's got two passengers–three month old Irish Wolfhounds. We'll need two sleds and one hell of a big box for those pups. Can you handle an Arctic cat?"

"Sure, but I don't have any gear. Only boots."

"No problem, there's extras in the kitchen store room. Something's bound to fit."

Soon the two men were sloughing through drifts of thigh high snow to the equipment shed where the snow mobiles were garaged. Luke hooked a flat bed sled to his machine and tied a large packing crate to the side rails. "There won't be a trail," he warned. "So hang close."

The sleds turned over with a roar. Luke pulled out into the drive, then cut off cross country. Heavy snow was still falling and the wind was picking up causing a true white out.

The going was slow. Twice the sleds stalled in deep drifts and had to be man handled free. Finally, they hit a sheltered area and the pace picked up.

Nature's fierce beauty surrounded them. The trees were glorious frozen sculptures. The white expanse of open country was incredibly beautiful and equally treacherous. Even with the warm clothing, the bitter wind driven cold seemed to penetrate to the bone.

Once they reached the main highway, there was evidence of other sleds. Just as Simon spotted the roof of a utility vehicle, Luke turned into the drifted rest area. Simon followed suit. As the two men dismounted, a woman in a long sheep skin jacket climbed out of the Jeep. A stocking cap was pulled low over her forehead with big sun glasses concealing much of her face.

Luke gave her a resounding kiss and picked her off the ground in a bear hug. "Welcome home, cuz." He sat her down and called to Simon. "Come on over and meet my cousin, the infamous Clara. Clara, Simon Hawk."

"Clara, my pleasure."

"Hawk. I understand Grandmother bludgeoned you into . . ."

"Not at all. I'm glad to help."

From the Jeep came sharp barks and two furry faces appeared in the rear window.

"Someone is impatient," Simon pointed out. "What say we load those pups and get the hell out of here."

Clara called a warning, "The rear doesn't open, bring them out the front."

Simon opened the passengers' door and was greeted by yips of joy and wet kisses. He laughed at their antics and picked up one of the squirming puppies. "Hey, could one of you give a hand here?"

Luke came to his rescue. They managed to get the two puppies into the waiting box. Clara pulled an old quilt from the Jeep and using a bungi cord to hold it in place, covered its top.

Luke tossed Clara a pair of snowmobile pants. "Put those on." He ordered and handed her a helmet. "Come on, move it. I'm freezing. You can ride double with Simon. I'm hauling the pups."

Gail Elloian

Clara sat on the edge of Luke's sled and pulled her boots free so she could put on the pants. Once dressed, she put on the helmet. "Let's head directly to Hawk House. I've got to get the pups settled."

Two more sleds roared into the parking area and pulled up along side. "Hey, Luke, heard on the CB that you were headed out here. Damn, Clara, you in trouble again?" the man joked.

Clara pulled off a glove and made a gesture that brought a roar of laughter from the men on the sleds.

"Welcome home, Clara," the man on the lead sled said, "Follow us. We'll break a trail back for you."

"Thanks, Art," Clara said with a smile.

"Luke," Art said. "The gangs ready to ride. They'll be at The Haven about the time the bar opens."

"Yeah, yeah, we're set. Let's get the hell out of here."

Simon's sled roared into life and Clara climbed on behind. He glanced over his shoulder. "Ready?"

Clara nodded and leaned into his back.

The wind had died down and clearer visibility made the return trip easier. As they neared The Haven, the lead sled cut off and headed toward the river. It wasn't long before Simon had his first look at Hawk House.

Even though he knew its conception had been his great grandfather's, he thought the house looked like it might have been designed by Franklin Lloyd Wright. The house was of stone and glass with grey slate for the roof. It appeared to rise like a living entity out of the snow–profound isolation, perfectly preserved.

He braked to a stop in front of the wide front entrance. In the stained-glass fan window above the door was a hawk with outspread wings. It was not unlike the one he had so long ago carved into the oak tree at the New Orleans Hawk House. It was irrational but for reasons beyond his comprehension. He wasn't' ready to go inside the original.

Clara freed the Irish wolfhounds and they bounded in joyous release through the drifted snow. In the distance, Simon could see the roof tops of The Haven. "Luke, I'm headed back. Catch you later."

"Wait. I'll ride with you. Clara will need a sled. Clara," he called. "Powers out. I sent Rudy over to start your generator. When you get squared away, come on over. We'll be busy as hell."

Luke climbed behind Simon. Simon glanced over his shoulder. "Busy?"

"Absolutely. Everyone knows we have a generator. Snowmobilers will be out in force. Business as usual."

Back in his suite, Simon pulled on a heavy sweater and jeans. The hot shower had pulled the cold from his body. He was warm and intended to stay that way. The sound of the telephone startled him. "Hello."

"Simon, Luke. Just letting you know that the kitchen is open."

"Thanks, I've got food in the fridge."

"There a problem? You sound out of it."

"I didn't get much sleep last night. Today's writing went nowhere. I'm going to hang here, try the Baton Rouge number. I'll let you know if I find out anything."

"Okay, and thanks for this morning."

"No problem, catch you later."

Outside the wind still howled and snow came in flurries. The storm wasn't over yet. Simon decided he might as well make the Baton Rouge call. He punched in the Louisiana area code and the Toussaint number.

A low timbre voice with a soft Southern drawl answered. "Toussaint residence. Henri speaking."

"Mr. Toussaint, my name is Simon Hawk. I'm calling from The Haven in New York State."

"The Haven . . . why my wife and I honeymooned there nearly thirty years ago. What can I do for you, Sir?"

"I'm trying to find the family of a Jacques Toussaint who spent time in the St. Lawrence river area around nineteen twenty-two, twenty-three."

"This being my birthday, I have imbibed rather more of the bubbly than normal. But I do feel I should ask why you're inquiring."

Simon decided on a variation on the theme. "An old journal has come to light. Jacques Toussaint is prominently mentioned."

"In just what context might that be?"

"The journal suggests he was in partnership with a man named Andre Belmont."

Henri Toussaint chuckled. "That would be my great grand-daddy, 'the bootlegger' as he's fondly referred to at family reunions."

Simon was amused by his candor. "This comes as no surprise."

"Within our family circle it's common knowledge. Old Jacques is why my honeymoon was spent among Yankees. I wanted to see where the family fortune had its beginnings."

"Do you know anything about his partner?"

"Belmont, very little. Would he be the primary reason for your inquiry?"

"As a matter of fact, he is."

"My great granddaddy referred to Belmont as a sadist. He told my father that he once pulled him out of the river–saved his life I believe. Old Jacques smuggled booze but he said Belmont and his Irish counterpart dealt in a more deadly cargo. I understand old Jacques regretted having saved Belmont's life."

"Would you know who this other man was?"

"No, I don't think granddaddy knew either. He preferred not to profit from death."

"Then if your great grandfather's smuggling past came to light it wouldn't trouble you?"

"Mr. . . ."

"Hawk, Simon Hawk."

"Mr. Hawk, I'm a college history professor. Great Granddaddy's fortune allows me the freedom to not publish and not perish. Essentially, I do as I damn well please. His smuggling activities trouble me not at all. It surely didn't damage the Kennedys, nor for that matter the Toussaints. In fact in my reckless youth, I wrote a historical novel, quite well received about just that subject. There surely isn't anyone I know who'd be at all surprised."

"Would you have any idea where Belmont was from or where he might have settled after the bootlegging days?"

"No. It's my understanding that great granddaddy met Belmont through mutual acquaintances in Boston. Tell me, are you Simon Hawk, the novelist?"

"I am."

"Well, Sir, this is a true pleasure. You've given me many hours of enjoyment. I'm proud to make your acquaintance, albeit by telephone. Would there be anything else?"

"No, I think not. If you should remember anything about Belmont, I can be reached at The Haven. Thank you for your help."

"Then if there's nothing more, I'll say goodnight."

Simon put the phone down. Toussaint apparently had nothing he cared to hide. There didn't seem to be much known about the second partner except that he was Irish–guns, Fenians, IRA. Easy enough to perceive gun running as a continuing scenario from then even into now. But did it have any bearing on Libby's death? He'd talk to Luke, let him know what he learned from the Toussaint call. Maybe he'd have a different take.

Simon glanced at his watch. This time of day, Luke would either be in the dining room or taproom. He tried the taproom first. The bar was full, the loud, raucous crowd mirroring the turbulence of the storm. From behind the bar, John caught Simon's eye.

"Luke around?" Simon shouted above the din.

John pointed toward the back entrance. "Office."

Simon maneuvered sideways through the crush at the bar. His way became blocked by Lucinda Melrose. She intimately leaned into his body and pulled his head down for a kiss. Simon took her arms and stepped away.

Luci grabbed his hand. "I've finally found you. I'm not about to let you get away. Where have you been keeping yourself?"

"I've been putting in computer time. I have a deadline to

make," Simon told her with polite resignation.

Luci giggled drunkenly. "All work and no play." Her hand stroked his thigh. "Come on, let's go play."

"Not now, Luci, another time," Simon said.

As he tried to step around her, she insistently moved into his way. His patience at an end, he gripped her shoulders and lifted her out of his path. She stared after him in shocked surprise.

At the taproom's exit, Simon nearly ran into Luke. "Got a minute," he asked?

"Sure, let's go into my office. Can't hear yourself think out here."

Simon followed him into the office and closed the door, grateful for the quiet.

"Make yourself comfortable," Luke offered as she sat down behind his desk. "So did we dig up the right Toussaint?"

Simon sprawled into a chair. "We did. Henri is the great grandson of Jacques. I told him about the journal and he was kind enough to fill in what blanks he could."

"Did he know Toussaint was a bootlegger?"

"Yeah, couldn't care less. The family never has had any interest in nor need to conceal the past. They find the old man colorful."

"What about Belmont?"

"Toussaint thought Jacques hooked up with Belmont in Boston. Jacques saved Belmont's life and regretted it–called Belmont a sadist. So Sylvia may well have been right. It probably was Belmont whom Ethan saw in Georgia."

"Belmont alive and kicking. No wonder Ethan had a heart attack." Luke sighed. "Damn, still nowhere."

"Not quite so fast. Belmont also ran guns with a second partner who is as yet, nameless. But Toussaint said he was Irish–a starting point. I don't know if I mentioned it but a while ago, Susan Fowler pointed me in a different direction. She mentioned the French who came here to escape the French revolution may have shortened or Americanized their names. I've called a friend in France and asked him to run a check on Belmont. If there's anything to find, he'll find it."

"Interesting. And Clara is home. Now you can talk to Joseph Cloud. See if he can make anything out of those drawings. Who knows, they might turn out to be more important than all the rest."

"I'm no expert but the drawings have a different feel than the rest of the journal."

"Keep in mind. Ethan had a massive heart attack."

"It could be that simple," Simon acknowledged. "But Sylvia said he died a few days after returning to Hawk House. Doesn't seem likely he would have had the strength. Even if he did, why drawings?"

"No point in speculating," Luke commented. "Join me for a drink?"

"I'll take a rain check. Lucinda is in there loaded for bear. Just not in the mood."

"Clara begged off too. Maybe it's my deodorant."

"If it's possible, I'd like the three of us to get together tomorrow. I'd like Clara to hook me up with Cloud as soon as possible."

"Works for me. I'll set it up with Clara."

Hawk House

Clara curled in the cushioned seat of her bedroom bay window. In summer the river view was spectacular. Now the river was hidden, concealed beneath the thick, smooth ice, it's frozen surface blanketed by a pristine white cover of new snow. On the floor at the foot of her brass bed, the puppies were curled together sound asleep.

Out of the quiet came a whisper, a soft sigh. The air hung still and expectant. Clara lifted her head, waiting. The strange, haunting silence held her motionless, defenseless against its commanding presence. She closed her eyes. Breathing evenly, she diminished her inner energy.

Images flashed. The glint of flame on a steel blade, splashes of blood like paint on an artist's pellet. The knowing's message washed through her senses. A shadowed face faded in and out. An image slipped away before becoming fully formed. She saw eyes filled with madness, an incomprehensible fury. Who would die? If only she could see.

Down river from Hawk House, the roof of Joseph Cloud's log home barely peeked above the drifts. Smoke came from the chimney and light shone through the frosted windows. As Joseph filled the stove with enough wood to take him through the night, he thought of Clara and of how her discovery of the journal had brought Simon Hawk to The Landing. It was as if the wheel of life was coming full circle.

He picked up Simon Hawk's latest novel. From the reading of his previous books, Joseph felt he and Simon Hawk were already old friends. He would like this Hawk just as he had Duncan and David. Simon's conception of life and death and the futility of war had touched Joseph's very being. It was as if Simon had read his mind.

Joseph Cloud, like Simon Hawk, like Duncan Hawk hated the useless, senseless slaughter of war. He thought of his and Duncan's war. Only those who had lived in the green jungle morass of Viet Nam could understand. One had to have breathed the cloying stink of death, felt it underfoot, seen the streams run red with blood. Only then could the power of nightmares whose presence brought shrieks of anguish be understood. He remembered the many times he had awakened in a cold sweat with tears running down his face. How even in daylight, the demons could still own ones mind. Duncan had said that in Viet Nam death had a life of its own–the eternal paradox. But Duncan was gone and Joseph fought his battle alone.

Joseph shook his head and took a deep breath. Long ago, he

had come to terms with that which was lost. It had taken time but he had managed to climb out of the desolation of the past and was content with his life. His home was his alone. It wrapped around him with the comfort of a warm quilt in winter. With pride, he looked around the large open room with its shelves of books. The wide plank floors he laid with his own hands, a sleeping loft, and on the wall was the painting of the river that Libby had given to him.

Though his life was complete, it was far from what he had once believed his future would be. As a young man, he had viewed his life as a canvas already painted. He would teach, write, raise a family. But this wasn't to be.

Once there had been many women but only one that he had loved. Their love had become bitter and twisted, ending in rage. But after Viet Nam, he no longer had need of a woman. An exploding land mind had taken away his dream of children–of family. His time was shared with no one. It was his alone, and he used it wisely–to study, to write of his ancestors, learn from their past, and their mysticism.

Joseph made himself comfortable in a chair by the wood stove and turned his attention to the Hawk novel. As he read, he heard the humming roar of snow machines climbing the trail along the ridge. Strange, one of them seemed to be pulling into the yard. He got up and reached for the loaded, double-barreled shotgun that hung on a gun rack within easy reach of the front door.

A soft knock came. He opened the peep hole to see who was outside. It could not be, yet it was. He leaned the shot gun against the wall and opened the door. Firelight glinted on the blade that slit his throat. His arms reached out and clutched for his killer. A strong arm pushed him away and he fell backwards, sightlessly staring into the black abyss.

Dead, pitiless eyes watched the pooling blood drain the life from his body. "You always were too trusting."

Clara pressed her head against the cold window pane of her bedroom at Hawk House. Her breathing was shallow from the tightness in her chest. Her body trembled. Death had come, a ghost from out of time who had been one with the past and was now claiming the present. She grieved but knew not for whom.

The Haven

In the Haven's small family dining room, Luke rearranged the white lilies on the table for the third time. White linen, candles, crystal, china, silver. Fire in the fireplace. Perfect. Since neither Clara nor Simon cared for red meat, Bouillabaisse was a safe choice. Hot cheese bread, garden salad. White wine–a pouily fussie would do. For dessert . . . cheese cake. No, he decided, too heavy. Cloud cake–filo dough layered with custard and cream and topped with delicate lemon sauce. Just right. No doubt about it, he was a master.

Satisfied, Luke went out into the lobby where the bellhops were doing their best to settle in the arriving members of the New York State Bar Association. This was their annual midwinter conference. Three days of more play than work. Given the storm, it was surprising how few had canceled. He made a mental list of their needs. Welcoming fruit baskets and fresh flowers were already in their rooms. Conference rooms reserved and set up. All the bases were covered.

Sam Maitland, Luke's assistant manager who only moments before had made it back from a wedding in London, crossed the lobby. "Sorry, Luke. Flight out of Heathrow was delayed and for some unknown reason we circled Syracuse for over an hour."

"No problem. The storm has everything screwed up."

"How did the wedding go?"

"Great. It was good to see family." He glanced around the lobby at the semi-organized turmoil. "Well, best I get to work."

"Good to have you back," Luke told him. "We'll catch up later," he said and went on into the taproom.

Simon waited at the bar nursing a drink. "So, I'll finally meet Clara."

"Meet her? You met her yesterday."

"Not exactly. I was introduced to a sheep skin coat and sun glasses."

"No time like the present. She's coming in now."

Simon turned and saw her walk into the barroom. Gunnar Lindquist had been right. She radiated magnetism and something else–a vital kind of aliveness.

Clara held out a slim, white hand. "Hawk, at last we meet. Yesterday all I saw was a helmet and your back."

Simon took her hand. "I'm glad we've rectified the oversight. May I get you a drink?"

"I think John is just bringing me one."

John handed Clara a glass of white wine. "Missed you, lady." And with a conspiratorial wink at Luke, he went back down the bar to quench the thirst of a group of lawyers ready to unwind.

Simon watched Clara. Sea green eyes in a bold, sculpted face. Pale flawless skin with a strong mouth that was both determined and sensual. Hair that was an indescribable shade of red falling to her narrow waist. Yes, she was beautiful but a beauty he couldn't categorize. Her ankle length black dress was of soft wool belted with an intricately wrought silver concho belt. Simon touched the silver. "Beautiful belt."

"Thank you."

"How are the pups doing?"

"Rambunctious but fine. As yet unnamed."

Luke put his arm around Clara's waist. "What say we three adjourn to the dining room."

Dinner was superlative as Simon had known it would be. Yet he found himself concentrating far more on Clara than on his food. Luke poured each of them a second glass of wine. "Clara,

Simon thinks the drawings in the journal might be of Indian origin. I suggested Joseph was the man to talk too."

Clara nodded. "Jospeh is the man . . . unfortunately, he hasn't as yet had a chance to read the journal. He's been up in Canada researching myths and legends of the people."

"Luke mentioned he's written several books on Indian lore."

"Yes, well received. An off shoot of his life style. Joseph doesn't believe that the earth belongs to man but rather that man belongs to the earth. He lives close to nature, values his privacy. Which isn't to say he doesn't have friends, just that he picks them carefully."

"An individualist," Simon commented. "But then everyone's world is based on personal impression. We all have our own truths."

"I've a feeling you and Joseph will hit it off," Clara said without surprise. "He likes your books. He said you write with incisive knowledge, but without the necessity of proving yourself right."

Simon found that he immediately felt comfortable with this woman. There was risk in that, danger in the attraction she held. "Someone once said the ultimate paradox is that the man who thinks he knows, doesn't. He who knows that he doesn't know, knows."

"Sounds familiar," Clara said.

Luke kept his face expressionless. His gut had told him that Clara and Simon would like each other. In fact would be perfect for each other. He had promised Simon that he would respect his privacy but if nature took its course, Simon couldn't blame him. "Gosh, Luke, great meal." "Why thank you." He tossed his napkin on the table. "You will excuse me while I tuck in the bar association. I'll be back for coffee and dessert. Try not to miss me."

Clara smiled at Simon. "All my life, I've heard about the Hawks. You're the first one I've met."

"I thought you knew my grandfather."

Clara shook her head. "Adam, no we've never met. We did all our business via the telephone." She paused and looked speculatively at Simon. "Outside of your books, I don't know anything about you."

"Come on now, I'd wager your grandmother has brought you up to speed. Let's say that what I write pretty much reflects who I am. How about you?"

Her green eyes had a smoky softness. "Me. . . let's see. Growing up I was two people. I used to feel like the characters in the story of the city mouse and the country mouse. The city me lived in a world of intellectuals and idealistic goals. I was taught to define the fights worth fighting."

"How about the country you?"

Clara's eyes lit up. "The county me spent summers right here at The Haven."

"So tell me about life here in The Landing."

"Here life was the river and nature. A discovery of my more spiritual side . . ." Her voice trailed off and she fell into silence.

Simon instinctively realized that her thoughts had drifted into areas she didn't care to discuss. Easy enough to perceive what it was. "Luke and your grandmother mentioned the knowing. How does it factor in . . . and if you don't mind what is it?"

"Omnipresent. Anywhere I lived there was always the knowing."

"Is it difficult to live with?"

Clara shrugged in dismissal. "It can be." The previous night's knowing replayed in her mind. Flames on a blade, eyes filled with fury–death.

Simon watched her eyes grow sad and wanted to somehow ease her distress. "Clara can you tell me a little of what happens? How it happens?"

"It comes when it wills and in different ways. I see events, things that will happen, things that have been. The knowing shows me flashes but usually not enough to change or prevent what I've perceived." Tears stood in her eyes. "It's all so useless." She felt Simon's warm hand on her arm. She didn't draw away or acknowledge the touch. "I know when people are lying. It's not that I can read minds. It's more subtle, like distant whispering where you hear only fragments."

"How have you handled it?" Simon wondered aloud.

"For a time, not well. I couldn't understand what was happening. I only wanted it to stop. I tried drugs, alcohol, anything to make it go away."

"Obviously you've found a solution."

"Yes. Thanks to Joseph Cloud."

"How so?"

"One night I was drunk, out of control, underage and surfing at Sailors." Clara looked at him and smiled. "Have you been surfing yet?"

"Not yet, but I've been told it will be an experience. Go on with your story."

"Joseph hustled me out of Sailors and took me out on the river in his sloop. He kept me there until I was straight. Out on the water there was only his world. He made me see that fear is the greatest destroyer of self. That I had to find a way to balance the knowing, to live courageously and decently in the way of nature."

"The balance between the physical and the metaphysical," Simon softly added. "The yin and the yang."

Clara nodded. "Joseph suggested the martial arts. Eventually, once I learned to control my mind and my body, the knowing became manageable. In college I studied Eastern mysticism and its philosophy. It helped, too." She toyed with the ends of the silver concho belt. "Joseph gave me this in acknowledgment of my first black belt."

Before Simon could comment, Lucinda Melrose strolled into the room. "Clara, I heard you were back."

"Hello, Luci."

"I see you've already corralled the sexiest man around. I guess we'll have to share. Hello, Simon."

"Lucinda."

Uninvited, Lucinda sat down at the table. "We girls are frolicking Wednesday at Molly's. Care to join us, Clara?"

"Probably, it's been awhile."

"The inference being?"

"None, Luci. I'm looking forward to it."

Lucinda stood. "Well, I'm with Mother. We're planing a surprise birthday bash for Father. And Clara, be careful. This one hits and runs. Ta."

Clara took a deep breath. She glanced at Simon and looked away. It was as though she had been punched in the stomach. What had prompted her to tell this man, this stranger, so much about herself? She wished she had kept her silence.

Simon was angry with himself, with Lucinda. A meaningless interlude but one which might cut him off from a woman who could conceivably mean something to him. He waited until Clara again faced him. "Since I've been here, it's been my observation that everyone screws everyone. If that sounds coarse or crude, I apologize. Lucinda is a consenting adult. As am I. Obviously, she wants me to consent to more than I choose to. When I met you tonight, I thought . . ."

She tersely cut him short. "I don't play that game."

"You didn't let me finish," he mildly censored. "Unfortunately, I'm afraid Lucinda just set up a barrier I won't be able to penetrate." He lifted his wine glass in a toast. "Morality and honor are on the endangered list. You're a rare species." He sat the glass down. "I'll leave you to your wine."

Clara's solitariness was a weapon against emotion but Simon Hawk caused a stirring deep inside. She wanted to trust him. Simon looked into her eyes and saw something fathomless and terribly, terribly sad. He involuntarily reached for her hand. His fingers' hard and calloused protectively covered hers.

Clara heard the beat of wings and a fading chant. Her voice was a whisper to be heard only by him. "Stay if you wish."

Simon slowly withdrew his hand and took a long swallow of his wine. His eyes never left her face.

"Why are you staring?"

"You're extraordinarily beautiful," he told her as though the admission came as a surprise.

"Don't."

"No, no," he said with raised palms. "It wasn't intended to coerce you into bed. I've been so busy listening, learning who you really are that how you look became incidental. I've a feeling I can know you for the rest of my life and never complete the puzzle."He smiled a hesitant half smile.

Clara listened. His voice, his compassion made her feel vulnerable, chipping away at the wall the knowing had built around her. She found herself smiling back as he continued to speak. "Please give me time to try."

Luke approached the table and sat down next to Clara. "Clara, honey. I'm afraid there's bad news."

Simon saw the distress in Luke's eyes, head the tender concern in his tone, and knew a tragedy had occurred.

Luke took both of Clara's hands in his. "Damn, Clara. I don't know how to tell you . . . Joseph's dead, murdered."

The color left Clara's face. "How did he die?"

Luke knew Clara would only be satisfied with the truth. "The chief said his throat was cut."

Clara's eyes went blank. The knowing was done. Joseph was dead. "Last night around eleven."

Neither Luke nor Simon needed to ask how she knew.

"Who found him?" Clara said in a choked voice.

"Mike said the Kensington boys were riding sleds down on the river trail. When they went by the cabin, Danny saw Joe's dog howling at the door. He went to see what was wrong."

"Where's Dog?"

"Mike had to call Doc Coons. Dog wouldn't let them touch Joe's body. Doc used a tranquilizer dart to put him asleep for a while. He's out in the car. Can you take him?"

"Of course," Clara said as silent tears ran unnoticed down her face. "Have Mike take him to my house. Luke, would you please call the reservation and let Joseph's friends know. Tell them we'll get together tonight about midnight, surfing at Sailors."

"You're sure, Clara?"

"Joseph thought of death as a new beginning. He always said when he died he wanted music and song. A celebration of life."

Luke gave Clara a hug. "I'll be there. Maybe Simon will come. His is an objective eye. He might see something you and I would miss."

"Yes, of course. Joseph would want a Hawk."

Simon followed Luke's directions and turned right toward the St. Lawrence. In the plowed space in front of Sailors, banks of snow rose above the roofs of the pickup trucks. Snow machines were scattered among them like abandoned toys.

Luke pointed to an empty spot at the side of the ramshackle log building. Simon parked and shut off the Cherokee's engine. "Quite a place."

"Our local den of iniquity. Every town's got one. A late night place where a semi-respectable crowd shows up for what is generally known as slumming. 'Course we're to high class for that, we surf," Luke smugly said. "Rock and Roll, country music, and if your stomach is up to it, breakfast."

A Lincoln Continental pulled in next to the Jeep. Simon recognized Lucinda Melrose. The put-together blonde older version must be her mother, Corrine Melrose. "Luke, who's the older woman leaning on Lucinda's arm?"

"Anne Soames, the first Molly's sister. She's got to be in her nineties."

Simon watched the women make their way to the front entrance. "Why would they all be here?"

"Joseph put himself through college working at Molly's. Anne Soames took care of him like a son. Corrine and Joe were part of the group who hung together–Hawks, Dunns, Pillards and so on. Luci. She's probably here because she hates to miss a party."

Inside Simon looked around the crowded room. Quaint was his kindest thought. The tables were made from barrels with stained plywood tops. Chairs were of batter proof metal. The walls and ceilings were grayed with smoke. The long mahogany bar was already three deep with only a few tables left open. At the further end of the room, a band hammered out Bob Seger's 'Old Time Rock and Roll'.

Simon and Luke found standing room at the bar. "You're right," Simon admitted. "I've seen a reasonable facsimile of this bar in every town I've ever been in. You can't miss the pungent aroma of old sweat, stale tobacco, and beer."

"Let's not forget the underlying aroma of ode 'de old cooking oil," Luke added. "And behind the bar we have Jumbo, bartender and owner."

Simon glanced at the man behind the bar. He was no more than five feet two or three and whippet thin. "Jumbo?"

"Refers to the size of his heart. Jumbo's the softest touch in town."

Simon looked around and saw that Lucinda Melrose and her group had managed to find a table. Simon recognized a number of people–a doctor, two lawyers, an accountant, several teachers. He thought that Joseph's Clouds friends were an eclectic mix. Indians from the reservation. Women he had seen at The Haven were here in their designer jeans and imported hand knit sweaters. Other men and women dressed in flannel shirts and Levi's represented the working class. Doctors, lawyers, truckers, boatmen, construction workers, teachers. Joseph Cloud had been well loved.

Late arrivals grabbed a drink from the bar, and leaned against the log walls. The volume of the music lowered and attention turned to the stage where Clara stood. She held a microphone in one hand, a beer in the other. Her face was composed but her voice was husky with emotion. "We're all here tonight to celebrate the life of Joseph Cloud. Joseph always said that death is a myth. The body a prison which inhibits us. He believed that once liberated from this body, we merge with the endless sea of pure knowledge.

"Tonight, Joseph's spirit is free to sing the world song. To walk the spirit path, to rest awhile upon the wind." She raised the beer in a toast. "To Joseph Cloud."

All glasses rose. "To Joseph Cloud."

Clara spoke again. "Tonight its open bar. Drinks are on me. The food later is on Jumbo."

The lead guitar player stepped forward. "You all know Joe's favorites. So get your dancing shoes on. We'll play 'em. Clara'll sing 'em. You folks just jump in when you feel like it."

Clara and the guitar player sang together, playing one off the other. The walls seemed to rock with voices joining in on the chorus. The first song ended and flowed directly into John Denver's Rocky Mountain High.

Simon was enthralled. Clara's voice was like warm honey, low, pleasing, and sensual. Lucinda jealously watched Simon and saw that he looked only at Clara. She finished her drink and motioned to the waitress for another.

The light's dimmed and the guitarist raised his hands for attention. "Listen up folks. Clara'll sing Joe's favorite, a Garth Brook's song. The Dance. If the spirit moves you, sing along."

The guitarist switched to an acoustic guitar and played the opening bars. Clara sang with plaintive sadness. The song reached deep into the hearts of the audience. The words giving meaning to each of their separate memories. By the time Clara reached the chorus, the crowd, voices choked with tears, joined in and sang, " I could have missed the pain, but I'd have had to miss the dance."

The touching song ended and with a grin the guitarist said, "And a second favorite of Joe's . . ." The band changed tempo and the guitarist sang, "I've got friends in low places. Where the whiskey flows . . ." The song was greeted with hoots of laughter and the dance floor began to fill.

Clara wove her way through the tables and grabbed Luke's hand. "Dance with me."

Corrine Melrose came to Simon's side. "Mr. Hawk, please allow me to introduce myself, I'm Corrine Melrose. I knew your father and uncle well."

"Mrs. Melrose."

"Corrine."

"And I'm Simon."

"Do you plan on being in the area long?" She asked.

"Possibly. I've been toying with the idea of making The Landing my home base."

"How nice. You'll be a permanent resident. It'll be wonderful to have a member of the Hawk family back in town."

"Thank you."

"Luci told me you've found a journal of Ethan Hawk's. Do you honestly think there might be a connection to Libby's murder?"

"It's a possibility."

Corrine eyes grew sad with memory. "I don't think I'll ever forget that time. Libby dead, Duncan gone."

"Were you and Libby friends?"

"Oh, yes, for most of our lives. My family always summered here. They have an island just off the point. Of course, since I married, The Landing has been my home."

Lucinda intrusively joined them. "Gee, now that Joe's out of the picture. It'll be amusing to see whom Clara fucks next."

"Lucinda, that was uncalled for," Corrine snapped.

Simon picked up his beer. "Nice meeting you, Corrine." He walked past Lucinda as though she didn't exist and leaned against a wall at the edge of the dance floor.

A tall, dark-haired man in jeans and a red and black plaid flannel shirt cut in on Clara and Luke. Luke relinquished her and joined Simon. "I need a cold one. How about you?"

"No thanks. I'll coast. This looks like a long night."

Luke looked around at the crowd. "By the time I get waited on you'll be ready."

The song ended and the band announced a break. Blaring music from the juke box filled in the vacancy. The side door slammed open and a group of men piled into the room. A tall barrel chested man in a down jacket and jeans, shouted, "came to celebrate. It's time somebody took out the stinkin' breed."

He swaggered across the dance floor shoving people out of his way. "And here's Clara. The grievin' widow." He grabbed Clara's arm and pulled her to face him.

Before Simon could react, Luke handed him a beer. "Here drink this and stay cool. She'll handle it."

Clara looked up into the bearded face. "I'll ask you just this once. Take your hands off me."

"Watch it bitch. You ain't got a protector to save your ass."He obscenely jerked his hips. "What you need is a real man. I'll teach you what fuckin's all about." He grabbed for Clara.

She wasted no time with another warning. Her hand chopped into his throat, transforming laughter into a gasping gargle. Before he could counter, Clara had spun out of his reach. She came down on her right foot, and with her booted left foot snapped a kick into his groin. Shock and pain doubled him over. On his way down Clara delivered a backhand fist to his face. Blood spurted from his nose and he collapsed to his knees holding his crotch.

Clara stood in front of him. "Touch me again and fucking anyone or anything will be permanently out of the question."

Jumbo came out from behind the bar. "Okay boys, take out the garbage. And Clara, next time skip the blood. It stains the floor."

The band played a riff and kicked into high gear. The dance floor filled and the incident was soon forgotten. Clara danced first with one man then another, leaving the dance floor only long enough to grab a quick beer.

Luke and Simon found space at the bar. Simon watched Clara. "Is she going to all right?"

"Not right away," Luke said honestly. "She'll drink tonight. Tomorrow she'll hide. Nobody will see her until she works her way through it."

"Who was the guy she put away?"

"Red Delaney. He's one of the Flat's ass holes. He's had the hots for Clara for years."

"The Flats?"

"Stay east on the main road out of town about three miles. On the right there's a run down trailer park. Losers, boozers, druggies–bikers hang there in the summer."

"Who's the guy in the red and black shirt that keeps asking her to dance?"

"John Cloud. He's Joe's nephew. Simon, why not just go and dance with her."

"I'm not sure I'm up to it."

Luke grinned. "She isn't easy, just worth the trouble. But

you'll have to figure her out for yourself. She's always been something of a mystery. Even to me."

Corrine Melrose came to the bar. Tears stood in the corners of her eyes. "Simon, may I impose on your good nature and ask you to dance with me? The way you're standing there . . . you could be Duncan. All the good ones are gone. Duncan now Joe."

Simon held out his hand and smiled. "It would be my pleasure."

The music was Cajun country. A sound that for Simon called up memories of the Louisiana bayous. Corrine easily followed his lead. "You dance Cajun style very well," he complimented.

"Your uncle taught me far more years ago than I care to remember."

When the song ended, Corrine smiled her thanks and disappeared.

Simon turned and through the crowd saw Clara at the bar. He caught her eye and mouthed, "Dance?"

She walked toward him and into his arms. Her body was slender, but Simon could feel smooth muscle over flexible bone. He thought of what he knew of her. From what he had seen and heard, some held her in awe because of her strangeness. He suspected that even those who had known her since childhood professed to an intimacy never achieved. Clara was an enigma whose separateness created myth.

They danced in silence. When the song ended, Clara slipped from his arms and was gone. Simon watched her sidestep through the crowd making her way toward the back door.

Luke joined Simon. "Where's she going?"

"She didn't say."

A few minutes later, Chief Mike O'Connor joined Simon and Luke. "Just saw Clara outside. Said she had to go check on the dogs."

Simon took a long pull of his beer. "Can you tell us anything about the murder?"

"Not much. When Danny found Joe rigor mortis was complete. He'd been dead twelve, fourteen hours, probably longer.

Throat slashed deep from left to right. Wide blade, razor sharp, likely a hunting knife."

"So we know the killer is strong. About the same height as the victim and right-handed" Simon reflectively said. "Where was the body found?"

"Just inside the front door. His shotgun was resting against the wall."

Luke frowned. "Doesn't play. If Joe opened the door and put the gun down, it had to be someone he knew and trusted. Why would anyone what him dead? Where's motive?"

Chief O'Connor put his foot up on the brass rail and leaned against the bar. "If there'd been a break-in, signs of a struggle. Then I could think of possibilities. Joe tagged a bunch of smugglers out on the river. Damn fools were smuggling drugs. Cigarettes, Joe would've looked the other way."

"What do you mean," Simon asked?

"Around here it's a time-honored tradition. Most Indian kids buy their first truck with the money they make smuggling cigarettes. Drugs are a different story. Joe's testimony put them away. Red Delany. He's hated Joe's guts ever since Joe kicked the shit out of him for plaguing Clara."

Simon glanced at Luke. "Did you mention to anyone other than Clara that we wanted Joseph to read the journal and see what he could make of the drawings?"

"Nope."

The chief frowned. "You trying to tie this to the journal?"

"Let me ask you this," Simon said. "How many murders have there been in The Landing since Libby Hawk was killed?"

The Chief thought for a moment. "Couple drug related. One out at the Flats. Another on a boat docked out back of here. Five, six years ago, Jimmy Smith shot his wife and her lover. Caught them buck naked in his bed."

"The weapon in each was?"

"Gun. One dealer was beaten to death."

"Joseph Cloud was killed with a knife. Didn't the knife that killed Libby have a broad blade, razor sharp?"

Luke's tone was thoughtful. "The Clouds have been around here at least as long as the Hawks and the Dunns. In the early days, what happened to one pretty much happened to all. Maybe there's something in that journal that the killer wouldn't have wanted Joe to see."

The Chief took a swallow of his beer. "Simon has suggested that maybe Libby or Duncan was the first to find the damn thing. Are we headed in the direction of the journal being what precipitated Libby's murder and Duncan's disappearance?"

Simon enlarged on the Chief's trend of thought. "The killer also trashed Hawk House. If we follow the same line of reasoning, he or she was looking for the journal but didn't find it. It was too well hidden. In the present, Clara discovers it. It follows that Libby's killer would still be concerned about the contents of the journal."

Luke shook his head. "I don't see it. Joe is killed to prevent him from reading the journal. Makes no sense. We've all read it."

Simon took a swallow of his beer. "Maybe the killer thinks there was something in the journal that would've had meaning to Joseph. Something meaningless to the rest of us."

Corrine Melrose tapped the Chief on the shoulder. "Mike, forgive me, but your car has mine blocked in. Luci is having a hissy. She wants to leave. Oh, Simon, before I forget. Anne Soames would like to speak with you in private."

"Now?"

"No, she said tomorrow. Anytime it's convenient for you. Her house is on Riverwalk and Oak. The corner lot."

"Tell her I'll be there at one."

The Chief finished his beer. "All set, Corrine. Simon, Luke, be seeing you."

Hawk House

Clara dozed on the couch. The puppies had romped them-selves into exhaustion and were sleeping on the rug in front of the fireplace. Dog. Still, groggy from the tranquilizer was curled next to her on the floor.

The party would still be going strong. She should go back and honor Joseph's memory. No, she decided. Too much to drink, too tired. Her breathing slowed and she drifted in the netherworld between sleep and dream. Soon the knowing came. This time she bore witness to a past that though familiar was not as yet complete.

The night was suffocating darkness as if with the absence of light all oxygen had gone from the air. Madeleine's lungs labored to breathe. She could feel him out there in the menacing silence waiting, watching. As she ran down the incline, her feet slid on the damp pine needles and she stumbled heavily against a tree. With her arms protectively cradling her rounded stomach, she rested against the pine's rough bark. Nowhere left to run. She would die because her own sense of honor was in conflict with his purpose.

Once she had loved him, trusted him until the old man with his stories of the past had forced her to see the truth of the present. The old man was gone now. He had died in the flames of his burn-ing cottage. So many dead, dead because they like she had believed in him.

A breeze came across the water and cooled the sweat on her body. She fought against her rising despair. He hadn't come for her but for the baby. He wanted the child and he would have it. Even if it meant her death.

The stench of a decaying animal wafted from out of the under-brush and made her stomach churn. A far off rustle in the brush startled her and her head snapped toward the sound. She stared into the darkness, listening, waiting, afraid to move in any direc-tion. Move. She had to move. To stay meant death.

She pushed away from the tree and cautiously made her way along the track made slick and dangerous by the rain that whispered through the pines. Sharp pain radiated from her lower back and down her legs. Dear God, she would lose her baby.

Again came a sound, then another each closer than the last. She picked up her pace and awkwardly ran toward the river. The effort brought sharp, stabbing pain that drove her to her knees. Panting to breathe, she struggled to her feet and staggered down the slope to where the path followed the edge of the bluff. Her feet slid on the gravel and she grabbed at a bush to slow her descent. She glanced back and saw a rustle of movement. A shape came into view. He had found her.

His voice came out of the fog. "Come now, darling girl, don't move, stand still. You're close to the edge. Please stay still. I promise I mean you no harm."

"Stay away. Stay away."

"I cannot. You'll fall. Just walk toward me. You'll be safe." He reached out a hand."

His face swam before her eyes. "No. Stay away," she gasped. "You can't have my child."

He stepped closer, arms out reaching. Then she was falling.

Clara shivered and came awake. How terrible the knowing had been. She had felt evil . . . the man, but who he was hadn't been seen. The knowing had been very detailed but for that—and strange and terrible. Strange in that she had never known her great-aunt Madeleine had been pregnant. Terrible that in all probability Madeleine's greatest fear had been realized and she had lost her baby. One aspect was clear. Tonight's knowing would have bearing on an event yet to be.

Simon drove slowly down the drive for Hawk House. Clara hadn't come back to Sailors and he wanted to be sure she was all right. Not quite the truth. Fact of the matter was that he wanted to see her. Talk to her—to know her.

As he rounded the bend, he could see that the lights were on in the house. Grey-blue smoke ribboned out of the chimney streaking the clear night sky. He shut the engine off and got out of the Jeep. The limbs of trees twisted in dark definition against the white landscape. As he slowly walked toward the house, he heard the snow creak beneath his feet. His breath came in frozen puffs.

The closer he came to Hawk House, the more reluctant he was to enter. Why? Why this persistent feeling that if he went inside, he would never leave? He raised the door knocker.

From inside the house came the menacing growl of a dog. He banged the knocker again and the growl became a rumbling, deep throated bark accompanied by the excited yips of the Irish wolfhound puppies. The second knock pulled Clara from the couch. She flicked on the outside lights and opened the door. "Simon," she said. "Come on in. I must have fallen asleep."

Simon frowned at her carelessness in opening the door before finding out who was on the other side. He forced a smile to take the sting from his words. "Clara, there's a killer out there some-where. Might be a good idea to know who's on the other side of the door before you open it."

"Warning taken," she sleepily acknowledged.

The Irish wolfhounds circled Simon begging for attention. He bent down and tumbled them onto their backs and scratched their stomachs. Dog paced the perimeter making certain the stranger was welcome.

"That's it guys," Clara told the puppies. "Back to bed."

"You heard her," Simon said. "Where do you want them?"

"By the fire."

Simon walked to the fireplace and snapped his fingers in invi-tation. The puppies ambled to his side and discovering that play-time was over laid back down.

"How about an Irish coffee," Clara asked as though his pres-ence was natural and expected. "I got chilled when I was sleep-ing. Something warm would hit the spot."

"Sounds good." The house captured Simon's attention. The main floor was open space–great room, dining area, kitchen, and a curving, open stairway that seemed to float up to a balustered balcony. Oak beams along with the furniture defined the living space with broad windows facing toward the river.

The house had the presence of a great legacy–an immortal statement which transcended time. "You wouldn't want to sell Hawk House would you?" He asked with a smile.

Even though Clara knew his question was rhetorical, she answered, "No, never. But feel free to look around. I'll fix the coffee."

As Simon wandered through the main floor, the house cast its spell ensnaring him with its all encompassing peace. He understood why the New Orleans house had never seemed like home. This was where the Hawks belonged.

Clara handed Simon a tall, crystal mug. "Shall we sit down?"

Simon followed Clara to the long leather couch and sat down. "Clara, this is a wonderful place. You're fortunate to have it."

"Hawk House has always meant more to me than any other. I can't tell you why." She impishly grinned. "In fact when I was a teenager I used to sneak in and hang out. I had a stash of food, sleeping bag. That is until Grandmother found out."

"I can imagine–grounded. Clara, if you don't mind my asking. Where did you find the journal?"

Clara sat her coffee mug down on a marble topped stand. "Follow me."

At the book shelves to the right of the fireplace, she bent down and removed what appeared to be a particularly long nail. With a light touch of her hand the book case swung out from the wall. Carved into the stone wall was a recess large enough for several books.

"How did you happen to come on this?" Simon said.

"By accident. The hardwood floors were water damaged, badly in need of refinishing. I tackled the job myself. When I was sanding this area, the sander hit a loose peg. I pulled it out with the intention of gluing it back in place or replacing it. You can see it isn't an ordinary peg. Only its head is wood the rest is steel."

"Ingenious." Simon pushed the book case back and replaced the spike.

"Would you like to see the rest of the house?"

"Very much."

Simon again followed Clara. She led him up the open stair-case. At its top was a long, wide gallery its shelves filled with books, and CD's. Overstuffed chairs created an area of comfort. In between the shelves was an oval stained glass window running from floor to ceiling. "I could spend a lot of time here," he said as if to himself.

Clara opened a door at the end of the loft. "This is the mas-ter bedroom, my room."

Simon stepped inside. Spacious with a fieldstone fireplace. A large brass bed was against one wall. In an alcove was a Queen Anne vanity and pier mirror. Opposite the bed was a broad bay window underneath which was a deep cushioned window seat and pillows. "I'll bet you sit there and watch the river."

"Yes, you're right I do," she said. "This is the only room in this wing. In the other wing there's three guest suites. You can explore them another time.

"Let's go down. I'd like you to see my addition. It's the only structural change that I made. I took great pains to be certain the integrity of the original design wasn't compromised."

Behind the staircase, Clara opened a double set of doors into a vast room with an enormous skylight. The floor was of oak, much of which was covered my mats whose color had faded in the sun to a grey blue luster. "My personal dojo," she needlessly explained.

To Simon the space was as familiar as self. A space that exuded discipline and humility, sanctity and solemnity. "You cer-tainly got this one right."

In Clara's mind she could hear Joseph Cloud telling her to share her life only with those who could understand and know her true self. She wanted to believe Simon Hawk would be able to do just that. "You're welcome to work out here. I've free weights, a treadmill. The gym at The Haven gets very crowded."

"I'd like to," Simon told her as they walked back into the great room.

"Party still going on?" Clara asked as she curled into the corner of the couch.

Simon seated himself at the opposite end. "Still people around but it was getting pretty drunk out."

"Joseph would be amused."

"Would he be amused by the gossip linking the two of you?"

Clara stared into the fire. "No. He never was. And the answer to your unspoken question is, no. No, we weren't lovers."

"But he was important to you."

"Yes. He meant more to me than I can say. He was not only my friend but my mentor . . . he was family and I loved him."

Simon watched the play of shadows across her face. "Clara, why did you let people think you were lovers? You're very forth right. It's hard to believe you'd let it slide."

Clara wondered how he perceived a truth no one else had ever questioned. He deserved an honest answer but could she trust him? She was afraid her judgment was centered more in need than in reality. But there was a certainty that she could neither lie to him nor evade the question. Joseph would understand. "Joseph did a tour in Viet Nam. He was damaged. His injuries rendered him impotent."

"How tragic. It must have been a horrific adjustment for him to make."

Clara nodded. "You can see why he'd rather it wasn't common knowledge. Still, once he was back home women sought him out. Through the years each seemed to think he was committed elsewhere because there were no rumors, at least not concerning his sexual prowess. In fact one woman even went so far as to claim he had fathered her child."

"How ironic. Did he have to go through the blood test scenario?"

"Sure. Consequently when he and I became friends, even with the age difference, people were quick to assume the obvious."

"So you decided to let their assumptions be a public truth. And Joseph retains his pride and dignity." Simon gave Clara a salute. "You are a very wise and compassionate woman. Joseph was lucky to have you in his life."

"I'm lucky he was in mine. Even being as damaged as he was. Joseph lived life more fully than anyone I've ever known."

Simon felt a stab of envy. "The true rapture of being alive. I envy him. Living, loving . . ." his voice trailed into silence.

"Joseph said that before we're able to love, one must come to terms with whom we are–flaws and virtues. All my life the knowing kept me apart. How do you explain to someone that most of the time, you feel like a culmination of many women? Of the first Clara, of Aunt Libby, of my great-aunt Maddy. I dream their dreams. Sometimes I think it's my obligation to fulfill their destinies."

"You just did."

Clara looked startled. "I did what?"

"You explained. I understood." Simon thought that he had been waiting a long time for Clara. They had only just met, yet he felt he knew her, knew the person hidden in the closed private space of her soul. "I think our problem is that you and I need more than . . ." he gestured aimlessly as if their surroundings were less than nothing. "We need passion but haven't as yet discovered for what or whom. Maybe our truths aren't much different." He fixed Clara with a piercing look. "Have you ever been in love? Passionately loved someone?"

"No, not in the sense you mean. I've had a few passionate affairs but no one I couldn't live without or for that matter with."

Simon was amused by her evaluation. His story wasn't much different. "We must be kindred spirits. Years ago a woman I thought I loved married my father. As I experienced more of life, I could see that many relationships evolve out of a biological itch. When she and I met again, I realized I couldn't care less."

Clara laughed. "Married your father. I can see where you might have been a trifle miffed."

"At the time. Now Dad and Nicole are about to have their first child. I'm very happy for them."

Clara abruptly changed the subject. "Simon, Joseph's murder. Do you think it's connected to the journal?"

"At least to the journal's first appearance."

"First?"

"Luke and the Chief and I were speculating earlier that Libby and Duncan may have been the first to find it. The ring worn by Belmont or one similar was found in her studio."

Clara frowned. "Yes, but that was a long time after Libby's death."

"True. But it seems likely that Libby's fingers were broken trying to hold on to it. In the struggle the ring fell through the floor boards."

"And when it was found it meant nothing," Clara mused. "Now with the journal surfacing it does."

"Exactly."

"Before Joseph was killed, I was going to ask you to forget the whole thing. I was concerned that dredging up the past would cause more harm than good. It seems I was right. Now I'm afraid that without a resolution more people will die."

"Afraid or is it the knowing?"

Clara shrugged. "A little of both. Simon, I know, as Joseph would say, that you walk your own path."

"Do I hear a question?"

"Before writing became your profession what did you do?"

"Our illustrious government recruited me right out of Harvard. I had the required credentials for the post. The right schools, the right background." The contempt he felt for a life he had put aside was defined by the bitterness in his eyes. "My job was to move, blend in if you will with the upper echelon. To do this, it was necessary to modify my morals. When I began to see the battle wasn't between right and wrong but between right and right, I quit."

"And so began your career as a writer." Clara speculatively watched Simon. "Our families are bonded by blood, by values, by intertwined finances. What happens to one happens to the other."

"Clara, say what you mean. What does the knowing tell you?"

Clara shivered and rubbed her arms. "Lately it's becoming stronger and comes more frequently. Nothing is clear. Revenge, a struggle for power, deaths yet to come. So much is hidden. I think the Dunes and the Hawks are going to need all their considerable resources to survive. But beyond our personal survival there is something far more important."

"I sure as hell don't have the answers." Simon finished his Irish coffee. "Anne Soames asked to see me tomorrow."

"She's a remarkable woman. She and Joseph were very close. She thought of him as a son."

"Do you know her well?"

Clara smiled and nodded. "She used to call me her wild child."

"Go with me tomorrow?"

"If you like, sure."

From outside came a low, muffled roar.

"Sounds like a snow machine pulling in," Simon said.

Clara pulled the curtain aside and looked out the window. "It's Luke. Must be important or he would have just called." She opened the front door. "Aren't you out a little late?"

Luke came into the house carrying a bottle of champagne. He saw Simon seated on the couch. "I figured you'd be here and it's you I came to see. I am the bearer of glad tidings of great joy. Clara, three glasses please," he requested as he kicked off his boots and removed his jacket.

Clara brought three crystal flutes from the armoire. Luke poured the champagne, handed Clara and Simon each a glass. He raised his. "To the newest Hawk–Duncan Joseph. Eight pounds, twenty-two and a half inches long. Born about an hour ago."

Simon broadly grinned. "A brother. Can you believe it? I've got a brother." He raised his glass. "To Duncan Joseph."

Clara raised her glass. "To Duncan Joseph."

In stocking feet, Luke warmed himself in front of the fire. "Simon, it was your sister who called. She insisted Sam Maitland wake me up so you'd be sure to know right away. Pushy girl, real pushy."

Simon teasingly glanced at Clara. "But not quite as aggressive as Clara. Judith rarely beats guys' up."

Luke grinned. "Anyway, I also spoke with your father. I told him about Joseph's death. Hence Duncan Joseph. Your father wants you to call him first thing in the morning. Then just when I thought I was out the door, a second call came. This one was from a frantic Frenchman. Jean-Claude somebody. He said call him, then a lot of French which I think meant like now."

Simon finished his champagne. "Clara, may I use your phone?"

She handed him a cordless phone and he punched in the French exchange.

"*Allo.*"

"Jean-Claude, Simon. Hold on for a second. Clara, speaker phone?"

"Put it in the holder and punch the bottom button."

"Jean-claude. I've put you on a speaker phone. I want my friends to listen."

"Okay. Count Andre Joaillier Le Belmont de Pillard."

"Pillard."

"*Oui,* Pillard. I know the de Pillards. So I imposed on our acquaintance and as you Americans say, dug in."

"Did some digging," Simon corrected.

"What I said, some digging. Andre Belmont is the skeleton in the family closet. He was a womanizer, a gambler, and a drunkard. The de Pillards put the shoe to him."

Simon raised his eyes. "Gave him the boot."

"This is true. This Andre Belmont as he call himself left France in disgrace. He came to your country in the twenties. The de Pillards felt well rid of him. Later they heard he made a fortune in gun running, smuggling how you say scotch, vodka . . . ah, hooch. The de Pillards they feel much shame."

"The French de Pillards. What do they do?"

"Small winery. Excellent wine but only in France."

A woman's voice came through the phone. "Simon, it is Elise."

"Hello, beautiful."

"Your American friend tells us you are not in your suite. So late it is your time. Shame, shame, and whose bed are you warming? I'm afraid I must be angry with you. You did not confide of his new love. I warn you. No more this musical sheets game. You hear, my friend?"

"I hear, Elise. So did Luke, Clara, and three dogs."

Elise gasped. "Simon, you are bad. I must hang up so you do not see my red face."

Jean-Claude came back on the phone. "If I learn more, I'll let you know. Stay in touch, *mon ami.*"

"Thank you, Jean-Claude. Kiss Elise for me and tell her that even with a red face she is beautiful." Simon hit the pound button and terminated the call. "You heard. Belmont was a ruse. Pillard as in all probability Marcus, Harmon, Corrine now Melrose Pillard."

Clara thoughtfully flicked her finger nail against the crystal of her wine glass. "When Aunt Libby was murdered, Corrine was the only Pillard here in The Landing. That Harmon and Uncle Carson are and have always been at odds is a given. Harmon is a bastard, but he's not a killer. As for Marcus–according to my Mom, Libby and Marcus agreed to disagree. No bitterness on either side."

Simon shrugged. "You may be right, but I still want to talk to the Pillards. At least to Harmon and Marcus."

Clara's eyes narrowed. "Aren't you displaying just a hint of male chauvinism?"

"I am, how?"

"Corrine is a Pillard. She is the one who was here at the time of Libby's death. Do you think that because she's a woman, she isn't capable of murder?"

"Libby's fingers were broken. She was repeatedly stabbed. Her face was slashed. It would take a very strong woman."

Luke pulled on his boots. "Or a very determined one in a murderous rage. Corrine's not the type."

"A woman could have killed both Libby and Joseph. Especially if she was someone they knew," Clara insistently said.

Simon spoke sharply. "Based on what?"

"In this there is a woman. I know there's a woman."

Luke zipped up his jacket. "Must be the knowing. I wouldn't dismiss the possibility. I'm out of here. Some of us have to be up early. Simon, don't forget to call your father." With the final admonishment, he was out the door.

Clara hadn't moved from her curled position at the end of the couch. Yet Simon sensed something had changed. He spoke softly. "It's late. I'd better be going and let you get some rest."

She turned her head to look at him. Her eyes were sleepy green pools, her voice a husky whisper. "No, don't go. Please stay."

"Clara . . ."

She smiled. "I know, say what I mean. Tonight I'd like to celebrate life, celebrate being alive. I don't want to think–just feel. I want you to stay and make love to me. Honest enough?"

Simon pushed himself from the couch and walked to the fireplace. He added wood to the dying fire. Clara's face seemed to float in the flames. He envisioned the haunting, slanted green eyes. His mind trailed the length of her body–the long neck on proud shoulders, firm breasts, graceful limbs. He turned from the fire to face her.

"Clara, I'm sure you know that I want you. You're unique–strong and fragile, and smart. I love the way your mind works."

Clara listened intently as if her life depended on his decision.

"Men look at you and see only your beauty. Few will ever perceive your intelligence, discover your strength." He thoughtfully paused. "In the past years, I'm sure there have been men in your life. Just as there have been women in mine. There were other women that I was attracted to but stayed away from because they weren't casual people. Not the sort of women who are available for one night. I wasn't ready for the commitment they needed and deserved.

"You, too, are not a once person. With you I know I can't get up in the morning and walk away. So tell me now. What do you want? Are we exploring possibilities or is this to be a right time, right place, get me through the night thing?"

Clara came to him and touched his face. "You want the truth. The truth is tonight when I saw you it was oh, good, you're here. It felt as if I'd been saving you a place in my life."

Simon groaned and deep inside himself knew he was lost in her, in the moment. She lived her life at the center of a force she was barely able to control. What he wanted was to make love to her–to love her and keep her safe. He coiled his arms around her and felt her relax into his body.

Touching and kissing, they slowly made their way up the stairs and into Clara's bedroom. Simon's lips bruised hers. His tongue explored her mouth and he tasted their lust. As he gently removed her clothes, her body trembled. Arms outreaching, she encircled his body and pulled him tightly against her. His lips moved to her neck, the hollow of her throat leaving a heated trail against the cool satin of her skin. He lifted her to the bed and stepped away to quickly strip off his own clothes.

He lay down next to her. "Clara, you have only to say so and this stops now."

"Ah, Simon," she breathed. "We have only just begun."

He tenderly cupped her face in his hands. She looked up at him with eyes that were heavy with passion. Yet she waited, and he realized that in this she wanted him to take charge. His lips found her breasts, her thighs, her wet sex. His mouth and tongue bringing sensation to every part of her body. He kept them totally connected with the touch of his hands, with murmured words of tenderness, the clean masculine scent of his body. His breath warmed her skin as he kissed her neck, his lips softly touching her eye lids.

The scented musk of her inflamed him with a yearning that was far more than physical. When he entered her, she cried out with joy. Her body moving of its own volition against his.

Groaning with pleasure, Simon felt as if he were plunging into the dark, bottomless sea, and swimming upwards into the light of a transformed reality. Good, oh so very good . . . never like this, never before. He gasped and arched even deeper into her.

Clara cried out with delight. Everything grew brighter, refracting like sunlight through cut crystal. "Oh, Simon . . ." With closed eyes, she lay on the bed. Her body seemed to float free of physical boundaries. Its only anchor was Simon's hand resting flat on her stomach.

Tonight Simon had torn down the barriers thrown up by the knowing. The knowing had kept her apart from people, from truly feeling anything. With Simon's touch, her fear of what the future held had wafted away like mist chased from the river by the dawn. Their lovemaking had taken her beyond the knowing and brought her into bliss.

Her training in the martial arts had taught her to trust her instincts. Most certainly thought had played no role in their love-making. She intuitively trusted Simon, but nothing had prepared her to love him. She now saw how the refining of her spirit had distanced her from the good in life as well as the bad.

Because of Simon, she had rediscovered a part of herself that she never again wanted to live without. And wrapped in his arms, she slept.

The first light of dawn drew Simon from sleep. He turned to his side and watched Clara. It was as if she was far away, dream-ing. He wanted to hold her, too simply be with her. His original discernment had been correct. If he entered Hawk House, he would never want to leave. His fingertips toyed with the silken strands of her hair. "Clara, time to wake up," he whispered.

She sighed and slowly stretched.

"Clara, are you awake?"

"Hu huh."

"Awake enough to listen for a moment?"

"In a manner of speaking," she mumbled.

Simon softly laughed. "Open your eyes so I can be sure."

Clara pushed herself up against the pillows. "I am awake."

"Clara, I want you to listen closely. You and I can do the tra-ditional wine and dinner thing. I can bring you flowers. We can spend a year or two getting to know each other or we can cut to the chase and get married." "I love you. Time can only intensify the feeling. Will you marry me?"

Her expression was tender and mystified. "Oh, Simon . . . it's as if we're renewing an old love. The knowing. It shows me fragments of events, people, myself–you. You as many different men, yet you are always the same man. Me as many women who are actually the same person. What we will be to each other is what we have always been. It's as though you and I have always been together, will always be together." Her smile was wistful. "Here we are only hours after having met and we're talking about a lifetime commitment."

Simon brushed her hair back from her face. "Clara, you still haven't given me an answer."

"In my heart, I know I have always loved you. Yes, I'll marry you." She lightly stroked his groin and ran her nails down his chest, his legs, coming upwards to again tease the inside of his groin.

When he thought he could stand no more, her tongue slowly retraced the same path. His body arched and his breath caught in his throat. She slid lower and took him into her mouth transforming his desire into excruciating need. She swung her leg across his hips and positioned herself above him.

Prolonging his agony, her fingers teased his nipples and she slowly lowered herself onto him. He felt the muscles of her vagina contract and release. Simon's breath caught in his throat and he gripped Clara's hips. But it was Clara who controlled the moment keeping him suspended at the peak of pleasure.

Her eyes gleamed mischievously. "Is my meaning clear?"

When it was nearing time for Simon's appointment with Anne Soames, he went outside and started the Jeep to warm the interior then began to clean the night's accumulation of snow from the windshield. It was a beautiful winter day cold, and sunny. As he brushed away the snow, he thought of the previous night. There was no explanation for how he felt about Clara. He knew only that Clara made him feel vitally alive, and ready to begin a lifetime of commitment that was as natural and right as the morning sunshine.

The front door of Hawk House opened. For a moment Clara was framed against its backdrop. Dressed as she was in a long, Logan green cape and boots, she seemed to be a medieval figure bridging the threshold of time.

"We'd better get a move on. Anne will be waiting," she said as she climbed into the passenger seat.

Simon put the Jeep into gear and started up the drive. "While you were in the shower, I spoke with my father."

"I'm sure he's a very happy man."

"That he is. But what he wanted to talk about was Duncan's disappearance."

Puzzled, Clara asked, "Does he think Duncan is alive?"

"He didn't have time to get into it. A conference call was waiting. I was going to tell him about us, but I thought better of it. Luke should have first dibs."

Clara smiled. "I can't wait to see the expression on the big bozo's face."

"Trust me in this. He's going to gloat." Simon glanced at Clara. "Luke gave me a tour of your school's training facility."

"Then you must have met Gunnar. He's a most remarkable man. Such presence, he dominates a room."

Simon chuckled. "I see you two have a mutual admiration society. The schools–you've hit on quite a concept."

"I only wish we could do more. Something is very wrong in the world. Spirituality is ignored for the material or as Joseph put it. No one is listening to the world song. The schools are at least a tiny light in the darkness." Her eyes lit with pleasure. "These kids can really kick butt–intellectually as well as physically. In fact," she smugly added, "you know one of our first graduates."

Simon raised an eyebrow. "I do?"

"You do. John Gramoli."

"John, the bartender at The Haven?"

"The very same."

"An inner city kid?"

"Hell's Kitchen. That's as inner as it gets. He and his brother were heavy into gangs. His brother got gunned down in a rumble over turf. John wanted out and heard about the school on the streets. He found us. Now he's at Clarkson working toward a degree in environmental engineering."

"Remarkable. He should be proud of all he's accomplished."

Clara stared off into space. "Somehow . . . sometime in the future, I think the schools will have a function that isn't as yet perceivable."

The sign for Riverwalk flashed by. "Damn," Simon said. "Missed the turn."

"Take the next left, then right," Clara directed.

Simon made the turns and found they were on Riverwalk. He drove slowly looking at the houses. "Beautiful homes. They've certainly stood the test of time."

"And to think our ancestors built them."

"Yes," Simon agreed. "The Dunns and Hawks certainly knew their stuff."

Clara pointed to a large white Victorian house. "Driveway on the left."

Simon parked by what had once been a carriage house and was now a garage. He followed Clara up the broad slate steps and onto a wide roofed porch which ran around the sides and front of the house.

At the front door, they were greeted by a tall, distinguished, middle-aged man expensively dressed in a tailored three-piece suit. "Please come in. Anne's been waiting for you. Clara, good to see you." He extended his hand to Simon. "You must be Simon Hawk. Please allow me to introduce myself. I'm Oliver Melrose."

Simon shook his hand. "A pleasure, Sir."

"Oliver, please. Well, back to the office." He picked up his top coat from a Deacon's bench. "Have a good visit. You'll find Anne in the parlor."

Clara took off her cape and gloves. "Good to see you, Oliver. It's been a while. Be sure to say hello to Corrine for me."

Simon shrugged out of his leather jacket. "Parlor?"

As they walked across the marble floor of the foyer, Clara explained. "Here in The Landing it's still referred to as a parlor–especially in this house. You'll see what I mean."

They walked through an open doorway into a large, square room. Hanging at long, narrow windows were rose velvet draperies straight out of Tara. The sofa and chairs were vintage Victorian. An oriental rug which belonged on a museum wall graced the hardwood floors. A woman wearing a blue velvet dressing gown reclined on a chaise lounge near the fire.

"'Arsenic and Old Lace', Act I," Simon irreverently whispered.

Clara hid her amusement and went to Anne and kissed her cheek.

Anne smiled in delight. "And here's my wild child."

"I hope you don't mind that Simon asked me along."

"Mind. It's a wonderful surprise." Tears filled the old woman's eyes. "How are we to live with the loss of our Joseph?"

"He would say that his spirit is always with us. But I miss him, I always will."

Anne's voice quavered. "His death must not go unpunished."

"The Chief is doing his best."

"I know. I know. It isn't enough. Even if he finds out who did it, Joseph will still be dead."

"Life isn't fair," Clara huskily said. "Anne here's Simon."

"Come closer young man," Anne ordered. "Let me take a look at you. I heard you had a great behind." She took her time looking at him. "Great everything. For once the rumors are true."

Simon brushed her hand with a light kiss. "Thank you. A compliment from a beautiful woman makes my day." And beautiful she still was, Simon thought. High sculpted cheekbones, glorious blue, blue eyes. Her skin was lined but nothing could really detract from the finely formed head and the perfect oval of her face.

Anne laughed softly. "Watch out, Clara. I may steal this charming rouge away from you." She gestured toward a tray. "Simon, if you will, please pour the sherry. I gave George the afternoon off so we'd have some privacy. I don't know why I bother. The man had been with me so long, he probably knows me better than I know myself."

Simon poured a sherry for Anne and Clara and sat down on the couch next to Clara. Anne took a sip of her sherry and fixed Simon with a gentle look. "I promise you this won't be the rambling of an old woman. Though I'll soon be ninety-two, my mental faculties remain strong. My hearing and eyesight may not be what they once were but they serve. I admit, there are days when arthritis keeps me right here on this chaise, but overall I'm healthy as a horse."

"Personally," Simon said. "I can't imagine anyone being bored in your presence."

"Ah, handsome and charming. Tell me Clara, is he smart?"

"He is."

"Intelligent, too. My, my, he's quite a package. An irresistible combination, as I well know. Just such a man is in the story I'll tell you. And like all stories, this one has a beginning, a middle. It's the end that isn't clear.

"Ireland was the beginning. At the time I speak of Ireland was in turmoil. People were starving. My family was small—only Da, Mother, and my sister, Molly. My brother, Terrance had died when he was just a babe. There was little work to be had. Da did the best he could but it was never enough. We were always hungry.

"But in the houses just a few blocks away where Da sometimes found the odd job, there was no poverty. These houses were mansions of brick with walled gardens. I use to hide in the shadows and watch the elegant ladies and the handsome men. At one house, I'd often see men going in and out and heard music. The woman who opened the door was beautiful and always wore silk. I wondered about the place. So I asked my mother. She said wicked women lived there. Women, who used their bodies for sinful purposes, flesh pots of the devil.

"That year winter came early and stayed late. We froze. All we had to eat was potatoes and cabbage. Potato soup, cabbage soup. Potato and cabbage soup. To this day I can't stand the stink of cabbage. My mother became sick with consumption. There was no money for a doctor, no money for medicine. She coughed herself to death. The day she died, I swore I wouldn't end like her."

Anne smiled. "And so my path was set. I was only fourteen. A well-developed fourteen and some said beautiful. I don't say this immodestly, just as a fact. Men looked at me and when you live in a Dublin tenement with paper thin walls you surely learn early what their interest is. Flesh pots of the devil be damned. God wasn't going to put food on the table.

"One day when Da was at work. I bathed and dressed in the best I had and presented myself to the beautiful woman with the wicked ways. Soon I was warm, fed, and cared for. And making enough money to care for Da and Molly. I told Da I was a kitchen maid, but truth was I sold my body. My soul I kept for myself. I saved all I earned except for the little my family needed.

"When I was sixteen, I attracted the interest of a man." With a wicked gleam in her eyes, she added. "A charming, handsome, intelligent rogue of a man. Sound familiar, Clara?"

Without waiting for an answer, Anne went on with her story. "This man became my protector and set me up in my own house. I was his sole property, but any money I made from the house was my own. His name was Harry Devlin. His business partner's name was Belmont, Andre Belmont."

Simon knew a gauntlet had been thrown. "Then you must be aware a journal of Ethan Hawk's has been found and that Belmont plays a prominent role."

Anne nodded. "And so he did."

"Do you know," Simon asked? "That Ethan Hawk and Thomas Dunn believed they had killed Belmont?"

"Yes, but he survived. I know because I was in his company many times in the late twenties when I was still with Devlin. Let me go back some ways. In nineteen twenty, Harry and Belmont talked of The Thousand Islands and the new prohibition law. They saw it as an opportunity to make money.

"The river was a smuggler's delight–islands to hide them, hidden coves, and the river itself the border between two countries. Belmont was what you here called a bootlegger. Harry was certainly willing to make money from the hooch, but his main interest was guns for the Irish.

"By this time, I had enough money to be financially independent. I became convinced that this Thousand Islands would be a place for a new beginning. I sent my sister, Molly, here to buy a house. I taught her how to deal with permits. Who to pay so she could conduct business–a speakeasy, and a bit more."

Clara smiled. "And so Molly's came into being."

Anne nodded. "I spent a few more years under Harry Devlin's tutelage learning all I could of business. By then, between Molly's and other investments, I was as they say a woman of independent means."

"Was this when you came here?" Clara asked.

"Not right away, I traveled. Saw what I wanted to see of the world. Harry was angry so it was best to stay out of his reach. I came to The Landing the summer of nineteen-thirty. Here I've been ever since."

"How did you learn of the attempt on Belmont's life?" Simon asked.

"Molly told me. I never mentioned that Belmont was still alive. There was no point. Ethan and Thomas would only have wasted their lives seeking useless revenge."

Simon watched the fire. "Suppose Belmont wanted payback for the attempt on his life."

"Oddly enough, he was relieved to have so easily disposed of the Belmont persona. He never returned to the Islands. Harry did. He bought an island near Gananoque. Our liaison was comfortable, familiar, and safe." Anne smiled. It was a wise knowing smile. "I know. I left him once. But not because I didn't love him. I did. The difference was that later we came together as equals."

"An important distinction," Simon agreed. "Anne, at this juncture was Devlin still running guns?"

"I imagine so. He was up to his eyebrows in the Irish thing. I'd venture a guess that the Devlins still are. In fact, the last I knew Harry's son, Roger surely was."

"Why? Aren't the Irish and the English on the fast track toward peace?"

Anne shrugged. "I've heard that song before. Will be a long time, if ever." Anne glanced at Clara. "It's Roger who I want to speak of, and of your great-aunt Madeleine.

"Was nineteen thirty-six. Madeleine Dunn had her eighteenth birthday bash at The Haven. I remember it was July first. A perfect summer day. There were ice sculptures, a champagne fountain, and food, incredible, wonderful food. During the day we danced on the terrace and that night in the ballroom.

"It was a truly memorable event. It was also when Maddy met Roger Devlin. Maddy was drop dead gorgeous–like you Clara. Roger was like his father, my Harry–black Irish with blue eyes and handsome. Roger played polo, sailed, raced sloops. Maddy was smitten. I think she fell in love the second she set eyes on him.

"When the summer ended, Madeleine was invited to visit Ireland. Needless to say, Nicholas and Eleanor wouldn't let her go without a chaperon."

"Let me guess," Clara said. "Aunt Maddy convinced you to go along."

Anne laughed and nodded. "Harry's wife had died and we'd have time together. Madeleine could get to know Roger. In late August, she and I sailed on the Queen Elizabeth out of New York harbor." Anne's eyes grew sad. "At first it was a happy time, a glorious adventure. But by the time we came home, Madeleine was a transformed young woman, no longer a girl. In Ireland she saw a side of life which for her had existed only in the abstract."

Clara's lips tightened. "People starving, violent death. She saw people killed. Bombs explode, dead children lying like rag dolls on a school yard . . . and she was pregnant."

Simon listened mystified. Anne with her eyes closed said, "The knowing?"

"Yes, out of the knowing. Last night, other times, too. Last night it seemed so real."

"Real it was, my wild child. To, too real. Roger had underestimated Maddy's moral fiber. He took Maddy somewhere in Northern Ireland to meet his uncle, Sean. Harry's brother. When she returned to Dublin the joy had gone from our Irish adventure.

118

Roger had made the mistake of letting her see too much. Once she knew of his terrorist activities, she walked away from him. There was nothing he could say to change her mind. In a strange way I felt sorry for him."

Clara's voice was a lament. "Madeleine was pregnant. He came for her and she fell."

Anne's eyes filled with tears. "Maddy fell from the path that takes you down to Clara's Cove. Was Roger who brought Maddy here. She lost the babe right upstairs in the front guest room. Roger returned to Ireland. To the best of my knowledge he never came back to The Islands. Harry still came every summer until his death."

"A few years later Aunt Maddy was dead. Grandmother said she foresaw her own death."

Anne sighed and shifted painfully on her chaise. Clara saw her discomfort and came to her. "Lean forward. Let me get the pillows for you." Clara plumped the pillows and put them behind Anne so could rest more comfortable. "If you're tired. We can do this another time."

"No, child, I'd like to finish. Roger quickly married an Irish girl and they had a daughter. In the spring of . . . I forget the year but it was in the late fifties. Harry brought his granddaughter, Lilith with him. She was an absolutely stunning young woman. Long black hair, grey eyes with long lashes and the pale, ivory complexion the Irish are famous for."

Anne looked at Simon. "This is the middle of the story where the Hawks play a role. Joseph, our Joseph met Lilith and fell hard. But for her it was no more than a romp in the hay.

"When the Hawks came for the summer, Lilith saw Duncan and her fling with Joseph was over. Duncan was a glorious man. At any rate, Lilith took one look and went for him like a bitch in heat. Of course, Duncan had no idea of Lilith's affair with Joseph or of how much Joseph loved her. Duncan and Lilith's affair was very hot, and very brief."

"I always knew someone had hurt Joseph but I never knew who," Clara said. "Quite the little player wasn't she? Did Duncan find out about her thing with Joseph?"

"Duncan found out. I can't say how, but he ended it with Lilith and went back to New Orleans. Harry told me Lilith didn't take Duncan's rejection well. It sent her into a rage. In Harry's words, she went crazy. Smashed dishes, literally tore her bedroom apart. Harry quickly packed her back to Dublin. *The coup de grace*–Lilith was pregnant."

"The baby," Simon asked?

"I never knew whose it was nor what happened to the babe. It could have been Joseph's or Duncan's or someone else. Harry never spoke of her again."

Simon stood and began to pace. "Anne, who besides you would know of Lilith's pregnancy?"

"No one here. Neither Joseph nor Duncan knew. Of that I'm certain."

"Did you ever see Harry Devlin or Andre Belmont wear a silver ring with male and female figures intertwined?"

Anne thought for a moment. "Not that I recall. Harry occasionally wore a diamond ring. Are you speaking of the ring found in Libby's studio?"

"Yes, but it was also described in Ethan's journal. Belmont was wearing it or one very like it."

"Then the answer is definitely no. Mike O'Connor showed me the ring years ago. I'd never seen one like it." Anne rested her head against the back of the chaise lounge. "So as you can see, we have the beginning and middle of the story but not the end. Suddenly I'm very tired. Simon would you help me to my room?"

"Of course." He bent down and picked her up. Under the blue velvet robe, he could feel her fragility. "Where is your room?" he asked.

"The first door on the right at the top of the stairs. Clara, this one's a keeper."

"I know, Anne. Would you like me to come along and help?"

"No, child. There's something I want to show Simon."

Simon carried Anne to her bedroom and gently lay her on the canopied bed. The satin comforter and sheets had already been turned back. He pulled them over her as one would tuck in a child.

"Thank you. I've always loved being fussed over. Women today don't know what they miss. What with this independence thing, they carry it too far. Simon, behind the Flemish tapestry is a safe. It's open. Please bring me the velvet ring box."

Simon crossed the room to the safe. The velvet box was atop a stack of papers. He brought it to Anne. She snapped the top open. Inside was a pear shaped diamond. "The stone is a flawless blue white. It's more than three carats," she said. "The setting is platinum and twenty-four carat gold." She handed it to Simon. "Look at the sides. A pair of hawks hold the stone."

"An incredible ring."

"I had this designed in London at Duncan's behest. It was to be a special gift for Libby. I brought it back with me the week after she was killed." Anne sighed. "She never got her present."

"It must be very valuable."

"It's worth nothing sitting in a safe. I want you to have it. A ring worthy of a Hawk to be given to a Dunn. You can't fool an old romantic like me."

"Wouldn't even try," Simon said with a warm smile. "Thing is, I'm having trouble understanding it myself. If anyone had ever mentioned me and love at first sight in the same breath . . ." He shrugged. "But there it is."

Anne pressed the ring into his hand. "Was the same for Harry and me. I saw him and never saw another. Take the ring."

"Anne, I can't accept this," Simon objected.

"Simon Hawk, I love that wild child. I had no children of my own, but I had Joseph, and Maddy was like my own. You and Clara deserve the chance taken from Libby and Duncan. Is because of him, I've told you of Lilith. I've never known for certain but in my heart, I've always believed Lilith's child was Duncan's. The Hawks have a right to know."

"I have to wonder why you waited so long to bring it up."

"Ah, my dear, you are the first Hawk to come to The Landing in many, many years. I said nothing when Libby was murdered.

A love child. It would only have given the authorities more fodder in their lynching of Duncan. No, then was not the time. Duncan was already the only suspect, and he was gone. Your family already had a full plate of grief."

"I see. But if Lilith's child was Duncan's, my grandfather and father would want to know. I'll have to check it out before I say anything."

Anne nodded wearily. "That would be best. As for the ring, if you must, contribute its worth to the Lindquist/Dunn Schools. In the safe, the top envelope has the receipt. Now go away. I need to rest.

When Simon and Clara stepped outside they were surprised to find that the sun had disappeared and storm clouds were settling in. Simon took Clara's arm and helped her down the icy steps. "What say," he said. "We head for The Haven and . . ."

"Tell Luke we're going to a plight our troth."

"Plight our troth–gad zooks. Sounds positively decadent."

Clara fastened her seat belt. "Drive on. Your future awaits."

Simon chuckled and backed out onto Riverwalk.

Clara fell silent. So much had happened so quickly. Joseph's death. She and Simon. Somehow her feelings for Simon were tied to the knowing. To those men she thought of as protectors and to the one man who seemed to be many.

Simon pulled the Jeep into The Haven's parking area. Clara glanced out of the side window. A blue and gold village police car was parked in front of the main entrance. "Police car. Look's like something's wrong."

"No shit, Dick Tracy," Simon said with a smile.

As they entered the lobby, Luke hurried to greet them. "Where in hell have you two been? I've called everywhere."

"At Anne Soames," Simon explained. "You were there when Corrine told me Anne wanted to meet with me, remember?"

"Right, damn I forgot. Listen, Simon, someone broke into your suite. A woman from housekeeping was hit from behind. She's been taken to the hospital. I just called over there. She's unconscious but stable. Looks like concussion. The Chief wants to see you. He's up in your suite."

Simon started toward the elevators. "Clara please wait for me in the taproom."

"Come on, cuz," Luke said. "Join me for a toddy. Today's been a real bummer."

Inside the suite, Simon saw that an oak table had been overturned. Fresh roses and carnations were scattered on the rug. He saw Mike O'Connor speaking to a man in a business suit. He had cop written all over him. Probably from the state's Bureau of Criminal Investigation. "Chief."

Mike O'Connor turned. "Simon, finally. Take a look around. Anything missing?"

Simon gave the room a cursory examination. "Nothing out here that I can see. It isn't likely the intruder would have much interest in my socks and underwear. Let me check my work room."

In the study, Simon saw that his book manuscript had been moved. The computer keyboard seemed closer to the screen than usual. He picked up the keyboard and saw minute scratches on the plastic of the screw holes that held the back plate in place.

Using the Swiss army knife that he always carried, he carefully removed the screws and cautiously lifted the cover. Plastique was wired to the enter key. "Chief," he called. "Better take a look."

The Chief appeared in the doorway. "They get the journal?"

"In a manner of speaking." Simon pointed to the plastique. "It would have taken me and anything in the room out, including the journal."

Mike O'Connor wiped sweat from his forehead. "What in hell is going on?"

"I think it's very clear that somebody doesn't want me poking around in the past. I'd better thank the lady that got hit. If that hadn't happened, I might not have noticed the manuscript and keyboard had been moved. Even if I had, I'd likely have chalked it up to housekeeping. I've have booted up per usual and ka boom."

"Let's get this room sealed off," the Chief said. "Come on back into the other room." He called to his men and gave them instructions on how to precede then walked on into the living area. He nudged a heavy crystal vase that was lying on the carpet in a pool of water. "Woman was bludgeoned from behind. Looks like she fell against that small oak table."

"Poor woman. She was unlucky–wrong place at the wrong time."

"Yeah. But no one knows why she was in here. Luke said she had no business on this floor. Simon, I'm bringing in a bomb squad. I want this suite gone over with a fine tooth comb. Mind staying out of here for a while?"

"No problem. Me casa Su casa."

The Chief stared at him. "What's wrong with this picture?"

"What do you mean?"

"You haven't speculated as to whether or not this is connected to Joseph Cloud's death, the journal."

Simon chuckled. "I don't have to. You've done it for me. But I admit it did cross my mind."

The Chief glared. "Don't be smug. There's a killer on the loose and I'd say you're on his hit parade."

In the taproom, Clara took a swallow of ice water. "Luke, what time did the break-in happen?"

"Shirley's shift began at midnight. She'd set the small dining room for breakfast. Helped out in the laundry." He paused and thought for a minute. "I'd say anytime after one-thirty, two. I've no clue as to why she'd be in Simon's suite or for that matter, why she'd be on that floor."

"Maybe she saw something wrong and went to check," Clara suggested.

"Possible. Shirley's been here ten years or more. Anything out of sync, she'd spot it. And she's honest as the day is long. If she was in Simon's suite, she had a good reason."

"Funny," Clara said. "I can't seem to place her."

"You probably wouldn't know her. She's always worked the midnight to eight. A behind the scene's person."

"Did anyone else see anything?"

Luke shook his head. "Everybody we could spare was at

Sailors for Joe's wake. Sam Maitland worked the reception desk until two in the morning. Night clerk had the flu so he covered until Jim Tully could get in from Massena. Sam said that about one fifteen a pair of drunk lawyers stumbled through the lobby. They were the last people he saw. Jim didn't see anyone, nada, until around six this morning. A few early checkouts."

"Seems odd. It would be very difficult to slip unnoticed up to the second floor."

"Agreed. When Shirley comes around, she might be able to fill in the blanks." Luke toyed with his glass of beer. 'Say, Clara. What's going on with you and the Hawkster?"

Before Clara could formulate a reply, Simon pulled up a chair and joined them at the table. From the bar, John questioningly caught his eye. "Coffee," Simon answered.

"Anything missing," Clara asked?

Simon shook his head. "Nope, nothing."

Clara shivered and closed her eyes. An image came. A man falling, blood pooling on a stone hearth. The sound of waves rushing against rock.

Simon took her hand. "Clara?"

She shuddered and opened her eyes. "They killed you once."

He kissed the palm of her hand. "Not this time."

Luke decided it was time to lighten the mood. "Okay, one more time. What's going on with you two?"

John came from behind the bar and set a large mug of black coffee in front of Simon. He leaned down and with a conspirator's whisper, said, "Yeah, what?"

Simon took a deliberate sip of his coffee. "Clara, Luke, wait ten minutes and join me in the family dining room. John, I hate to exclude you but unfortunately you're on duty and out of the loop. You'll be informed at the appropriate time."

John clicked his heels. "Yes, Sir." And returned to the bar.

Puzzled, Luke looked to Clara for clarification. She smiled and shrugged. "We'll just have to wait and see."

Simon lit the final candle and stepped back to survey his efforts. A romantic fire flickered in the fireplace. The champagne was iced, flowers on the mantel. He looked toward the door and saw Clara and Luke come into the room.

Luke eyed the candles and champagne. "Oh, oh. Something's up."

Simon pulled out a chair. "Clara, please sit here. There should be gypsy violinists but they're hard to come by on short notice. Luke, please stand to the side."

When Clara was seated, Simon dropped to one knee and took her hand. "I, Simon Hawk. Ask you, Clara Dunn Eaton, to marry me. To be my friend, my lover, my partner, my wife." He reached into his pocket for the green velvet box. "Clara, will you marry me?"

Tears stood in her eyes. "Yes. Yes, I'll marry you."

Simon opened the box and slipped the diamond onto her finger. The fit was perfect.

Luke broadly grinned ignoring the tears in his own eyes. "Hot damn! And I didn't even have to break my blood oath." He grabbed Simon in a bear hug. "Welcome to the family." He released Simon and kissed Clara. He lifted her hand. "That's some rock. It's the ring, huh? You're marrying him for the ring."

"Yep. Without the ring, I'd have probably refused."

Simon poured champagne. "By the way, Luke, I'll need a best man. You game?"

Luke raised his glass. "But of course."

A voice came from the doorway. "Is this a private celebration or can anyone stop by?"

Simon turned and saw his sister, Judith hesitantly standing in the doorway. "Judith. What the devil . . ."

Judith hurried across the marble floor to give him a hug. "Dad and Nicole are bringing Duncan Joseph home from the hospital tomorrow. Grandfather is in Geneva on business. It's the perfect opportunity for the new parents to have time alone with the baby. So here I am. I hope it's all right."

Luke watched this female Hawk with trepidation. He most definitely didn't need another complication in his life. Between The Haven and the schools, his plate was full. But he couldn't take his eyes from her face. She was absolutely gorgeous–honey tanned skin, those incredible yellow/green Hawk eyes. Black hair shining like a seal's pelt. A showgirl's figure encased in a red jersey dress–and those legs. Shit, he was in trouble.

Simon hugged Judith tight. "Your timing is perfect. Allow me to introduce you to my fiancée, Clara Dunn Eaton. Clara, this is my sister, Judith Hawk."

"I'm very glad to meet you," Clara said warmly. "This must come as quite a surprise."

"It's a pleasure to meet you. And yes, your engagement is a surprise but one of the best kind. I wish you all the happiness in the world."

Simon sensed his sister's confusion and drew her off to one side. "You okay?"

Judith swallowed back tears. "I just get you back and already I'm losing you to another woman." She punched his arm. "Not just any woman but a very beautiful one, and a Dunn to boot. How long have you known her?"

"Not long," he ruefully admitted. "But long enough to know I want to spend the rest of my life with her." He bent his head and kissed Judith's forehead. "No matter what, you'll always be my favorite sister."

Judith grinned feeling more at ease. "Big deal," she teased. "I'm also your only sister."

Luke impatiently cleared his throat.

Smiling, Simon took the hint. "Judith, may I present my friend, my soon to be best man. Clara's cousin, Luke Dunn. Luke. My sister, Judith."

Judith held out her hand and smiled. "Hello, Luke."

Luke took her hand and held it just a little to long. "Judith, this is truly a pleasure. Champagne?"

"I'd love some," she answered in a soft melodious drawl.

Luke quickly poured her a flute of champagne.

Clara held up her ring. It seemed to sparkle with a life of its own. "Simon, where did you find this extraordinary ring?"

"By way of Anne Soames. Duncan had it designed for Libby

127

in London. Anne picked it up for him as a favor. But by the time she got home from her trip Libby was dead, Duncan gone. Somehow the ring seems very fitting. I hope you don't mind."

"It couldn't be more perfect."

Sam Maitland paused in the doorway not wanting to interrupt. Luke waved him into the room. "Please forgive the intrusion, but I'm afraid I'm the bearer of more bad news. Chief O'Connor just phoned to say that Joseph Cloud's place has been torched."

Clara's eyes blazed with outrage that quickly faded to fear. "John. John Cloud was going to stay at the cabin while he packed up Joseph's papers and books."

"Do you want to go over there?" Simon asked.

"Please."

"Don't worry about Judith," Luke put in. "I'll get her settled. Keep an eye on her."

"Thanks, Luke." Simon turned to Judith. "I'm really glad you're here. We'll have a second celebration when Clara and I get back."

"I'm sorry to have to leave you like this," Clara apologetically said. "We won't be long."

"You go, I'm sure Luke will take good care of me."

"Not too good," Simon warned as he and Clara went out the door.

As Simon and Clara approached the river, they could see black smoke from the flames licking through the log house and the sides of the ancient wood boat house.

"Oh, Simon, the bastard has burned it all. Even the boat house."

Police and volunteer firemen swarmed over the area. Firemen hauled the heavy hoses, shouting for more pressure from the tanker. The spraying water turned the white snow into a slippery black morass.

The color faded from Clara's face as she watched a body bag being loaded into The Landing's Volunteer Rescue Squads' ambulance. "Let's talk to Mike."

Hands on his hips, Chief O'Connor stared at the burning

cabin. He glanced at Simon and Clara. "Son-of-a-bitch, what next? I feel like I'm in over my head and about to go down for the third time."

"Mike, was it John Cloud?" Clara asked.

"No, honey. John's fine. He and some of the firemen are down by the boat house. They're trying to save Joe's ketch. I'm afraid it's pretty badly damaged."

"The man?" Simon asked.

"No idea. He was badly burned. We'll know more later."

"Chief, I'm going to take a quick look around. That is if it's okay with you," Simon said.

The Chief waved him on and walked over to the fire chief.

Clara stared down at the river. "I'm going to talk with John. I'll pay to have Joseph's ketch restored."

"Of course you will," Simon said. He started toward the snow-mobile trail. "Catch you later." He followed the trail and found a track that seemed newer than the others. It led up the bank behind the log house to where it crossed the main trail. From there the track continued across a field and on up into a heavily wooded area of tall pines.

Once Simon was in the open, the drifted snow became too deep to wade through. But there was still enough light to see where the track led. He turned and retraced his steps and found the Chief leaning against a pine tree and watching the fire. "Chief, right of the cabin. There's a fresh snow machine trail that heads up the bank and into the woods."

The Chief waved a deputy over and pointed. "Grab a sled. Follow the trail that heads up toward McKinley's woods. Whoever it was is long gone, but it might tell us something." He glanced at Simon. "You're good. My men must have missed it."

"You've had other things to do."

The Chief shook his head. "No excuse. What in hell is going on? Joseph murdered, a man dead in his cabin. Your suite broken into . . . more than that, someone wanted to blow you up. And I haven't got a clue."

"Can't be coincidence. It all has to tie together."

"Care to venture a guess?"

"No guess. Joseph's killer must know the area, probably come in on a sled. Ditto today. Knew how to approach and leave without being seen."

"I said I didn't have a clue," the Chief bristled. "Not that I was the village idiot."

"Sorry, Chief. I was thinking out loud. I didn't mean to imply . . ."

"I know," the Chief cut in. "We're all getting edgy. Shit, maybe it's time we got scared. We got a killer who has no compunction about killing anyone who gets in the way."

"Chief, the plastique–let's keep it between us. Clara's had enough bad news."

Judith Hawk watched Luke as he leaned over the rail of the hospital bed. "Shirley, I'm here." He took her work worn hand in his. "Shirley, It's Luke. You asked for me."

The woman on the bed seemed small, diminished by the sterile surroundings. An intravenous tube ran into her hand. She licked her lips. "Dry . . . mouth dry."

The nurse picked up a cup of ice chips. "Let me give her some ice. It'll help."

Shirley Johns gratefully sucked on the ice swallowing against the dryness. "Luke," she said, her voice oddly loud. "Luke."

Luke patted her hand. "Right here, Shirley. Can you tell me what happened?"

"I came out of the laundry, saw the door . . ." Her voice trailed off and she seemed to drift briefly into sleep. She forced her eyes open. "The door wasn't locked. Something was wrong."

"Which door wasn't locked?"

"Service door . . . elevator door wasn't open. Should've been open."

Luke frowned in confusion. "Shirley, the service door was unlocked?"

Shirley nodded her head. The motion brought pain and she gasped.

"Take you time," Luke compassionately told her.

"I'm okay," she said with a weak smile. "It only hurts when I laugh. Anyway, the service door wasn't locked. Elevator was going up . . . shouldn't have been. Only for service. Never used at night."

"The service elevator was going up. What did you do then?"

"Tried to lock the service door . . . couldn't. Tape."

"Damn," Luke said. "That's why no one was seen in the lobby. Whoever it was came in through the service entrance. Someone taped the latch so it wouldn't catch."

Shirley's eyes grew wide. "Didn't do it. Didn't."

Luke patted her hand. "Of course you didn't. What did you do next?"

"Elevator stopped on two. I took the stairs. A Suite, the one where the famous writer is staying, the door was just closing. I waited in the hall . . . listened."

"How did you come to be inside?"

Shirley's head restlessly moved from side to side. "Door opened . . . someone grabbed me . . . pulled me inside." She tried to smile. "Woke up here."

Judith found herself admiring Luke. From the deferential manner in which he spoke to Shirley Johns, he obviously viewed her as an equal deserving of respect. She wasn't just an interchangeable employee without an identity.

"Shirley, one more question. Could you tell who it was?"

She slowly shook her head. "Face was covered."

"How so?"

"A helmet," she said. "Like snowmobilers wear."

"Could it have been a woman?" Luke wondered aloud.

"Maybe . . . yes, I suppose . . ." She thought for a moment. "No, not a woman. Big, big hands–a man."

"Thanks, Shirley. You rest now and don't' worry. You're still on the clock. When you're well enough, your job will be waiting."

Shirley's eyes closed. "Thanks, boss," she murmured as she slipped into sleep.

Luke took Judith's arm and led her out into the hall. She

smiled up at him. "What now, Sherlock?"

"Well, Watson. What say we explore downtown and find the dazzling duo a smashing engagement present?"

"Luke Dunn, you're really a nice man."

"Damn, who told. I've been working on my man of mystery persona. Should've known better. Simon's got that one tied up."

"You really like my brother, don't you?"

Luke pushed the elevator button. "I do. He and my cuz are right together. You can just feel it."

Judith thought that her brother had always been her ideal man–strong, intelligent, compassionate, and fun. Luke seemed to have those same qualities. No wonder they'd became friends.

As Judith and Luke came out of the hospital's main entrance, Clara and Simon were pulling up the curved drive. The Jeep braked to a stop in front of them. Clara lowered her window. "Sam told us you were here. How'd it go?"

Luke shrugged. "Pretty much what you'd expect. Let's get somewhere out of this cold and I'll fill you in."

"That's why we've tracked you down. Would you two like to join us at Hawk House for dinner?"

Luke looked inquiringly at Judith. She nodded. "That's a tentative yes," Luke said. "Depending on whose doing the cooking. It's my day off."

Clara batted her eyes. "Why the little woman will cook, serve, wash the dishes, and . . ."

Simon raised the window. "Say goodbye, Gracie."

"Bye Gracie," Clara said just before the window closed.

Simon followed the three frolicking dogs into Hawk House. The Irish wolfhounds were all gamboling legs sliding on the hardwood floor and crashing into Dog. Dog tolerated the pups, playfully pawing them to the floor. When he was bored with the game, a low growl sent the pups scurrying for the relative safety of the rug in front of the fireplace.

"You tell em, Dog." Simon walked out to the kitchen where Clara was chopping celery. "Want me to start a fire?"

"Good idea. I'll bet Judith is freezing. Sunny Louisiana is a far cry from the North Country cold."

Simon stacked kindling on the grate and topped it with wrist thick logs. Soon flames licked at the bark and the puppies snuggled closer to its warmth. A tantalizing aroma came from the kitchen.

"Smells good," Simon told Clara and kissed her neck. "So do you."

"Why thank you, you charming devil. Now release me. I've cooking to do."

"What are we having?"

"New England Clam Pie. Ever had it?"

"No, can't say that I have. How do you make it?"

"Celery, onion, potatoes, clams, clam broth, and water. Cook together, thicken, bring back to a boil. While boiling place biscuit dough over the top, seal pan and bake. Voila!"

"Thank you, Julia Childs. Want me to make the salad?"

She handed him a knife. "Salad stuff is in the bottom bin of the fridge."

They worked in companionable silence. Clara rolled out the biscuit dough and, using the pot cover as a guide, cut it to size. She placed the dough on top of the boiling mixture and put it into the oven. "I'll set the table," she said. "Why don't you pick out the wine?" She gestured to a door at the end of the kitchen. "Wine racks' in the basement."

Simon went down the broad fieldstone steps and into the huge basement. Simon was surprised to see a copper ceiling and was impressed by the three-foot thick fieldstone walls. He thought that Ethan had certainly built the place to last. The temperature controlled wine cabinet was against a wall across from a workbench. He selected two bottles of a white Chardonnay.

When Simon emerged from the basement, he saw Judith bundled in a huge, grey wool sweater and sweat pants huddled on a stool by the fire. "Whoa, nice outfit, sis. A real fashion statement. Who designed it, Nanook of the North?"

"Fashion be damned," Judith answered. "I was freezing.

Luke helped me out. Tomorrow I'm buying insulated underwear."

"Not sexy, better rethink it. Sexy is as sexy does. Speaking of Luke, where is he?"

"Bringing in a package from the car."

Clara held the door open and Luke swaggered in. He set the balloon-festooned box on the oak table at the side of the fireplace. Judith got up and stood next to Luke. "Now," she whispered.

"Now." And in unison they shouted, "Happy Engagement!"

Simon took Clara's hand. "What do you think? Is it safe to open?"

"Don't worry. Anything dangerous jumps out. I'll protect you."

"Come on you two. Get with the program," Judith impatiently ordered.

"Oh, by the way," Luke put in. "The gift's from Judith and me."

Clara pulled the balloons free and let them float upward. Simon attacked the wrapping paper and careful lifted the bronze sculpture out of its wrappings. Clara pushed the box away so he could set it down.

The bronze sculpture was of an inextricably intertwined male and female whose stillness seemed a prelude to movement. Simon was the first to speak. "Exquisite."

"It's absolutely wonderful . . . incredible." Clara gave Luke a hug. "I love you, Lucas Dunn. Thank you." She turned to Judith. "Only a truly loving and generous spirit could give something as wonderful as this as a gift. This sister-in-law thing is going to be terrific. Thank you, Judith."

Simon touched the cool bronze of the unique sculpture. "I really don't know how to thank you."

Luke smiled. "You just did. If I recall correctly, we were invited to dinner."

Clara started toward the kitchen. "Simon, quick pour the wine. Put the salad on the table. I don't want them to take their gift back."

Dinner was served, accompanied by wines, conversation and much laughter.

Judith sighed with contentment. "Delicious, but I think I've stuffed myself."

Luke raised his eyebrows. "Acceptable. But wait until you sample my cooking–a true gourmet delight."

"Hah," Simon put in. "Wait until Judith and I cook up some Cajun. "We'll put you to shame."

Clara swatted Simon with her napkin. "You are hereby challenged to a Cajun cook off. Right, Luke?"

"Indeed. My mother taught us and believe me, she knows what she's doing."

"Hah," Judith imitated her brother. "Our teacher came from the bayous. We be smokin'"

"So who was this famous Cajun chef?" Luke asked.

Simon eyes warmed with memory. "Lena Dubois. She was our cook. She was from Iberia Parish where her family lived right on the bayou. We called her, Ena."

Judith sadly smiled. "She died a few years ago. A very special person. Warm, loving with a laugh like molasses." Judith glanced at Simon. "I always thought her and Grandfather had a thing going."

"Could be. If so, I hope it brought them joy."

Dog suddenly growled low in his powerful throat and went to the front window. The pups trailed behind unsure of their mission but willing.

Simon frowned. "Someone's out there. Luke, go upstairs where you can get a broad view," Simon said as he got up to make certain the front and back doors were securely locked.

As Luke started up the stairs, Clara called, "There's a pair of night binoculars hanging on a hook in my bedroom closet."

After a moment, Luke called. "Simon, back by the garage, there's someone on a sled. A couple of more riders down by the river. One closest is moving along the tree line . . . and out of sight. Looks like it's just a rider admiring the house."

"Clara, do you have a gun?" Simon asked.

"Sorry, no guns. I don't like them. Besides there's no need."

Simon snorted his disgust. "You seem to forget that there's a killer on the loose."

"Simon, take a look around. Every window in the house is of bullet proof glass. I forget the more scientific name. The roof is slate and the walls are fieldstone."

Luke came back to the table. "Now how about some brandy and coffee?"

"In a minute," Simon snapped. "I'd like to hear why Clara turned this house into a fortress?"

"The house has a lot of windows. When it was empty, it was a target for vandals. I'm often away for extended periods of time. I had to do something."

"Wouldn't you call bullet proof glass overkill?"

Luke laughed. "You wouldn't at the price she got it for. Some rich smuck ordered it for his island estate and went belly up. Contractor got stuck with it. Clara bought it for a song."

"Certainly has eliminated the strain of replacement," Clara smugly commented.

The puppies snuck into the room and crowded against Clara's knees begging for a handout. Dog waited patiently, tail wagging. "What's wrong, the babies get lonesome?" She scratched their ears and got up to give each of them a dog biscuit.

Simon watched as Clara fed Dog. The fierce animal growled low in his throat in pleasure. Most people couldn't get anywhere near the huge mastiff but he was putty in Clara's hands. He got up from the table and put his arms around her. "Sorry . . ."

She kissed his cheek. "Don't be. You're just acting out of concern. Now stop worrying. We're going to be fine."

The lights from a vehicle cast a shadow across the wall. Simon went to the front door and looked through the peep hole. "Mike O'Connor," he said as he opened the door. "Chief."

"Hi, Mike, come on in," Clara called from the kitchen. "I've got clam pie. Hungry?"

The Chief took off his jacket. "I've always liked you, Clara. You know the way to a man's heart. I am. And I will. And since I'm on a roll and off duty–got a cold beer?"

"I do." Clara opened a can of beer. "Mike. This is Judith Hawk, Simon's sister, Judith, our police chief and good friend,

Michael O'Connor."

Judith held out her hand. "You must be the Mike O'Connor who helped my father and uncle tie the boy to the tree and forgot about him."

The Chief chuckled. "I plead guilty. Funny, I'd almost forgotten that. Jerry Taylor. . . good ol' Jerry. He was the town bully, had a gang of followers. We decided to teach them a lesson. Duncan, David, Joseph and I raided their clubhouse. Kidnaped Jerry, took him out into the woods and tied him to a pine tree. If his father hadn't come looking for him, he'd have spent a very uncomfortable night. Worked though, Jerry never bothered us again."

"To think you enforce the law," Clara said with a smile as she set a salad and a plate of clam pie in front of him.

The Chief reached for a soup spoon. "Smells great. By the way, Simon. The track ran out up in the Flats. Deputy Martins did find a yellow gas can tossed in the underbrush a stone's throw from the trailer park. Maybe there'll be a viable print. Even if there is, it won't mean much. We can't connect the can to the fire but it might be a way to shake something loose."

"Chief," Luke put in. "Shirley Johns said the service entrance door was taped. Must be how the guy who broke into Simon's suite got in."

"Yeah, I got your message. He must have gotten out the same way because I checked that door myself and there wasn't any tape."

Luke tapped Judith on the shoulder. "Come on, Judith. I'll show you the rest of Hawk House."

Simon picked up a yellow legal pad from the counter. "Clara, may I use this? I'd like to make some notes while the Chief has dinner."

"Sure. Pen's in the drawer just below."

Judith leaned on the balcony rail and looked down into the great room. "What a wonderful house."

Luke nodded. "Ethan Hawk was a remarkable man." He took Judith's shoulders and turned her to face him. "How long are you staying?"

Judith nervously stepped back. "A week, ten days, coming here was very spur of the moment."

"I'd like us to get to know each other."

Judith's emotions were strung like fine wire. Luke Dunn was too much too soon. But before the thought was finished, she heard herself say, "I'd like that."

Luke took Judith's hand and led her back downstairs. Simon, Clara, and the Chief were seated around the fireplace. Clara leaned against the floor pillow with Dog's head in her lap.

With a yawn, Judith said, "I'll say goodnight. It's been a wonderful day but I'm bushed."

"A pleasure meeting you, Ms. Hawk," the Chief said.

"Judith. And I'm glad we've met."

"I'll take Judith back to The Haven," Luke volunteered. "You can bring me up to speed in the morning."

Clara waved goodbye from the floor. "Goodnight. Oh, Judith. Tomorrow night I'm joining some friends for drinks. Would you like to come along?"

"Sounds like a good time. Thanks for asking."

Luke opened the front door. "Button up. It's cold."

"The man is smitten," Simon said with a grin. "I'm grabbing a beer, anybody in?"

"Get us all one," Clara answered.

Simon handed Clara and the Chief their beer. "Let me run a few things by you."

The Chief leaned back in his chair. "Go ahead, but prod me if I doze off."

"Fair enough. Let's begin with the journal. Ethan and Thomas believed they killed Andre Belmont. According to Anne Soames, they failed. One of Belmont's partners in bootlegging was a Jacques Toussaint. His great-grandson, Henri Toussaint told me that Jacques despised Andre and regretted having saved his life.

"Belmont had a second partner who is referred to as Irish. Again, after talking to Anne Soames. I believe Irish was probably

Harry Devlin. This partnership dealt in guns for the Irish for profit. Toussaint doesn't seem to be part of this second equation.

"Ethan believed Belmont was part of a larger picture having little or nothing to do with bootlegging or gun running. According to Ethan's journal, Belmont wore an unusual ring. The same ring or one similar was found in Libby Hawk's studio years after her death. The ring gained significance only after the journal was discovered by Clara."

Simon paced while he talked. "Now here's where it gets interesting. I've learned from a source in France that Andre Belmont was in actuality, Andre Joaillier Le Belmont de Pillard. The Pillards still have ties to The Landing. Corrine Pillard Melrose is a resident. Her brother's, Harmon and Marcus Pillard, summer here on their island. The Devlins own a place down river. But to the best of anyone's knowledge it hasn't been occupied since Harry Devlin's time.

"Now I need to digress. Harry Devlin's son, Roger met Madeline Dunn at The Haven. Eventually they became lovers. Madeline visited Roger's home in Ireland. While in Ireland, Madeline became pregnant. Roger wanted marriage and their child, but he had made the mistake of allowing Madeline to learn of his IRA activities. She apparently couldn't forget nor forgive what she'd seen. She rejected Roger and returned home. Ultimately, Madeline miscarried. Exit Roger.

"Years later, Harry Devlin brought his granddaughter, Lilith to The Landing. She had affairs with both Joseph Cloud and Duncan Hawk."

Startled, the Chief took a long swallow of his beer. Simon now had his full attention.

"When Duncan found out about her affair with Joseph, he ended his relationship with her. Betraying a friend wasn't in Duncan's makeup. Lilith didn't handle Duncan's rejection well. So Harry shipped her back to Ireland–pregnant. Where she is now, parentage or sex of her child is unknown.

"Some years later, Libby is murdered. Duncan disappears. Present, Joseph Cloud is murdered and his cabin and boat house are destroyed by arson. A man as yet unidentified is found dead inside the cabin. My suite is broken into."

The Chief noted that Simon hadn't mentioned the attempt on his life. Clara should be told. It was dangerous for her not to have all the facts. Not knowing might make her careless.

"There has to be a commonality," Simon continued. "A thread that ties all of these events together. If we're to prevent more tragedy, we damn well better figure out what it is."

"Goes to motive–if I may point out the obvious," the Chief said.

Clara stared into the fire. "Revenge? Unlikely. Money, power? Money doesn't seem to be an issue. Power–could be but power in what form? To keep what one already has or to in some manner become even more powerful. Love or hate? Sometimes it's hard to tell where one begins and the other ends . . . or fear? Fear that the past won't remain past."

The Chief taped the top of his beer can. "Keep in mind. The Pillards are rich and powerful. No way I can justify an official inquiry. Better you blind side them. As a private citizen you can ask any damn thing you want. Who knows? Maybe you'll put one of them off balance and they'll make a slip. That is if they're involved." He shrugged. "As for the Devlins, they're really out of my jurisdiction."

Clara stretched out her legs and Dog groaned in protest. "The Devlins. Anne would know how to find the family." She raised her left hand and wiggled her fingers causing the diamond to sparkle in the light from the fire. "Ireland would be a perfect place for a honeymoon."

Mike O'Connor leaned forward. "Damn. Would you look at that rock. A Dunn and a Hawk. Whoa, the old Landing will really have something to talk about. Congratulations, best wishes."

"Thanks, Mike," Clara said. "But keep it to yourself. Only Judith, Luke, and now you know. We haven't made an official announcement."

"No problem." The Chief forced a smile as he remembered Libby and Duncan and the tragedy that their lives had become.

"Chief, any development's in Joseph's murder?" Simon asked.

"I'll have to ask for the same from you two–keep what we discuss under your hat, so to speak. Simple fact of the matter–this is an ongoing investigation. I shouldn't be discussing it with civilians."

"Mums the word," Clara said with a grin.

Simon put wood into the fire. "I do believe I can do that. I've had quite a few years experience in just that venue."

The Chief chuckled. "So you have and Clara isn't exactly a blabbermouth. Truth is, we've got nada. The only prints were Joseph's, John Cloud's, and yours, Clara."

"Ah, am I a suspect?" She jokingly questioned.

"Sure, so is John. I suspect both of you of being devastated by the death of someone you loved. As I said, we've got no leads. No murder weapon. Simon, any thoughts."

"We can figure out why. We can figure out who."

Clara became perfectly still. "Maddy. Maddy divined their purpose. She figured out what they were planning and she died."

"Clara," Mike said softly. "Madeline died in an accident."

Clara blinked and sighed. "So the story goes. There was no reason to think otherwise. But suppose she kept picking away at what she had learned in Ireland? Did anyone ever consider it to be anything but an accident?"

"Clara, she was skiing down the mountain. Hit an icy patch and went head on into a tree. Broke her neck."

"Did anyone see it happen?"

The Chief raised an eyebrow. "Before my time. Thanks a lot, honey. Another possible murder to check out . . . should be a piece of cake. What was it? Fifty, sixty years ago?"

Simon rubbed his forehead. All they had was a spider's web of supposition. "Initially, I thought Sylvia was grasping at straws–events from the twenties having bearing on a death and disappearance some forty years later. Now we've taken it all and projected it another thirty years forward into the present."

"Your point?" The Chief asked.

"Andrew Dunn brought his bride, Moria Killarney here from

England in what . . . ?"

"Eighteen forties." Clara answered.

"A member of the British aristocracy married to a daughter of an Irish tenant farmer."

Clara pushed Dog off her lap and began to pay more attention. "Go on."

Simon feigned an Irish brogue. "If the hatred ran deep, it could run long. Sure and the Irish are not a forgiving race."

"You're putting me on," the Chief put in. "A damn grudge running seventy years."

Clara tossed her hair back over her shoulders. "Aye, but was an Irishman tried to murder me great, great, great, grandfather Andrew when the Hawk saved his hide."

The Chief began to play their game. "Sure and I can see you're not joshing me. The babes in Ireland are taught from the cradle to hate the English. When you bide long with violence and death . . . for some, the killing becomes second nature."

Clara covered the Chief's hand with hers. "There's something more isn't there, Mike?"

He patted her hand. "You're right. Ireland was damn near the end for me. My senior year at St. Lawrence, I decided to see the places my Grandfather had talked about–get to know the Irish O'Connors, learn about my roots.

"Once in Ireland, I was welcomed with open arms. The O'Connors were from the north but I wanted to see all of Ireland. My three cousins, Kevin, Brian, and Matthew offered to travel with me. Violence seemed to follow us everywhere." The Chief's eyes were distant, lost in the tragedy that was Ireland. "I saw a man go into a church to make his confession. The penitent and the priest whose words brought absolution and death, meaningless death.

"My cousins did their best to convince me of the rightness of their cause." For a moment he fell silent. "Rightness . . ." he said softly. "What can be right about blowing up a school bus full of children?"

Simon exchanged a glance with Clara. "Your cousins?" he

asked.

The Chief nodded. "No one wants to rat out their own family but the deaths of those children were . . . I couldn't look the other way. I knew Kevin had planted the bomb. He'd bragged about it. My testimony put in prison for life."

"Testimony you gave from a wheel chair," Clara added. "I remember Uncle Lucas talking about it. He used it as an example of knowing what fights are worth fighting and those that are not. I never forgot."

"Kevin's brothers nearly beat me to death. Left me for dead in an abandoned shipyard. A bunch of kids found me or I'd have bled to death. I was weeks in a Belfast hospital. My parents came and stayed with me through the trial. When they brought me home, I was six more months in an orthopedic clinic in Boston." The Chief finished his beer. "'Course, Kevin spent his life in less comfortable surroundings. But that's why until tonight, I didn't know Lilith Devlin had ever been here in The Landing."

Simon looked puzzled. "You knew Lilith Devlin?"

"Met her in Ireland. The O'Connors, Killarneys, and Devlin were all from the same area. The Devlins being the most upscale–bankers, bankers who most likely helped bankroll the IRA. Lilith was the most visible of all the Devlins, a frightening species. The kind of woman you wanted the second you laid eyes on her, and at the same time knowing if you had her, she'd destroy you. That was Lilith, sure and it was."

Simon speculatively looked at Clara. "The knowing. Doesn't it come through the Killarney line?"

"Yes," she answered. "From mother to daughter and so on. Where are you going with this?"

"When I first spoke with your grandmother, the knowing was at the forefront of her concerns. Maybe it's central to everything."

Clara thoughtfully closed her eyes. "I've always believed the knowing would eventually provide us with the truth. It's just that it's unreliable in that sometimes what I see isn't clear."

The Chief sipped his beer. "The knowing. I'm not surprised nor would I dismiss it as a possibility. I've seen too much to doubt that such a force exists." Dog raised his head and growled. A moment later a car door closed. Simon went to the windows. "One of your deputies, Chief." As the police officer drew closer, he added, "Your son." Simon opened the door. "Hi, Mike, good to see you. Come on in."

"Mr. Hawk."

"Simon, please."

"Simon." Mike O'Connor the fourth kicked the snow from his boots. "Clara, Dad."

"Grab a beer on your way," Clara called.

"Thanks, Clara. Can't. I'm on duty. Dad, I just came from the country coroner. Shall I give you what I got?"

"Simon and Clara are okay."

Young Mike nodded and opened a plastic envelope and handed his father a ring. "This was found under the body. Thought you might want to see it. Doc said the man was dead before the fire, hit from behind. The blow literally opened up his skull. Doc was able to get a clear set of prints from the hand lying under the body. Maybe it'll get us a name."

The Chief stared at the ring turning it round and round in his fingers. Heavy silver, nude figures of a man and woman embracing. "Same design as the ring described in the journal and the one found in Libby's studio."

Clara held out her hand for the ring and slipped it on her thumb. "Large. A man's ring. Its design must have some significance–but what?"

Simon leaned on the fireplace mantel. "Symbolic of . . . say a brotherhood, monks, an Order of some sort, a sisterhood?"

"Joseph might have known," Clara said with sadness in her voice.

"Dad," Mike said. "Delaney's over at Sailors spending big. Jumbo said he's tossing around a lot of cash."

"So?"

"He's also riding a different snow machine. The guy who died in Joe's cabin had no wallet, no identification. The track Simon found ended in Delaney's backyard. The dead guy had to have gotten into Joe's place on something and there was no vehicle left at the scene."

Clara handed the ring to the Chief. "Red hated Joe. He'd burn the place out pure meanness. He probably went there drunk and stumbled on the man who was in the cabin. Hit him, took anything of value, torched the place, and booked it out of there."

The Chief finished his beer. "Okay, son. Let's go ring Red's chimes. Clara, dinner was great." As he pulled on his jacket, he glanced at Simon. "Delaney may have torched Joe's place but he doesn't have the brains or the skill to have broken into your suite at The Haven. Whoever picked the lock to your room was a pro. Watch your backs."

Simon's cell phone beeped and he answered waving a good-night to the two O'Connors. "Hey, Luke, what's up?"

"How about the four of us have breakfast at The Haven?"

Simon feigned surprise. "Four of us. Who would that be? Clara, you, me . . . John? Yeah, John did want to know what was going on."

Luke sighed. "I acknowledge my besottment and place no blame on you. Tomorrow, breakfast."

Simon hung up the phone. "Luke says he's besotted. I never would have guessed."

Clara wiped tears of laughter from her eyes. "Besotted. Oh my, he's a goner."

Dog went to the door to be let out. "I'll take them out," Simon offered. "Come on, pups. Last call."

The wolfhounds dashed for the door clumsily crashing into Dog. Clara shook her head. "They need to be trained. Time they have names."

"I'll take it under advisement," Simon said as he followed the dogs outside.

Clara took the empty cans out to the kitchen and tossed them into the recycle bin. She rinsed out the coffee cups and glasses and put them in the dish washer. Names for the pups. Mickey and Minnie? Romeo and Juliet? George and Gracie?

Simon unlocked the front door and the three dogs herded in

front of him. "Scarlet and Rhett," he called.

"Sure and the pups are Irish, but do the names suit?"

"Rhett here is all male. Bold with a touch of arrogance. Scarlet, an Irish lass. She likes to have her own way and if pushed bites."

Clara grinned. "Okay, you work with Ms. Scarlet. I'll take Rhett–I like bold, arrogance in my male animals."

Simon pulled her close. "Woof, woof."

In a corner of Molly's, a revolving fan cast a repeating pattern across the white table cloth of the round table where Lucinda Melrose, Susan Fowler, and Holly Lawrence were seated. Lucinda toyed with her wine glass. "Are we going to The Haven or what?"

"Drinks here. Dinner at The Haven. We agreed, remember?" Susan's exasperation showed in her tone. "You're in a big rush to get to The Haven to see if Simon Hawk is there."

"Well, pardon me. I'm just a little out of sorts. Waiting for royalty to arrive always puts me off my feed."

Holly sighed. "Luci, don't start. Clara called to say she'd be a few minutes late."

"Mention royalty and her name just sort of pops out. What a surprise."

Holly set her wine glass down. "You're piqued because you saw Clara with Simon. Grow up. You went out with the man once. I repeat, one time. This does not a commitment make. I believe Simon's a free agent."

"Without Clara coming on to him . . ."

Holly shook her head. "He blew you off and that was before he met Clara."

"You wanted Clyde," Susan quietly interjected. "Because you thought, you were taking him away from Clara. Once you had him, he wasn't enough. Clyde's a good man and he loves you. There aren't many around like him."

"Take him, he's yours," Luci contemptuously said as she glanced toward the front entrance. "Here she is with some stranger in tow."

146

Clara and Judith removed their coats. Clara brought Judith to the table where the others waited. "Sorry I'm late. I had to speak with my parents and the call ran long. Holly, Susan, Luci. This is Judith Hawk, Simon's sister. Judith next to you is Luci Melrose. Then Holly Lawrence. And last but not least, Susan Fowler. We've all known each other forever."

A waiter came to the table and the five women ordered. Luci looked at appraisingly at Judith. "So Judith, what brings you to The Landing?"

"Simon is thinking about making this his home. I wanted to see the area and I had vacation time coming."

Luci mockingly snapped her fingers. "And here you are."

Holly shot Luci a look of disgust. "What is it you do, Judith?"

"Investment banking. I've been at it since college. You?"

"Interior design. I've my own firm."

Clara handed the waiter a bill. "Yours."

"Thanks, Clara," he said as he served the drinks.

Clara took a sip of her wine. "Susan's an architect. The house you admired on the hill just before we came into the village–her design."

"Sounds as though everyone's found their niche," Judith said. "How about you, Luci?"

"Oh, I'm more accomplished on the physical plane. As in fucking, as in your brother."

The table fell into shocked silence. Judith purposely emphasized her southern accent. "Why sugar, we're all adults here. Y'awl could've come right out and said you were a hooker."

Susan gasped with laughter. Holly patted Luci's hand. "Hoisted on your own petard."

Luci grimaced. "Right. Let's finish this one and head for The Haven. I'll even buy."

Clara drove the winding snow-encrusted road with an expertise born of familiarity. She glanced at Judith. "What do you think of my friends?"

"Two out of three ain't bad," she joked.

"Luci does tend to put people off. She's her own worst enemy. Men, material things, jobs–once she has them, she doesn't want them. She's really very bright and creative. Just doesn't know what to do with it."

"Clara, you hid your ring. Why didn't you tell them about you and Simon?"

"Luci has a little thing for your brother. I didn't want to embarrass her in front of the others."

Judith smiled at Clara. "You have a good heart."

Clara turned the Jeep down the drive to The Haven. ""Not always. I can only be pushed just so far."

"Clara, how long did it take for you to know Simon was the right man?" Judith softly asked.

"Before we ever spoke. From the first moment I saw him." Clara answered as she pulled into a parking space. "And each minute I spend with him makes me more certain."

Luke jogged across the parking lot and helped Judith from the Jeep. "Come on woman. We're off to parts unknown–at least to you."

"Hi, Luke."

"Oh, hi cuz. See ya."

"Have a nice night," Clara called after them.

Chief O'Connor pulled up along side Clara and lowered his car window. "Got news, honey. Bud Turner's prints were on the gas can. Caught up with him and Delaney while they were both drunk. Mike and I played them off against each other. They torched Joe's together. Delaney takes the fall for nailing the guy in the cabin. District attorney made a deal with Bud. Red's a lock."

"Still, we're no closer to Joe's killer."

"No," the Chief admitted. "Afraid not. Red and Bud aren't suspects. When Joe was killed, both of them were working in Toronto. The contractor verified their alibi. He said the day of Joe's death both Bud and Red worked overtime. After work, the crew partied together at a local bar. Plenty of witnesses."

"Chief, Simon's suite. The break in. Do you think he's in

danger?"

"Yes, to tell the truth, I do," the Chief warned. "He's the one stirring up the past. I warned you last night to watch your backs. This isn't some damn game. It's for real. Clara, when you see Simon get him to tell you what's up or I will."

Holly, Susan, and Luci parked and got out of their car. Clara called, "Go on without me. I've got to get home."

Luci hurried on toward the front steps. "Fine with me," she muttered under her breath. "Maybe Simon will be alone."

At Hawk House, Clara found Simon working at his lap top. "Simon, the truth about the break-in. You can tell me or the Chief will–I'd rather it was you."

Simon closed the lap top. "I suppose he's right."

"So give."

"Plastique. Somebody wanted to take me out."

Clara's eyes seemed to look inward. Her voice was a soft lament. "Was when I saw you dead on the stone . . ."

"Clara, that was another time, another place. I'm fine."

She took his face in her hands and stared into his eyes. "Simon, no lies not even by evasion. Promise?"

Simon was relieved to have it out in the open. "Sorry, it won't happen again. I was . . . sorry, no defense."

She kissed him and took his hand. "Come on. I'll show you how you can make it up to me."

Much later, Clara came awake and quietly slipped from the bed so as not to awaken Simon. She picked up a quilt, wrapped it around herself, and curled in the window seat to wait. The knowing came as she knew it would–first the stillness, and then the anticipatory quiet. Her breathing slowed becoming imperceptible.

Soon she was adrift in the darkness of the void. It was as if she was becoming that which she saw–who she had once been in a lifetime long past.

The house was dark and silent. Only a single room facing the sea was dimly lit by candlelight. Its shuttered windows were closed, and the heavy draperies were pulled so no one from the outside could see in.

She sat on a bench near the hearth. The flames from the peat fire seemed to be captured in the wild redness of her hair. Her slender arm drew the brush through its curling, silken mass.

A tall man came into the room. One hand rested on the hilt of a long sword. His clothes were rain soaked, the brown-made black by the dampness. Water dripped from his wide brimmed hat and he took it off and tossed it onto a table. He unfastened the clasp of his cloak and draped it over the back of a chair that was close to the fire to dry.

When he moved, she could think of nothing but a sleek, dangerous wild animal. His weathered face of planes and angles served to enhance the command of his presence. His eyes, grey and cold as the ice of winter ran over her. She felt as if he stroked her body with his rock hard hands. She smiled a shy welcome.

"The search is ended. They believe you dead, drowned in the sea."

Her smile slowly faded as she remembered how she had come to be here in this place of safety. Her voice was a lament. "At what cost?"

The man drew his sword and wiped the water from its blade with the edge of his cloak. "To protect and serve—to keep the knowing alive is all that matters. Torrin died willingly, just as I would."

Tears clung to her long eye lashes. "Is there no room left for love?"

He carefully laid the sword across the trestle table. "To whom is it offered? Between us love should not be."

"I love you, Liam Devlin."

"And I you," he answered with a distant look in his eyes. "But the knowing builds a wall between us. You are Claire Killarney, and all the Killarney women of the knowing who have come before, and all those yet to be."

She raised her arms. "I cannot change who I am. But I promise there will be no ghosts past or future in our bed."

150

Clara took a deep, gasping breath. Her body ached with long-ing. The same man. Different faces, different names, yet always the same man. Just as she was always the same woman.

The sound of Clara's ragged breathing drew Simon from sleep. He rolled over and saw her silhouetted against the moon lit sky. Her arms were upraised as though reaching for or pleading with someone he couldn't see.

From the haunted expression on her face, Simon knew she was lost in the knowing. Even though awake, he felt as if he too was captured in a dream. He heard the sound of waves beating against rock. Rain pounding fiercely on the roof. Yet at the same time, he knew full well that the ground outside was covered by snow, the river frozen over with ice.

Clara's eyes slowly opened, seeing but not the now. With another's sight, she watched Simon walk toward her. His long, lean muscles rippled with power under the skin of his naked body. "Liam," she softly whispered.

Simon sat down and gently stroked her cheek with the tips of his fingers. "Clara, it's Simon. Come back to me love."

Her bewildered expression faded into awareness. "Simon, I'm sorry. I didn't mean to wake you."

"Clara, we need to talk. Let's go downstairs by the fire. There should still be coals enough to get it going."

Minutes later, they were curled together on floor pillows in front of a flickering fire. Clara nestled closer to Simon. "What is it you want to know?"

"When I woke up and saw you in the window, I could tell it was the knowing. Was there rain, a sea, ocean with pounding waves?""

She sat up to look into his eyes. "Yes, yes it was raining. The house is one I've seen many times in the knowing. The same house where I see your body lying against the hearth. It's on a cliff above the sea. Could you see it, too?"

"No. But I heard rain and the sound of waves. Clara, when I

mentioned the knowing to the Chief . . ."

"I remember. You feel the knowing is relevant to this entire situation."

"Yeah, I do. And if you'll pardon the pun, I need to know more about the knowing. Tell me what you believe it to be?"

Clara sighed and shook her head. "I wish I could tell you with certainty but truthfully, I can only speculate."

"Good enough for me," Simon assured her.

"Okay, here goes. I think that at one time the knowing may have been stronger. It's only a feeling but the force itself, the power was once more controllable, contained . . . something to be trusted rather than feared. The women from out of the knowing— I feel as though I have all their memories in me. That I am these memories. You see," she explained. "When I'm in the knowing there are times when I'm solely an observer. Other times I'm both observer and participant, watching and being all at the same time."

"Was the man of tonight's knowing Liam?"

Clara nodded. "The woman was Claire. She loved him and he her, but I think they weren't supposed to become lovers. Tonight's knowing seemed to have evolved out of a previous one. They often come in segments. Some connected to the next. Others have no common ground. Some are of the past, others precognitive."

"Have you ever tried to direct it?"

"Yes, but not successfully. When it's forced nothing's clear. Just fragments, flashes of movement without any real meaning. I do think at one time that the knowing could be . . . ah, channeled for lack of a better word. That once it was a force to be commanded."

"What kind of force?"

"A natural force arising out of the elements of nature. Joseph used to speak of a spiritual current of energy which leads to all knowledge or what some call the universal mind."

"So what do you think happened to the knowing? Did it just grow weaker?"

"No. More like the power is still there but the knowledge to utilize it has been lost or . . . something."

Simon stared into the flames. "You mentioned precognition."

"Yes, but the foreknowledge comes in fragments. Rarely is it enough to allow me act on it. Like when Joseph was murdered. I saw the knife, flames, death but not whose." Clara rested her head on Simon's shoulder. "As I matured the knowing grew stronger and I was less able to control it. As I've said before, I can sometimes tell what people are thinking, when they're lying. So watch it, buster."

Simon grinned and stroked her breast. "What am I thinking now?"

She slapped her hand. "Too easy."

"Was it always difficult for you to live with the knowing?"

"No, it wasn't. That is not until I became aware that it made me different from my peers. My family understood. They'd been accustomed to it from way back. Moria Killarney, Aunt Kathleen who was also a Killarney, Aunt Madeline, Grandmother, my mother, Aunt Libby."

"And you, Anne's wild child."

"I was that. There's a dark side to the knowing. This need to experience the other side of self. The wildness comes from that. You lose control and your civilized self seems to slip away. Alcohol and drugs enhance it. You feel powerful. I've often wondered if some women of the knowing didn't try to resist this darker side. Maybe they even preferred it."

"You think that there are other women of the knowing?"

"Why sure. The Killarneys can't have been the only family with the predisposition. There had to have been others. There must be others now." She rested in his arms. Here she felt safe. "Oh, just before we went to bed, I spoke with Anne. I meant to tell you but . . . but let's say I was waylaid."

Simon hugged her. "That would be voluntarily waylaid."

"True. Anyway, I have the Devlin's Dublin address. She said it's their family home and likely a Devlin still lives there."

Simon thought again of what he had experienced during

Clara's knowing. Rain, pounding surf. Maybe Ireland, where the Killarney's roots were, would be a starting point in learning the what and why of the knowing. "Clara, let's set our wedding date. Honeymoon in Ireland. Your parents and grandmother are coming this weekend. Judith is already here. We can get everything planned then."

"I can see the wheels turning. Honeymoon in Ireland. Check out the Devlins . . . and would the Killarneys also be on your list of must does?"

Simon laughed aloud. "You're to smart a lass for the likes of me."

"Aye, laddie, and don't you forget it." She untied his robe. Her lips played down his chest leaving a heated trail. There was an exquisite quickening in his groin. She raised her head. "By the way, I know what you're thinking."

The Haven

Luke surveyed the private dining room. It was filled to over-flowing with family. There were fresh flowers and candles, gleaming china, and sparkling crystal. He intended to give Clara and Simon an engagement extravaganza they would never forget. Thus far, the party was right on schedule.

Luke's parents, Lucus and Gabeiele Dunn had flown home from Arizona and were laughing and talking with Clara's parents, Lydia and John Eaton. Sylvia, beautifully elegant in a grey silk dinner suit, was seated by the fireplace.

Luke observed that the Dunn women would turn heads any-where. Lydia's gown was of ivory crepe de chime and draped in the style of the forties. Hers was the glamor of a different era. His mother, Gabriele was in her favorite blue—a flowing gown of silk with hand embroidered flowers. He searched the room for Judith and saw her talking with Sylvia. Judith's tea rose gown was cut low in the back. Just the sight of her made his groin tighten with desire.

If Adam and David Hawk were able to make the party, the evening would be an assured success. He had spoken to Adam in London and he'd promised to do his best. David's wife, Nicole felt it too soon to travel with their new baby, but she had graciously suggested that her parents could stay with her. She said they'd leap at the chance to spend time with their new grandson leaving David free to attend the party.

Luke checked his watch. John should be picking up Simon's friends, Jean-Claude and Elise de Lameries at the Syracuse airport. They should arrive in plenty of time to dress for the ball. He gestured to the waiter to keep the champagne glasses filled

Lucas Dunn came to his son's side. "Luke, stop pacing. Everything is perfect. Once a party is underway go with the flow. You've got a wonderful mix of people, people I've missed. Your mother hasn't been this happy in a long time."

"Dad, I think you're going to like Simon."

"I'm sure I will." He glanced toward Judith. "I like her. Should we perhaps be considering a second wedding here at The Haven?"

Luke's expression was somewhere between elation and panic. "I don't think so. Long distance relationships never work. Between the schools and The Haven my cup run'th over."

"Luke, as much as I want you to take over the Dunn properties, I don't want it at the expense of your happiness. If your place is with Lindquist/Dunn Schools, so be it. If it means Judith Hawk, so be it. All your mother and I want is for you to be happy." He took a glass of champagne from the tray of a passing waiter and handed it to Luke. "Enjoy tonight. Everything else will work out in due time."

"From your lips to God's ear," Luke muttered under his breath. He watched his father rejoin his mother and put his arm around her waist. She looked up at him with a love-filled smile.

He wondered if they knew how lucky there were to have each other.

The double doors to the dining room opened. Adam Hawk followed by David Hawk entered the party. Their imposing presence drew all eyes.

Lucas Dunn raised his glass. "To the return of the Hawks– our friends, our family. Welcome home."

Glasses were raised, excited greetings were exchanged. Luke smiled in satisfaction. He had never seen so much hugging and kissing. Judith touched his arm with tears in her eyes. "How did you ever manage to get my father and grandfather here? It's a wonderful surprise."

"Think of me as a super hero," he said with a smile. Over Judith's shoulder, he saw the light above the room's entrance flash twice. He raised his voice. "May I have your attention?" Luke's request was lost in the conversational hum. He shouted. "Listen up! Clara and Simon are on their way."

Heads turned toward the room's main entrance just as the double doors opened to admit Clara and Simon. Lucas Dunn again raised his glass. "To Clara and Simon. May their lives be blessed and filled with love."

All glasses were raised in a toast. "To Clara and Simon."

Simon glanced around the room and saw his grandfather and father standing with Judith and Sylvia and his face broke into a broad smile. He took Clara's hand and whispered. "Luke is something else. Come on, let me introduce you to your prospective in-laws."

As Simon brought Clara to meet his family, David spoke in an aside to Adam. "My God, they could be Libby and Duncan."

Adam nodded. "Let's pray this union is blessed."

Simon smiled at his family. "Grandfather. Dad. This is Clara," he proudly said. "Clara. My grandfather, Adam. And my father, David."

David Hawk enfolded Clara in his arms. "I can't tell you how pleased I am."

Adam took both of Clara's hands in his. "My dear, thank you

for giving us the happiest of reasons to end our long exile."

"Thank you for welcoming me into your family," Clara said with a warm smile. She leaned toward Adam and whispered. "I think he's marrying me for Hawk House. He fell in love with it first."

Simon chuckled. "I heard that."

"What no denial, son," David joked.

"Take a look at her and tell me what you think," Simon rejoined. He bent down to kiss Sylvia's cheek.

Sylvia smiled up at him. "Welcome to our family. You and Clara are a perfect match."

"If I didn't know better, I'd suspect you'd planned the whole thing."

"What makes you so certain I didn't?" Sylvia answered with laughter in her voice.

John Eaton joined them and took his daughter's arm. "Clara, I'm sorry to intrude but the Pillards are at the door. They'd like to extend their best wishes to the happy couple."

"Excuse us for a moment," Clara said. "We won't be long."

As Clara, Simon, and John walked toward the door they heard Lydia greet the Pillards. "It's so good to see all of you again. It's been much to long."

John Eaton began the introductions. "Corrine, Harmon, Mark. I'd like you to meet my soon to be son-in-law, Simon Hawk."

Simon smiled at Corrine. "Corrine and I have met."

Corrine glanced at him, then at Clara. Simon was surprised to see something bitter and cold in her eyes. "I understand you and Clara are engaged," Corrine tersely snapped.

"Yes, we'll be married soon."

"I was right. You are indeed like Duncan."

Marcus Pillard put out his hand. "Simon, I'm Marcus Pillard. A pleasure to meet you. Congratulations, you're a fortunate man." He smiled warmly at Clara. "Best wishes, my dear. You grow love-lier every time I see you."

"Thank you, Senator," Clara said ignoring Corrine's rudeness that was so out of character.

"Simon, my brother, Harmon Pllard."

Simon nodded. Harmon's expression was bored and distant. "Hawk. Clara, you look magnificent."

Simon turned to Marcus Pillard. "Senator," he began in a low voice. "I'd like to speak with you and your family concerning a journal written by my great-grandfather, Ethan Hawk."

"Of course. We'll be dining in the main room. John has asked us to join everyone for dancing in the ballroom. Perhaps a good time would be immediately after dinner."

"Thank you." Simon turned to look for Clara and found her in the hallway speaking with Luci and a man who had been pointed out as her soon to be ex husband. He walked over to join them.

Luci seemed relaxed more comfortable in her own skin than he had before noted. She looked at him and with a genuine smile said, "Simon, I'd like you to meet my husband, Clyde Meridan. Clyde, Simon Hawk."

Clyde put out his hand. "A pleasure. May I say you're marrying a most remarkable woman."

"You may. And I'm pleased to know you."

Lucinda took her husband's hand. "Clara, I've thought over everything you said yesterday . . . that is after I got over being pissed."

Simon glanced at Clara. What was Luci talking about?

Luci saw Simon's puzzled expression. "Simon, yesterday your significant other invited me to lunch. It included a lecture on self-destructive behavior. As usual, I wanted to punch her out, but unfortunately or fortunately depending on ones point of view, she was right."

Clyde Meridan put his arm around Luci's waist and held her close. "Whatever Clara said is fine with me. We're putting our divorce on hold and see what happens."

"I'm not sure what to say," Simon answered. "Congratulations, best wishes, all of the above."

Luci tenderly looked at Clyde. "No one is more surprised than me."

Clara glanced at Simon with an expression much like that of

a cat who's swallowed the canary. "You two be sure and join us later in the ballroom. Bring Susan and Holly with you."

From the Pillard table in the main dining room, Corrine Melrose watched Clara and Simon return to the party–their engagement party. Old jealousies simmered beneath the surface and brought a flush to Corrine's face. Her eyes were dark with fury. Clara and Simon together. If they weren't careful, they were likely to end up becoming another tragedy in the Hawk/Dunn saga.

Marcus and Harmon joined her at the table. A hovering waiter quickly took their drink orders.

"Clara certainly has become the image of Libby, hasn't see?" Corrine pointedly said.

Marcus glanced at his sister but refused to rise to her bait. That he had never forgotten Libby was his own private anguish. His fate had been decided long before Libby had come into his life. His destiny was tied to a family heritage supported by a massive fortune. He had always been pursued by the stereotype women of his social strata. Women who viewed him as their stepping stone to high position and wealth. His mother had very early taught him that there was a crucial distinction between a woman one takes, and a woman one takes seriously.

Libby had been the exception to all the rules. He had loved her knowing full well that she wasn't the right choice for his political future. It was his destiny and he had never considered any other. Not even when it cost him the only woman he had ever loved. He took a large swallow of his drink. He envied Simon Hawk his Clara more than it was possible to say.

In the private dining room conversation swirled and ebbed touching on the past, catching up with the present. Joyful that their future would again include each other. Laughter and tears–the joys and sorrows of two families whose history encompassed nearly a hundred and fifty years.

Simon watched as his father proudly displayed pictures of

Duncan Joseph. "He looks just like Simon did as a baby. I only hope he turns out as well."

Simon placed his hand on his father's arm. "Could we speak in private?"

David excused himself and followed Simon out into the hall. "What is it?"

"You said you had something to tell me concerning Duncan."

David looked into his son's eyes. "When you were a kid growing up, I was hard on you. In your teens, later in college, I tried to force you to conform, to be whom I expected you to be. Now I see why. It really had nothing to do with you, but with Duncan."

"Sorry, Dad. I don't get it."

"It's just that you are as like him as another person could be. Your attitude, physical appearance, even the same strong moral values and a talent for something other than business. I saw Duncan in you and was afraid I'd lose you just as Duncan was lost."

"Dad, we've put all that behind us."

"I thank you. I just hope you know how much it means to me to have you back in my life."

"Ditto. About Duncan."

David glanced around to be certain they would not be overheard. "About a week before Duncan disappeared, he called and asked me to liquidate one of his accounts and convert the funds into bearer bonds. A half million in bonds. I did as he asked and sent them to a bank in Toronto. He signed for them so I know they were delivered. Through the years those same bonds have been cashed in various cities–Paris, Naples, Hong Kong. Never the same city twice. Never anything conclusive on the person who cashed them." David paused, then said, "I've never told your grandfather. I didn't want to set up any false hope. But it's why I've kept on looking. Why I've never believed he's dead."

"Why didn't you mention it at the time of Libby's death? Bearer bonds can be cashed by anyone. Might have gone to motive?"

"The police were already convinced of Duncan's guilt. Their

interpretation would have been that he took the bonds and made a run for it."

"I see. Dad, did you know Duncan may have a child?"

David was obviously astounded. "Hell, no. With whom?"

"A Lilith Devlin."

"I'll be damned. I remember her. She was gorgeous but on the wild side. Do you think this ties into Libby's death?"

Simon shrugged. "Haven't a clue, just gut instinct. As soon as Clara and I are married, we're going to Ireland. Some of the answers may be over there."

"Excuse me," a waiter said. "Senator Pillard asks if you'd care to join him for an after dinner drink."

Simon turned to his father. "Tell Clara I'll meet her in the ballroom."

"Be careful. If looks could kill, we'd be among the dead. Ever since we started to talk, Corrine Melrose had been glaring in our direction. When I spoke with her earlier, she seemed furious about your engagement. Why should it bother her one way or the other?"

"Frankly, I don't care what she thinks or why. Then again, maybe I should."

Before David could ask what his son meant, Simon was on his way to the main dining room.

As Simon came into the room, he heard a string quartet playing Valvaldi. Corrine ignored his presence refusing to make eye contact. Harmon was seated next to her absently swirling his brandy in its snifter.

The Senator gestured for Simon to be seated. "Now what is this journal? Corrine tells me Clara discovered it in Hawk House."

"Yes, she did. But I think it's possible that Libby was the first to find it."

"I see," the Senator answered. "What does this have to do with us?"

"One of your ancestors is mentioned rather prominently. Andre Belmont–bootlegger, smuggler, and gun runner. Are you aware of his existence?"

Harmon Pillard leaned back in his chair. "His name is Andre Joaillier Le Belmont de Pillard. Much to our dismay, old Andre was our grandfather. Later he took the name of Joaillier. He had two sons, Claude and Charles. Claude, our father, had no use for Andre and broke with the old man while he was still in college. It was around the same time that our father traveled to France and met the French de Pillards. With their blessing, he elected to return to our birthright–hence, Pillard."

Marcus continued the explanation. "Out of deference to our father, Harmon and me rarely came in contact with Andre." He paused and smiled at Corrine. "My sister was less circumspect and ignored father's decree of non fraternization."

Corrine sneered. "He was a charming, cultured gentleman of the old school. His was the greatest influence in my life. He exposed me to the theater, music, the arts. My parents never had time for anything but politics."

"According to Ethan's journal, your charming, cultured grandfather raped Clara Hawk Dunn. A rape which drove her to suicide."

"Somehow," the Senator put in. "I find it quite believable. According to my father, Andre was a monster who liked to inflict pain–especially on those weaker than him."

"Let me ask you, Senator. Politically, wouldn't you view Andre as a time bomb?"

"Strangely enough, he's never come to light. If he ever does our long time disassociation from him, our going back to our roots will keep my proverbial skirts clean." The Senator spread his hands wide. "Besides, politics has become a media free for all. If Andre did escape from the closet, he'd probably be seen as a glamourous adventurer."

Simon's eyes narrowed. "Would that have been true around the time of Libby's death?"

A red flush crept up the Senator's neck. "You are direct. No, it wouldn't have been true at that time. But I wouldn't have killed Libby to prevent it from coming out."

Harmon glared at Simon. "Andre was a bastard. But even at

162

that time, I could have put a spin on it that would have made him seem to be a tragic hero–a man escaping France just ahead of losing his head. It would quickly have become a nonissue. Hawk. I've let you have the floor. Now I'd like to change the subject for a moment. A while back, your official protests put me on the hot seat."

"People died. Don't you think someone should have been held accountable?"

"If you bureaucratic paper pushers ever followed through, they'd have learned a hot shot reporter looking for a Pulitzer sneaked the list of agents assisting the Chinese freedom fighters by the senior editor. On the other hand, had I been cognizant of the situation. I might have published it anyway."

Simon shook his head in disgust. "How can you take pride in such a statement?"

"Tell me, have you ever read The Fountainhead?"

"Ayn Rand's novel? Yes, I have, many years ago."

"Do you recall the character who buys out a newspaper and how he determined its policy?"

"Yes."

"He was right. Sensationalism sells. If I publish a story of five kids helping an old lady cross the street no one would read it. If five kids beat up an old lady and steal her purse, it's news. Truth–the rank and file don't want to know. They want to be titillated."

"There are still people who value the truth."

"Not enough of them to pay the bills," Harmon spat. "But then we're not here to discuss my publishing expertise."

"Or lack there of," Simon added. "The subject at hand–Libby Hawk was brutally slaughtered. A ring described in the journal as having been worn by Andre Belmont/Joaillier was found in her studio."

Corrine barked a laugh. "By the time Libby was killed, Grandfather was too old to be running around the country slicing up women. In fact, after his smuggling days were over, he left the islands and never came back."

Simon speculatively watched Corrine. Where was all this hostility and anger coming from? All evening her attitude had seemed out of step with events. When they had first met, he had enjoyed her company. What had changed?

"One more question–what became of the other Belmont/Joailliers?"

The Senator shrugged. "Andre's dead. As are our father and his brother, Charles. Joaillier Limited is run by Charles' sons, George and Robert."

"Joaillier Limited?" Simon asked.

"Import/export firm."

"One does have to wonder if they've kept up the family tradition of trafficking in illegal arms," Simon dryly said.

"Perhaps they do," Corrine snapped. "It's nothing to us. We've had no contact with them since grandfather died more than twenty years ago."

Marcus leaned back in his chair and sipped his brandy. "Simon, where are you going with this? Do you actually think Ethan's journal could have precipitated Libby's death?"

"Yes, I do. Andre had two partners. Jacques Toussaint, and Harry Devlin. Toussaint figured in the bootlegging side of the equation. Devlin in both bootlegging and gun running. Something stemming from that time gave rise to murder and a disappearance in sixty-seven."

"Hard to fathom," the Senator mildly said. "What leads you to believe this?"

"Probably Clara's knowing," Corrine bitingly injected.

Simon ignored her remark and said, "Hawk House was trashed. My guess is that the person was looking for the journal, but it remained hidden until Clara discovered it a few months ago. I think Joseph Cloud was killed to prevent him from reading it."

For the first time since the conversation began, Harmon's face revealed emotion. "Joseph was a good man. I was very sorry to hear of his death. But even if old Andre played the role of villain in Ethan's journal. What does it prove? Why, so many years after the fact would anyone care?"

Simon's eyes were hard and cold. "If Joseph Cloud hadn't been murdered, I'd have been inclined to drop the matter. First, Libby. Now Joseph and the man who were bludgeoned to death in his cabin. It's highly probable that the same knife killed both Libby and Joseph." He stood. "I intend to find out who slaughtered those people, and why."

Corrine laughed without humor. "It takes proof, Hawk. The legal system requires proof."

"Indeed it does. There is also justice which often isn't the same thing. But I can assure you, once I'm certain of the killer's identity he or she won't kill again."

Corrine's tone dripped with venom. "My, my. There's still a lot of savage in you, isn't there?"

Simon smiled. "We prefer Native American." And without a backward glance, he walked away.

The Haven's ballroom took up the entire third floor of the East wing. It was most frequently used for wedding receptions. The balls of the past hadn't been in vogue for a very long time. Luke had decided it was time to revive their elegance. He had imaginatively transformed the space into a romantic setting. The enormous room's corners and alcoves were filled with saplings in baskets, their branches dressed with tiny white lights. The three Waterford crystal chandeliers sparkled in the light from the candles on each table. On the bandstand, the orchestra played an old-fashioned waltz.

Simon stood on the sidelines searching the crowd for Clara. It seemed that the entire population of The Landing was in attendance. How Luke had managed to pull everything together in a few short days was beyond him.

Lydia and John Eaton danced past Simon's line of vision, and he saw his grandfather and Sylvia circling the floor. Gabriele and Lucas Dunn waved as they passed. Judith and Luke. Where was Clara? He saw his father whirl by with a delicate petite blond. She looked familiar but before he could place her, they were lost in the crowd. Near the bandstand, he caught a glimpse of a tall man, bald with skin the color of honey. A glimpse was all Simon needed to identify him. Jean-Claude de Lamerie was a compelling man with the powerful body of an athlete, lean face, and slanted oriental eyes. The product of a marriage between a French diplomat stationed in Singapore, and a beautiful Eurasian woman. His was a face that Simon would have recognized anywhere. Only Jean-Claude's appearance among this evenings guests was surprising.

As Simon started for the bandstand, he heard the sensuous tempo of the tango. The floor began to clear and through the separating crowd, he saw Clara standing next to Jean-Claude.

A small hand plucked Simon's sleeve. He glanced down into Elise's upturned face. It had been she dancing with his father. Luke. Luke must have gotten in touch with them.

"Simon, *mes ami*, you are surprised, no?"

"My darling Elise. I am surprised, yes. Come dance with me," he said holding out his hand. "Your husband is up to his old tricks."

Elise took his hand and they stepped onto the dance floor. At the opposite end, Jean-Claude smiled at Clara. "You see. The gauntlet is tossed."

"Thrown," Clara automatically corrected as she followed his lead.

"*Oui*, thrown."

Simon and Elise danced the tango with style and grace. Jean-Claude and Clara danced as if they had rehearsed. The men's faces were fixed in concentration. The dance floor cleared as the two couple danced toward the center of the floor.

From the sidelines the other guests watched the two spectacular couples in entranced silence. When the music began the final movements, Jean-Claude whispered to Clara. "At the end I will spin you out into Simon's arms. He will do the same with Elise."

"How do you know?" Clara asked as he bent her low to the floor.

"Trust me." He lifted her back up and made a quick turn.

Suddenly Clara was spinning toward Simon to end in his

arms. While Elise finished the dance in the arms of her husband. The guests broke into delighted applause. Jean-Claude with arms wide spread came to Simon. He enfolded him in a bear hug and kissed both his cheeks.

Applauding, Luke and Judith joined the foursome. Luke wore a satisfied grin. "I didn't know how to find all your friends but at least I managed two."

"Thanks, Luke. I find I like you more every day."

"Yeah, right. You're buttering me up because you're besotted with my cousin and you want the family on your side."

Elise and Jean-Claude looked at each other and in unison asked, "Besotted?"

Jean-Claude's brow furrowed. "Does one drink it or wear it?"

Elise patted his shoulder. "I think you are it."

"I think with all that dancing, I could use a drink," Simon said.

The group strolled to the service area while the party swirled around them. Jean-Claude drew Simon aside. "Are these American Pillards here?"

"Yes. They're seated to your right, third table. Two men and a woman."

Jean-Claude glanced over his shoulder.

"The blonde is the daughter?"

"Yes, why?"

"I fell over Pierre de Pillard at an art auction."

"Ran into."

"*Oui*, de Pillard speaks again of these American ones. He tells me how many years ago he helped the family put the daughter in a private clinic outside Paris. He says they wished to play this very close to the chest . . . vest. She was, how you say, spaced out–drugs, booze. He thinks even heroin. He calls her a lost soul, very, very bad."

"Did he say when this was?"

"*Non*, but the clinic I know, as do you."

"Le Chateau Evian?"

"*Oui*, where we took Elise." Jean-Claude's eyes clouded with memory. "So long ago. Now she is okay."

"More than okay," Simon agreed. He glanced toward the door to see John Cloud hesitating in the room's entrance. Simon excused himself and took Clara's arm. "John's just arrived. He looks a little nervous."

"He shouldn't be. He's the best of the best. John," Clara called. "Over here. Join us."

"Clara, Simon. Thanks for the invitation. This monkey suit takes some getting used to. It's a first for me."

"Find more reasons to wear one. You look absolutely fantastic," Clara assured him.

Simon chuckled. "Watch it. Keep this up and I'll have to challenge John to a duel."

John relaxed, comfortable with his welcome. "Clara, driving up here from the reservation, I had the strongest sense of Joseph's presence. I'm certain he'd bless your union."

Clara looked at Simon. "I know he would. He'd have liked Simon."

Simon saw Corrine Melrose look in their direction and leave her table. She walked with the careful, precise steps of the very drunk

She stopped in front of them, swaying ever so slightly. "Johnny Cloud. My you do look handsome. I remember the first time I saw Joseph in a tux. I simply couldn't keep my hands off him. And Duncan. Now there was a catch. Simon here is just like him. Sooo very much like him." Corrine squinted at Clara. "You resemble my dear, dear friend, Libby. But you're not like her. She was weak. There's strength in you." She ran her fingernail along the velvet vee of Clara's gown. "She would have worn this. It's her style."

Clara's face suddenly drained of color. Her eyes stared into the darkness of the knowing–a monastery with a walled courtyard. She heard the clash of steel on steel and the screams of the dying. Flames from the fire turned the sword's blades a fiery red. Her voice was a whisper. "Do you remember the mountains?"

Simon saw her eyelids flicker and caught her just as she

fainted. He carried her out into the hallway and lay her down on a Victorian sofa.

Corrine's mocking voice followed them. "Was it something I said?"

Simon gently brushed Clara's hair off her face. "Clara, come on honey. It's Simon."

Her eyes fluttered open and she gripped Simon's hand as if it were a life line. "That hasn't happened in a very long time."

Simon helped her to sit up. John Cloud handed her a snifter of brandy. "Here, Clara. Sip this."

She took John's advice and sipped the brandy. "I'm all right. It's gone."

Simon shook his head. "No, you're still pale. Sit for a minute. Take it slow."

Clara rested her head against the back of the couch. "I'm fine, really. It doesn't last long and when it's gone, it's gone. No dizziness. Honest." She held out her hand.

John helped her to her feet. "The knowing, huh?"

"I'm afraid so," she admitted.

Simon was tense with concern. "It happened when Corrine touched you, didn't it?"

"It's over. Let's just forget it," Clara dismissively said.

The elevator doors slid open. Anne Soames, her arms linked with those of two handsome men, stepped out of the elevator. One of the men was blonde and blue eyed with the look of a Nordic Viking. The second was a handsome black man with broad powerful shoulders, and the lean frame of a long distance runner.

Behind them a giggling Holly Lawrence and Susan Fowler appeared. Luci and Clyde followed. The group was obviously having a good time.

Anne waved a gay greeting. "Simon, close your mouth. You look stunned. Clara, this is Stephen and Pepe. They're crashing your party," she airily explained, and with a smile at Stephen and Pepe said, "Keep in mind, I expect a dance from each of you."

Stephen bowed and kissed her hand. "We are honored."

Anne favored him with a smile and with regal grace swept on

into the ballroom.

Clara tilted her head. "Simon, do you know these gentlemen?"

The Viking took Clara's hand and raised it to his lips. "Madame, I am Stephen Hammersheild. My friend here is Pepe Hawkins, not to be confused with Hawk. Though they do look remarkably alike. Once we were friends of your fiancee but alas, he neglected to invite us to the festivities. We were devastated."

"Yes," Pepe agreed. He beat his chest with a closed fist. "Devastated, totally. Then we thought how wrong it would be for a lovely lady such as you to marry this bounder without knowing of his dark and checkered past. So here we are."

"Don't be deceived by appearances, Clara," Simon said. "These two are no gentlemen. They are fools of the highest order. Trouble makers from the word go." Simon smiled broadly. "But damn, I'm glad to see them. How in hell did the two of you end up here."

"Jean-Claude gave us a call," Pepe volunteered. "Luke Dunn told him if he thought of anyone . . . and presto we appear."

Stephen put his arms around Holly and Susan. "And my, oh my, the ladies here are very easy on the eyes–most definitely tens. Shall we enter the fray?"

Simon lowered his head and whispered to Clara. "Most of our friends and family are right here in The Landing. Perfect time for a wedding. How about a candlelight ceremony Sunday evening?"

"I'm game if you are," Clara said. "But what about the blood test, license?"

"My darling, we are surrounded by movers and shakers. It can be done."

Clara and Simon found Lydia and John, seated with Adam and David, and Sylvia. At their approach Sylvia smiled. "Here they are. I forgot to tell you. Your Uncle Carson and Stephen are sorry they can't be here. Carson is in Japan, and Stephen is vacationing in Cancun."

Clara reached out for Simon's hand. "I'm afraid they're going to miss the wedding, too. Simon and I would like to get married

Sunday evening while Simon's friends and family are here."

"Clara, I wish you'd reconsider," Lydia said, trying to hide her disappointment. So many people who would expect to be invited will be left out. I know it's your wedding . . ."

"Mom, how about when we get back from our wedding trip, you and Dad throw us a big reception."

Lydia brightened. "In New York?"

Clara impishly grinned. "Yes, my darling mother–in New York. And I promise to be the sole of propriety. Although, I'm afraid, I can't speak for the groom."

Simon raised his hand. "I do so swear, sole of."

John Eaton nudged David. "I'd say that's that. We'd better round up the relevant people and get this thing off the ground."

Luke was pressed into service and managed to get all those to be included in the wedding party assembled at one end of the ball-room.

John Eaton drew Clara and Simon forwards. "These two impetuous people want to be married on Sunday. We need volunteers to pull this off."

Amidst gasps of surprise and applause, Sunday was agreed on. Holly, Susan, and Luci were pressed into service as bridesmaids with Judith as maid of honor. Luke would be best man with Jean-Claude, Stephen, and Pepe as grooms men.

The women began to discuss what to do about the proper attire. Gabby Dunn tapped her champagne glass. "I have a suggestion. The overall effect would be timeless."

Clara looked perplexed. "What do you mean, Aunt Gabby?"

"In the attic of our Riverwalk house there are trunks of gowns belonging to everyone from Moria Killarney Dunn on down. Clara, the first Clara's bridal gown is in one of them."

"Oh, Aunt Gabby. Wouldn't that be perfect . . . if it fits?"

"My dear, I'm a seamstress extraordinary. Trust me. If it's what you want, it'll fit."

David Hawk and John Eaton waited on the sidelines. David impatiently cleared his throat. "Ladies, have we reached a final decision?"

Lydia smiled. "You and John announce the ceremony and invite everyone. The ceremony will take place Sunday evening at six right here in this room."

Clara raised her hand. "I have a question. How do we bypass the rules and regulations? And who will marry us?"

David Hawk chuckled. "I do believe the license and a blood test can be pushed through. I've already spoken to the Senator. As for who will preside–John, any suggestions?"

"Judge Atler has known Clara since she was a baby. He and his wife are here somewhere. I'm sure he'd be happy to preside."

"I'll locate him," David said and made his way to the bandstand. Soon a page was heard and Judge Atler came to his side.

John Eaton came over to where Simon was in conversation with Luke. "David has the matter well in hand. Simon, could we speak privately for a moment."

Luke did a moon walk backwards. "I know when I'm not wanted. I'm gone out of here."

"John, what is it?" Simon asked.

John saw that Simon was concerned and quickly belied his fears. "I can assure you that I'm very pleased you and Clara are marrying." With an amused smile, he shook his head. "You two may well have the shortest engagement on record, but when it's right, it simply is. Simon, what I want to talk about is the knowing."

"Go on."

"Firstly, I know you were agented out with consular cover and were damn good at your job–too good for the taste of some. I'm glad you're out. What I want to say now is for your ears only. If Lydia and Clara knew I'd pursued this, they'd drum me out of the family. You know how independent they are."

"I do. I won't say a word," Simon promised.

"Years ago when Lydia and I were first married, her knowing was much stronger than it is now. It frightened her. Where Clara has sought to understand it, Lydia simply wanted it gone."

"Clara's is growing stronger."

"I rather thought it would. She's always approached it head

172

on. Had it not been for Joseph Cloud. I'm not sure where it would have taken her. But to get back on track, Lydia's knowing concerned me. As a result, I spent a good deal of time in university libraries searching for a clue to this curse, blessing, gift . . . whatever. At every duty station, I prowled through old manuscripts. I found several mentions of wise women, and of men who were defined as protectors. Nothing definitive. Some time ago, I stopped."

"Why?"

"I was afraid that by dredging up the past, I might be putting those I love in danger. After a time it became apparent that I wasn't the only one interested in these wise women."

"Clara believes there are other women with this knowing."

John nodded. "I think she's correct. What frightens me is that in all the tomes I've searched, there has been a single common thread. These wise women had protectors. What I question is why . . ."

Simon finished his thought. "Why did they need protectors?"

"Precisely. And if the women needed them in the past . . . maybe for a reason that isn't clear, they need them now."

Simon listened to John Eaton with growing respect. He knew John Eaton had a British father who was one of the landed gentry. Yet when John's American mother divorced his father, John, who at the time was in his late teens, had chosen to live with his mother in the states. A decision which had cost him his silver spoon. Through his own efforts he had graduated from Yale. His pedigree and background made him a candidate for the State Department where he acquitted himself with great merit. John Eaton was a fine and honorable man. A man Simon knew he could respect and trust. "It would seem our role is to protect and serve."

"And to love, Simon. To love."

Culzean Castle/Scotland

As Simon watched Clara sleep, their wedding replayed in his mind. The wedding party had all worn gowns in varying shades of white from cream to ivory to a tint of pearl. All had been pilfered from the treasure trove in the Dunn attic.

Clara had worn the first Clara's wedding gown. Its satin had aged to a soft ivory and fit Clara to perfection. It was as if the simple, classic style had been designed for her. Her only jewelry was a pearl and diamond choker. A family heirloom which had been worn by the Dunn women ever since Andrew Dunn had given it to Moria Killarney as her wedding gift.

Simon thought that nothing could equal the pride and love he felt when he slipped the wide, gold wedding band on Clara's finger. Now they were in Scotland staying at the famous Culzean Castle in Ayrshire near Turnberry–a wedding gift from Clara's parents. Here was the same quiet exclusivity one found at The Haven. A place where one was content too simply be.

Yesterday they had walked along the sea, lunched in a working man's pub, and shot darts with some of the villagers. In the evening they enjoyed an intimate dinner in their suite.

Simon slipped from the bed and went to the windows overlooking the Firth of Clyde. The sea swept against the base of the sheer cliff sending white froth spray into the air. In a few days they would be on their way to Ireland to find Lilith Devlin. All they had to go on was the Dublin address given to them by Anne Soames–an address that was almost fifty years old. The trip might well prove to be an exercise in futility.

Lilith Devlin's only connection to the journal was through her grandfather, Harry Devlin and his partnership with Andre Belmont. Still, she had affairs with both Duncan Hawk and Joseph Cloud. In all likelihood one of the two men had fathered her child. With so little else to go on, it was worth checking out.

Simon wondered what had really happened to Duncan. Was

he dead or did the cashing of the bearer bonds indicate otherwise? His thoughts drifted to Corrine Melrose. Her behavior at the engagement celebration, coupled with being a no show at the wedding, had struck a discordant note.

Having learned of Corrine's hospitalization for drug addiction made her a more viable suspect. Was she capable of murder? Would something in the journal have struck a cord in Joseph and he was murdered because of it? He sighed, questions with no answers. Behind him, Clara stirred drawing his thoughts to more pleasant possibilities.

Dublin, Ireland

The Dublin address Clara and Simon sought was finally discovered hidden in an obscure cul de sac. The house, a monstrous structure of no particular architectural school, squatted like an ugly frog in the midst of new commercial development.

Clara and Simon cautiously climbed the ice slick brick steps. Even the wrought iron rail was glazed in silver from the still falling rain. Clara shivered. The steady drizzle pushed by the wind chilled her to the bone. "I thought the North Country was cold."

Simon banged the door knocker. "So far Ireland had been fog, rain, and a royal pain in the butt. Let's hope things improve."

The heavy door opened inward and they were confronted by a small, thin man in a black suit who peered at them through eyes dimmed by time. "May I be of service?"

"I'm Simon Hawk and this is my wife, Clara. We were told that this was the Devlin family home."

"To be sure. May I ask who you wish to see?"

"We'd like to speak with Lilith Devlin."

A voice barked from out of the gloom. "Send them in."

The man stepped aside to allow Simon and Clara into the foyer. To Clara the room seemed oppressive–dark paneled walls, marble floor with an open stairway climbing one wall to the second story. She reluctantly removed her coat and handed it to the waiting butler.

Through an open doorway, she could see the library with shelves of leather bound books. Again, there were dark paneled walls and a hardwood floor covered with a nondescript carpet. Next to a blazing fire, a man was seated in a high-backed leather chair. His legs were covered with a heavy throw. "In here," he barked.

Simon and Clara entered the room and the man gestured for them to be seated. Clara's breath caught in her throat. There was a leering evil buried deep in the man's cold, agate eyes.

"I am Roger Devlin."

In that one split second, Clara knew he had murdered Madeline. How she must have hated him once she had learned his truth. "I am Clara Dunn Eaton Hawk."

"I know who the Dunns are," he snapped. "What do you want?"

Simon felt tension vibrating through Clara's body and sensed it would be best if he answered. "To speak with your daughter, Lilith."

"Lilith," Devlin said with menacing softness. "Lilith took my bank, destroyed my life's work. May she rot in hell."

"Where is your daughter?"

Roger Devlin stiffened in his chair. The cold, command in his eyes made him a formidable presence. "For me she is dead. Now get out of my house."

Clara thought of Madeline and of her unborn child. This man had caused their deaths. Anger and contempt brought her to her feet. "Dead would be better than living under the same roof with someone as despicable as you."

Devlin stared at her as if at an apparition. "A long time ago another Dunn bitch said those same words to me. I'm certain that in time she regretted them."

Clara smiled then–a dazzling smile that was out of place in

the context of their confrontation. "In all things there is a balance. I look forward to the day I can dance on your grave. Soon–it will be soon."

Devlin's face turned an ashen grey and he fumbled for a pill box on the table. It slipped from his fingers scattering small white pills on the carpet. "Pill," he gasped. "Need pill."

Clara stood where she was. Simon quickly kneeled and picked one up and helped Devlin place it under his tongue. He gathered the others from the carpet and put them back into the pill box and placed it on the table.

Clara's voice reached Devlin as if coming out of the wind. "She died only once. You. You've died a hundred deaths. Inch by inch, you're dying–in fear and alone."

Simon touched Clara's shoulder. "Clara, it's time to leave."

For a moment she stared at him as if they were strangers. "Yes, we should."

In the foyer, the butler waited with their coats. He spoke in a hushed tone. "She's north by the Irish sea near Cushendall. Ask in the village. They'll know."

Simon pulled on his top coat and glanced at the butler. "Why didn't you help him?"

"Madame only suffered his presence for a few minutes and she wisely chose not to offer assistance. I've known him for more than fifty years. Would seem I might have greater reason. Sure and he's been dying from this same condition for twenty years. Would be a blessing were he gone."

Clara with one hand on the door, asked, "Did you know Madeline?"

The butler slowly nodded and with great dignity, he turned and disappeared into the bowels of the house.

Simon silently drove the rented Volvo through the grey rain on the first leg of the long drive to Cushendall. He and Clara had gotten up before dawn and had been on the road since first light. Acting as copilot, Clara read the map and guided them out of Dublin. Now she stared blindly at the passing scenery.

Simon was worried about her. Since leaving Roger Devlin's house, Clara had been strangely quiet. Last night, for the first time since they'd met, they hadn't made love. This morning when he awakened, Clara had already showered and dressed. "Clara, are you all right?"

Her hands were clenched together in her lap. "The closer we get the more afraid I am," she reluctantly admitted.

"But you don't know why."

"No, just this feeling . . . dread. Simon, I'm sorry for what happened yesterday at Devlins. I know you were disappointed in me. But I couldn't help him. I couldn't. I wanted him to die." She wiped tears from her eyes. "Something's happening to me."

Simon pulled to the side of the road. "Clara, we don't have to go to Cushendall. We can turn around and go back to Dublin and catch a flight for France. Visit Jean-Claude and Elise. If you'd rather not be around people, we can find somewhere warm and lay on a beach all day. We don't have to do this."

"That's what frightens me the most. We do. I can't tell any more what's real or what's unreal. At Devlins it was as if I was seeing Roger Devlin as a young man. I knew all he'd done–all the people whose death's he was responsible for. Maybe in Cushendall we'll find some answers."

Simon understood her trepidation. The then and now seemed to be woven of the same thread. "Don't worry. Eventually we'll get it sorted out." He started the car. "You've been awake since before dawn. Try to rest, it's still a good three, four hours before we get to the village."

Clara nodded and leaned back and closed her eyes. The rhythmic slap of the windshield wipers lulled her to sleep. Hours later, Simon turned into the parking lot of a small pub on the outskirts of Cushendall.

When the car stopped, Clara came awake. "I really slept." She looked outside. "Where are we?"

"Just outside the village. I thought we'd stop and have a late lunch. Chances are someone here will be able to tell us how to find Lilith Devlin."

"The Sign of the Dove," Clara read from a sign hanging above the doorway of the stone cottage. "The Manhattan equivalent is just a wee bit different."

"Yeah, but I'll be the food here is better and cheaper."

Clara opened the car door. "No bet."

"I'm starving," Simon said as he locked the car. "Breakfast was a long time ago."

As they stepped into the pub, they were greeted by the delicious aroma of fresh baked bread. Clara took a deep breath. "If the food is as good as it smells, you've made a great choice."

The proprietor came over to them. "Sure and it's a miserable day. Would you care for a table near the fire?"

"Sounds fine," Simon answered.

They followed the man to a small round table covered with a red and white checkered table cloth that was next to the stone fireplace. A whaler's harpoon hung above its mantle and there were seascapes on the white walls.

Once Clara and Simon were seated, the proprietor handed them a menu. "I'm Tim Farrell. Me wife and me run the place. Would you be caring for a drink?"

"Anything on tap," Clara requested.

"Make that two."

Tim Farrell quickly brought them two frosty pewter mugs of cold beer. "Me wife just made a kettle of seafood stew. She serves it with her own soda bread." He paused in his recitation to sniff the air. "Ah, apple crisp just coming from the oven."

Simon took a thirsty swallow of his beer. "Clara?"

"Stew and apple crisp sounds great."

Simon glanced back at Tim Farrell. "Tell you what. Wait about fifteen minutes, then bring us the stew and apple crisp. Another beer wouldn't hurt."

Tim Farrell beamed agreement and by way of the kitchen returned to the bar where he visited with three of his regulars. A family of six came in and were seated. Soon after, a young man in work clothes entered and glanced around the room. He walked over to where Clara and Simon were seated. "Since you're the only strangers, would seem you'd be driving the Volvo?"

Simon nodded. "Yes, we are."

"Your headlights are on. I tried to shut them off but the doors are locked."

"Thank you," Simon said as he got up from the table. "I'll take care of it."

The young man stared at Clara. His scrutiny made her uncomfortable. "What is it?"

"Sure and you remind me of someone, but I canna put me finger on who. Americans, are you?"

"Yes. We've just driven up from Dublin."

"Not often we see Americans here in the north. Seems they prefer a more peaceful climate."

"May I ask your name?"

"Pat. Patrick Kelly. Same as me father and his father before him."

Simon sat back down and Clara introduced him to the good Samaritan. "Simon, this is Pat Kelly. Pat, my husband, Simon Hawk. I'm Clara."

Simon shook Kelly's hand. "A pleasure, Pat. May we buy you a drink?"

"Me works done for the day. I wouldn't mind a pint."

"Please join us," Clara offered.

Simon went to the bar for the beer. Pat Kelly pulled out a chair and sat down. "So, if you don't mind me asking. What brings you to the north?"

"We're looking for Lilith Devlin. I was told she lives around here. That anyone in the village could tell us where."

"Sure and the Devlins have been here as long as the Kellys. Take the road straight through the village. They'll be another pub on the corner–The Shamrock. There you turn right toward the sea. About two miles down the road it narrows and branches off. Stay right and go on up the hill. At the top, there's a track runs left. Take it to its end. You're on Devlin's doorstep–a big stone house that sets on the cliff above the sea."

"Do you know if there are any Dunns or Killarneys in the

area?"

Simon set a mug of beer in front of Pat Kelly. He nodded his thanks. "Dunns and Killarneys. The Dunns got run out by the Fenians long ago. Their big house was burned to the foundation. Tucked their English tails between their legs and got themselves out of Ireland," he said with satisfaction. "Seems I recall me Gran saying one of the Dunns married a Killarney. Wasn't a happy time for either side."

Clara nodded. "I can imagine not."

"The Killarneys were angry that the Brit took one of our own. Gran had plenty of tales about the Killarney women. They saw things others didn't. Knew things before they happened. Plenty of them buried in the cemetery, but I don't think there's any left alive–at least not in this area. Where they went, I canna say. Me Gran might know, if you're staying a time, I'll ask."

"At least over night," Simon answered. "Where's a good place to stay?"

Tim Farrell set two steaming bowls of stew in front of Clara and Simon and a basket of hot bread between them. "We've rooms upstairs. Not fancy but clean and comfortable."

Simon glanced at Clara and she nodded. "Sign us up," he said.

Pat Kelly finished his beer. "I thank you folks. If me Gran recalls where the Killarneys went, I'll have her give you a call."

Tim Farrell collected the empty mugs. "I'll get the register and bring you another pint."

He was quickly back with the beer and a cloth bound sign-in book. "If you'll just sign under that last signature. I'll get the license number off the car."

Simon signed their names and address.

"Enjoy your dinner."

"The stew is delicious," Clara complimented.

"I'll tell the lady of the house. She'll be glad to hear." Once back behind the bar, Tim Farrell went directly to the telephone.

Devlin Manor/Cushendall, Ireland

The man replaced the receiver. He stared at the familiar room as though seeing it for the first time . . . or the last. He had always equated his life here in Ireland with the changing of the seasons. The first years had been the ice of winter when his soul was frozen with grief. The spring thaw when he was able to focus in the present, to bond with his son, Carlton. The summer years when he had come to love Lilith. Now it seemed fall was upon him. Around him life as he knew it was dying, scattering like leaves before the storm.

Lilith and Carlton were at odds. No, their separation was far worse than a minor disagreement. There had been no communication between them for months. Lilith had become distant, unwilling to share her fears. No matter how hard he tried, he couldn't give her the reassurance she seemed to need.

His eyes wandered to the portrait of Lilith that hung above the mantel of the immense stone fireplace. Her face was nearly a perfect oval with high cheekbones and startling sapphire blue eyes. A slender hand rested on the bridle of a grey mare. A beautiful young woman then–an even more beautiful woman now.

Daltry, family retainer, houseman, and jack of all trades came to the doorway. "Did me brother call with trouble?"

"Tim called to say we're expecting guests."

"From the village?"

"From the United States."

"Trouble," Daltry muttered as he withdrew.

"Trouble indeed," the man said to himself. Lilith had always warned that someday they'd come. In recent months she'd become even more insistent, certain it would be soon.

A blast of cold air from the opening of an outside door sent flames dancing in the fireplace. Lilith Devlin came into the room. "Hello, my love." She warmed her hands over the fire. "Will this rain never end?"

The man laughed. "My dear, you say the same thing every year this time."

"That's because by this time every year. I'm half convinced the sun has died."

The man's smile faded. This time she might be right. There could well be nothing but grey days ahead. "Tim called."

Lilith absently leafed through the day's mail. "Tim. How is the old rascal?"

"There's Americans at The Dove. Simon Hawk and his wife, Clara. They should be here within the hour."

The mail dropped unnoticed from Lilith's hand. "Dear God, what shall we do? The studio–you can wait there until they're gone."

He silently watched as she paced back and forth. Her long black skirt danced with the quickness of her step. "Let's not panic. We'll hear them out. It may be nothing, nothing at all . . ." She abruptly stopped. "Listen to me, pretending there's nothing wrong like a child hiding under the covers to escape the monster. And to think, me with the knowing ignoring its truth."

The man pulled her into his arms. "I love you. No matter what, we'll survive."

Tears' glistened in Lilith's eyes and she softly whispered, "I pray you're right."

Simon cautiously drove through the open gates of the Devlin estate. Fog hung heavy and visibility was no more than a few feet. He wished they had waited for morning and daylight. Clara leaned forward peering out the windshield. "The drive curves here. The house is just ahead."

Simon touched the brake slowing the car to a crawl. "I can't see dit squat. How can you?"

Up ahead lights flashed on illuminating the immediate area. Simon followed the circular drive to the front of the Devlin house. He parked the Volvo and he and Clara got out. Simon stared appreciatively at the classical lines of the stone house. It appeared to rise out of the fog as though formed from the elements. "The artisans who built this don't exist anymore."

Clara didn't answer. Her eyes seemed to be searching for someone she couldn't find. She was startled when the wide double front door opened and Lilith Devlin invited them into her home.

The central hall, lighted by a crystal chandelier hung in the center of a vaulted ceiling, was warm and inviting. Chinese porcelain graced shelves which were set into the stone.

Daltry took this coats. "Madame," he said to Lilith. "I've opened the wet bar. There's ice in the bucket. Would you like me to serve drinks?"

"No, thank you, Daltry. We'll make do." Lilith gestured toward the great room where the family normally gathered. "Please."

Clara and Simon stepped into the room with its windows that overlooked the sea. Simon thought it was a room where people actually lived. A book lay open on the Chippendale couch. There were comfortable wing-backed chairs by the fireplace. A Persian silk rug seemed to float on the polished stone floor.

In one corner of the room was a life size bronze sculpture of a hawk ready to take flight. Simon walked over to take a closer look. The deft technique of the sculptor created a feel of impending motion. He traced the wings with a fingertip and felt a thread of excitement unravel.

"Mr. Hawk. Would you care for a drink?" Lilith asked.

Simon turned toward her voice. "I don't recall giving you my name."

"Tim Farrell let me know. No stranger comes here without my having been alerted."

"I see. Then you know my wife's name is Clara. I'm Simon."

Lilith smiled at Clara. "Yes . . . Clara Dunn Eaton now Hawk. I'm Lilith. Would you care for a drink?"

"Scotch with a splash." Simon answered.

"Nothing for me," Clara said without taking her eyes from the paneled wall to the left of the fireplace. "By the fireplace, the panel opens outward. Behind it there's a narrow hall. At its end there is a small square room with shuttered windows, and a huge fireplace as large as this one. On one wall there's a tapestry, against the other a four-poster bed."

Lilith's breath caught in her throat. "Just as you say. Would you like to see it?"

"Please."

Lilith preceded Clara down the hall and opened the door to the room. Simon stayed close to Clara. When he crossed the threshold, he heard rain and the crash of waves against rock.

Tears unaccountably ran down Clara's face. Lilith came to her and took her hands. "It's the knowing isn't it?"

Clara stepped away from her. "How?"

"Because I, too, was once a wild child. Only I didn't have Joseph Cloud to see me through it."

"How would you know about me?"

Lilith only smiled.

Clara seemed not to notice her question went unanswered. She wandered through the room touching a bed post, the back of a chair, running her fingers across the fireplace mantle. She stared down at the stone hearth. "Liam died right there. His blood seeped into the stone and made the stain." She turned away and opened the shutters of the window. She stared out at the murky, grey sky but saw the past. "Claire saw him fall and knew he was dead. She climbed out onto the ledge and jumped to the rocks below."

Lilith's arms hugged her own body. "She did. Betrayed by her own she was. By those who feared her because of the knowing."

Clara's voice quavered. "Do you know who?"

"I do. I'm ashamed to say it was a Devlin. Liam's cousin, Rory, who coveted this house, coveted all Liam was, all he had . . . including Claire."

Clara's breathing became labored. "I can't stay in this place. I can't breathe in here."

Simon gently drew her toward the door.

Back in the great room, Lilith pointed to a wing-backed chair. "Sit by the fire. Its warmth will help."

Simon tenderly touched Clara's cheek. "Clara, are you all right?"

"It's the room from the knowing. From the night you asked about the rain and the waves."

"I thought it might be."

Lilith drew up a foot stool and sat down to one side of the hearth. "Clara, according to family history, Liam and Claire had a daughter. One they sent away to be safe. With whom or where the babe was sent, I can't say." Her eyes grew distant. "I've spent a lifetime searching the past. There's much I can tell you about the knowing."

Simon handed Clara and Lilith a snifter of brandy. "I hope you don't mind my taking the liberty," he said to Lilith. "But you both look as if you need it."

Lilith smiled up at Simon and saw Duncan as he had been thirty years ago. Saw the man she had fallen in love with. The man whom she still loved. "Not at all."

"Lilith, before you and Clara get into the knowing. I'd like to speak with my uncle, Duncan Hawk."

Lilith gasped, a choking sound of desperation. Before she could answer, two men came into the room. Daltry paused at the room's entrance, a rifle in his hands.

Simon stared at the other man. This is how I'll look when I'm his age. "Duncan."

"Yes. I'm Duncan Hawk."

"I'm Simon Hawk, David's son. You, Sir, you owe your family an explanation."

"That may well be, but I'll not have you acting as judge and jury."

"Simon," Clara said softly. "We're all strangers to each other. Give everyone a chance to adjust. A few more hours can't make a difference."

Duncan turned toward the sound of Clara's voice and saw her hidden in the shadows. For a brief moment, Libby was alive. The blood drained from his face, and his legs refused to support him. He sat down heavily in a chair opposite Clara and closed his eyes in negation of bitter reality.

Lilith saw Duncan's anguish and hated him for it. She pushed back her anger and spoke to Simon. "Can't this wait?"

Duncan raised his head. "No. I've wasted far too much time wondering, dreading when this day would come. I want to be done with it."

Simon refused to temper his impatience. "Will you tell me what you know of Libby's death? Why were the two of you having very public disagreements?"

Duncan's hand gripped the arms of the chair so hard his knuckles were white. "I understand our arguments were the major reason I was the only suspect."

"That and your disappearance. The fights?"

"Libby and I very much wanted to have a child. But each time she conceived the pregnancies ended in a miscarriage—two miscarriages. With the second, she nearly died. We'd been to specialist after specialist. All agreed that the next pregnancy might well kill her. She kept insisting we try again."

"The night at The Haven when you shouted that if she did, she just might die?"

Duncan nodded. "That's what it was over. Libby's disappointment became magnified when I learned I had a son. It broke her heart, not that I had a child, but that we might never have one of our own."

Daltry brought a chair over to the group and said to Simon. "Better sit. The story's long. I'll be fixing supper."

"Thanks. Will you take the rifle with you?" Simon mildly asked.

Daltry grinned. "To be sure."

Simon pulled the chair into the circle around the fireplace. "My father told me you asked for a half million in bearer bonds."

"Yes I did. I wanted to set up a trust for Carlton, my son." With a smile at Lilith, he added, "Lilith's and my son. I didn't tell David because . . ."

"Because he wasn't sure the child was his," Lilith put in. "Duncan knew I'd had an affair with Joseph."

Duncan took Lilith's hand. "Once I saw those Hawk eyes there was no doubt."

"The time just prior to Libby's death–what was going on in your lives?"

"Nothing major. Normal day to day."

"Tell me of the day she was killed."

Duncan stared into the fire. "I left at dawn for an early meeting with prospective clients in Toronto. I picked up the bearer bonds from a bank there. I planned on discussing them with Lilith when I got back. She was staying at the island–Devlin island, near Gananoque."

"Duncan called me that night," Lilith said. "I came up river to meet him at the Hawk House dock. It was late, full dark, around eleven or eleven-thirty. We sat down to talk and he told me about the bonds. I was furious. I thought he was trying to buy me off."

Duncan's voice was low. "Lilith misunderstood my intent. I only wanted to protect her and our son."

Lilith rested back against Duncan's legs. "Once Duncan explained, my anger was gone. I told him I wanted to speak with Libby. To tell her I wanted both her and Duncan to play a role in Carlton's life. We'd share him and he would have the best of two worlds."

"You have a generous spirit," Clara remarked.

Simon thought the coldness of Clara's tone was strangely at odds with her comment. He wondered what she was thinking.

Lilith continued her explanation. "Duncan told me Libby hadn't come home from her studio. If I'd drop him there on my way back to the island, he'd walk home with her."

"Strange the things that stick in your mind," Duncan said. "That night the water was flat, like a sheet of black glass. When Lilith and I came up the path to the studio from the dock, I remember thinking it was odd that the outside lights weren't on. But knowing Libby, she'd probably gotten busy and forgot. The door was open. She, she . . ."

Lilith broke in. "Libby was dead. Her studio was demolished.

188

Duncan went to her and bent down and gathered her against his chest. That was then he screamed. A scream like nothing I'd ever heard before or since. Such pain and anguish it broke my heart. I went to him and helped him to his feet. The front of his chest was covered in blood. He stared at me but I knew he didn't see me. I took his hand and he came unresisting. It was as if he didn't know where he was, like he'd escaped to another world. I got him into the boat. I didn't know what to do. Call the police . . . run. I was afraid for Duncan. I went down river to Joseph Cloud's."

"Joseph helped you," Clara said with certainty.

"That he did. By the time we got there, I was shaking and crying so hard I could hardly speak. Joseph gave me a brandy and patiently waited for me to be able to tell him what had happened. He got Duncan out of the blood-soaked shirt and cleaned him up. The entire time, Duncan just sat staring into space.

"When I was calm, Joseph asked if anyone had seen us at the studio or if we had seen anyone. The answer to both questions was no. Joseph warned it was likely that Duncan and I would be suspects–former lovers with an illegitimate child."

Duncan got up and went to the bar. ""Can I get anyone a drink?" he asked as he poured himself an Irish whiskey.

"I think we're all set," Lilith answered.

Duncan took a swallow of his drink. "From this juncture, Lilith will have to give you your answers. For me the next three years are a blank canvas."

"The mind suffers. The body cries out," Clara softly murmured. And out of the emotion's of Duncan's deep, abiding sorrow the knowing came. Clara closed her eyes and looked into the past.

Angry voices. "Help. You need help." A voice ranting. "Bitch, so damn superior. Always have to be right. You tell about him, about me, I'll kill you." Shadows flowing like waves, disappearing, appearing. Streaks of light, a knife slashing, red blood. A woman falling, holding fast to a hand. A ring slipping free and rolling out of sight. The shadow of a body pacing back and forth. A whis-

*pered, "why?" Shadow bending, touching the blood. "You, you took
my love, destroyed my life. Now I take yours." Eyes staring up, the
blade flashing, darkness.*

Clara opened her eyes to see three concerned faces. Her voice
rasped. "I saw Libby die. I saw it all." She repeated the words
from out of the knowing. Tears ran unchecked down her face.
Her hand raised and she stabbed downward. "Now I take yours."

Lilith gripped Clara's hands in hers. "Let it go, be done with
it. Just let it slip away. Breathe deeply, breathe."

Clara's labored breathing slowed. She jerked her hands free.
"I know how to stop it. I hoped if I continued, I'd see the killer's
face."

Duncan's face was taut with strain. "Dear God, it couldn't be."

"What do you mean?" Simon sharply asked.

"Not now. Lilith, please tell them the rest."

Lilith frowned but complied. "Joseph said to let Duncan sleep
for a while, then take him to the island. He advised me to stay
inside and keep the draperies drawn so no light would show. It
would be best if the island seemed deserted. When it was safe,
he'd come for us and we'd decide what to do."

Simon felt compassion for their plight. "Do you have any idea
why Hawk House was trashed?"

Duncan shrugged. "None."

"I've read the police file. There never was any other suspect.
You were it."

"From their point of view it was a safe assumption. Years
later, Joseph explained that he'd been against turning me in. He
felt I couldn't have defended myself against a murder charge.
That there was too much stacked against me–Viet Nam vet, the
arguments, an illegitimate son. Everything pointed to me. Joseph
thought the real killer would be found and I'd be vindicated.
Unfortunately, it didn't work out that way."

Simon finished his drink. "Did you ever read Ethan's journal?"

"Ethan's journal," Duncan repeated. "You mean my great-
grandfather?"

190

Simon nodded. "Clara found a journal written by him hidden in Hawk House."

Duncan's brow furrowed. "Just a couple of days before Libby died, she told me she'd found something she wanted me to read. I thought it was more of the same. Some article about a new surgical technique or a drug which might convince me it was safe for her to conceive. Now that I know about the journal, I can't help but wonder if that's what she meant. I think I should read it."

"I've a copy locked in the trunk with my laptop."

Lilith stretched and got to her feet. "Would seem we've miles to go before we sleep. Perhaps it would facilitate things if the two of you stay here. It would be our pleasure."

Simon waited for Clara to answer. "If Simon agrees, it's fine with me."

Simon nodded.

"Then it's settled." Lilith went to the telephone. "I'll have your things brought from the inn."

Simon turned to Duncan. "Let me know what you make of the final pages. They're different from the rest–drawings, symbols that are similar to cave paintings. You see, I'm convinced there was something in the journal that would have had meaning to Joseph Cloud, and that it is why he was murdered."

"Joseph's dead. When?"

"Two, three weeks ago. His throat was slit."

"I was thinking about Joseph just a day or two ago. Every now and then, when he was away from The Landing, he'd call and give me an update on family, friends. Joseph was my only link with the past–the best friend a man could have." He rubbed his forehead. "I hope he didn't die because of me."

Simon shook his head. "I think not. I think the discovery of the journal set the wheels in motion."

"I've so much to pay penance for. I've put my family through hell. I don't know how they'll find it in their hearts to forgive me. How can I make right what I put my father and David through?" Duncan rubbed his hand hands over his face. "By the time I was able to face what had happened to Libby, Mother was dead. I was still a fugitive. The real killer was still out there. I thought if I contacted family, I might be putting their lives in jeopardy. Lilith and I spoke of it many times . . . but there seemed to be no options other than the path I had chosen."

"I make no judgments. Nor will the rest of your family. I think your brand-new nephew, Duncan Joseph Hawk attests to that."

"Duncan Joseph," Duncan repeated. "Joseph would have been as proud as I am. But I can't help but think Thomas Wolfe was right–you can't go home again."

"Metaphorically, perhaps, but I'd never had a real home until I went to The Landing and met Clara."

"The Dunn women can cast a spell," Duncan said in a voice filled with sorrow. "Simon, I'd like to read the journal?"

"Not a problem. You can get through it in a couple of hours."

"I was thinking of the symbols you mentioned. Libby used symbols in what we jokingly called her secret code."

"Clara believes a woman was involved in Libby's death."

"The knowing?"

Simon recalled Duncan's reaction to the words Clara had repeated from out of the knowing. "I'd rather you read the journal and then we'll compare theories."

"Fair enough."

Daltry came to the doorway. "Tim's brought the luggage. He's putting it in the guest suite."

Simon took the keys to the Volvo from his pocket. "There's a small case in the trunk. Would you mind getting?" he said to Daltry.

"Not at all." Daltry quickly left the room and within moments was back with the case.

Simon unzipped the leather case and handed Duncan a copy of the journal. Duncan leafed through the unbound pages and absently said, "Daltry, I'll skip dinner. I want to read this."

"I'll bring you some soup, a sandwich," Daltry offered and as he left the room, muttered under his breath, "I've a feeling you'll be needing your strength."

"If you'll excuse me," Duncan said to Simon. "As soon as I've finished reading, we'll talk."

Simon closed the attache case and glanced up to see Daltry in the doorway. "Is there something you want to say?"

Daltry nodded and stepped back into the hall. Simon followed. "What is it?"

"Your uncle's one of the finest men I know. The troubles here run deep, deeper then he knows. Do you think you can help?"

"It'll take finding a killer who's been hiding for thirty years. But something tells me I'm making progress."

"Simon," Lilith called. "I've something to tell Clara that I'd like you to hear, too."

Simon sat down in the chair vacated by Duncan. "I'm all yours."

"First, may I ask how you learned about me?"

"Anne Soames," Clara answered.

"Anne, of course, I should have known. Grandfather's only love. I remember she was a delightful woman. Lord. She must be getting up there in years."

"Ninety-two and going strong," Simon told her.

"How did you come to find me?"

"Anne gave us your family's Dublin address."

Lilith drew in a sharp breath. "You saw my father?"

"Yes."

"He's a despicable man. Far worse than you can imagine." Lilith appeared to slip back in time. "He's a dangerous, dangerous man, vindictive, cruel. He has an unquenchable thirst for power. My grandfather, Harry wasn't cut from the same cloth. Grandfather wanted a free Ireland but grew weary of the blood shed. When my father gained control of Devlin Bank, he became the IRA's paymaster."

"He said you stole the bank from him and destroyed his life's work."

Lilith's eyes lit up. "To be sure. When grandfather left me his shares, I had a chance to take control and I did."

Clara's expression was remote. "Did you know your father

once had an affair with my great-aunt Madeline Dunn?"

Lilith nodded.

"That she became pregnant by him but ultimately miscarried?"

"I know of it. But Madeline didn't lose the baby."

"You are Madeline's daughter," Clara said matter-of-factly.

"A truth that my father didn't trouble to reveal until I ousted him from the bank. His rage was so great that he blurted it out. He told me I should have died at birth as everyone believed I had." She hesitantly paused. "As my mother did when she crossed him."

"Roger murdered Madeline." Clara said without surprise.

"He taunted me with it. Bragged how he had her killed so it would seem an accident. He warned me to watch my back or he'd see me dead, too."

"But why," Simon wondered aloud. "Why would he have killed Madeline."

"I can't be certain. I think when she was here in Ireland, she learned too much about his involvement with the IRA. Maybe what she discovered made her a threat to my father. He needed respectability to shield his real purpose. Not only was she a threat . . . she was also his greatest failure. He was always quite a ladies man."

"Roger must be much like Rory Devlin who killed Liam," Clara softly interjected. "Evil does seem to sustain itself."

"Ah, but so does the knowing," Lilith said.

Simon leaned forward. "Can you recall your father or grandfather ever mentioning the names of Belmont, Pillard, or Joaillier?"

"Moria Devlin, my grandfather's sister married a de Pillard. He was grandfathers' partner back in the early nineteen hundreds."

Clara was curled in the wing-back chair. Simon saw that she watched Lilith with a strange intensity. ""Lilith," she said, "Tell me about the knowing."

Lilith started at the cold command in Clara's tone, but complied. "I began to take the knowing seriously when I became pregnant. I stopped drinking, no drugs, nothing to harm my child. The knowing all of a sudden seemed to blossom and I had no way to control it. It came in flashes. Broad strokes out of the past, murky darkness for the future."

"Tell me something about the knowing I haven't experienced . . . no, let me tell you."

Simon saw fear flicker in Lilith's eyes. "Clara," he began, then froze under the intensity of her gaze. Not the calm, smiling gaze of the woman he married but a warrior's fierce piercing determination.

Clara kept Lilith from interrupting by the sheer force of her will. "So much of the knowing has been lost. I can't say how. Anymore than I can say when or where it began. But I know that once the women of the knowing came together to learn and share. Now we are few, separate and apart, struggling to survive what we do not understand. I believe the power of the knowing can be found again–if we aren't afraid to search."

Simon was both mesmerized and filled with trepidation at Clara's revelations. This knowing was becoming more, evolving. He listened as Clara continued. "We are born with the knowing but lack the knowledge needed to use its power. All that remains is a small spark which could be fanned into a blaze if we choose to seek the source. But those of us who remain are diminished in both strength and will."

Lilith shuddered. "Where did you learn these things?"

Clara ignored her question. "The knowing is a stream of consciousness–past, present, and into the future. There exists within its force all of the elements . . . and the seeds of madness. Many have died. I survived, survived because I sought the source inside myself. From out of my own memory, from out of the knowing itself."

"Than you are far braver than I."

Clara tiredly shook her head. "Necessity."

Simon realized that Clara hadn't mentioned her background in the martial arts or her education in East Asian studies. It was as if Clara was refusing to give Lilith the benefit of her experiences with the knowing.

Daltry came into the room. "Madame, dinner is served."

Lilith unresponsively stared into space.

"Madame?" Daltry questioned. "Is something wrong?"

Lilith turned to look at him. "Dinner. Yes, of course." She abruptly rose to her feet as though jerked upwards. "Yes, dinner. Please, let's go into the dining room."

Simon held his hand out to Clara and together they followed Lilith from the room.

Scattered throughout the dining room were lighted candles which reflected in the prisms of the chandelier. Simon pulled out a Queen Anne chair to seat Lilith at the head of the table, the chair at her right for Clara. He seated himself at Lilith's left.

After serving the lobster bisque, Daltry unobtrusively slipped from the room. Simon and Lilith made dissolute conversation touching on art and music, the breeding of the famous Irish race horses. It was apparent that Lilith was distracted and had to make an effort to respond. Clara made no effort at all.

When Daltry came in with dessert, Clara favored him with a smile. "Daltry, dinner was marvelous but I think I'll forgo dessert. When you've served the others, I'd appreciate it if you'd show me our room. I'm suddenly very tired."

"Will be my pleasure."

Clara pushed her chair back. "Lilith, if you'll forgive me."

"Of course. Rest well."

"Simon," Clara leaned down and her lips brushed his cheek. They were as cold as ice. "Goodnight."

"I'll be up as soon as I speak with Duncan."

"Don't hurry. I'll probably go right to sleep."

Lilith toyed with the chocolate mousse. "Clara is seeing more than she's saying."

Simon saw confusion and sadness in Lilith's eyes–and something more. Something hard and cold that prevented him from feeling any sympathy for her. His response was noncommital. "Possibly."

"Simon. If you'll forgive me, I need to be alone. There are books and magazines in the great room. Please treat this as your home. Duncan reads quickly. I'm sure he'll join you soon."

Simon returned to the great room and occupied himself by reading from a volume of Robert Browning's poetry. When Duncan sat down across from him, he put the book aside. "Anything ring a bell?"

"First, the drawings at the end are Libby's. From what I can make out, she saw rage, madness, death. She might even have been foretelling her own death but not knowing who or how it would happen. God, I can't imagine her fear . . . or why she didn't talk to me about it. Probably because she realized I'd link it to her desire to become pregnant."

"I wish it were different," Simon said. "Clara too suffers in silence. Was there anything in the journal that stood out?"

"Obviously, the first Clara's suicide set in motion a chain of events. Because of my affinity with the Devlin family, I know of Andre Belmont. He was later known as Andre Joaillier. Had he not been disinherited, he would have been a count. Lilith's grandfather, Harry thought it was quite a joke."

"Do you know of any shadow organization he might have been involved with?"

"Other than Harry's affinity with the IRA, no, but I see why you'd ask. Ethan apparently thought there was more going on than bootlegging and gun running. Only the knowing comes to mind."

"The knowing . . . ever and eternally the knowing. What was there in the journal that would bring it to mind?"

The ring Ethan described is symbolic of the knowing–a representation of the never-ending circle of life. Belmont could have gotten his ring from Moria Devlin but I have no idea why he would have worn it. Lilith might know."

"Did you know a ring of that description was found under the floor boards in Libby's studio years after her death?"

"No. No, I didn't."

"Chief O'Connor told me he showed it to virtually anyone who knew the two of you and asked if they'd seen it before."

"But no one ever had."

Duncan's voice was so low that Simon was barely able to hear him. "What makes you so certain?"

"The rings are rare, unusual. You can't just go out and buy one."

Simon wondered if these rings were so rare, why another had recently been found. "Duncan, after Joseph was killed, a couple of goons burned his place to the ground. Found in the aftermath of the fire was a man's body. His skull had been caved in."

"And?"

"Under the body was one of those rare, unusual rings."

Duncan's face grew ashen. "Who was he?"

Simon shrugged. "No ID was found on the body. He'd never been printed in the states but I'm sure the Chief is checking other data banks."

"Please excuse me for a moment." Duncan picked up the telephone from where it rested on an oak wine stand. He punched in a number. "Hello, Joan. This is Duncan. How's my favorite almost daughter-in-law?"

"Oh, Duncan, I'm so glad you called. Have you heard from Carlton? He was supposed to be home a week ago. He hasn't called . . ."

"Why didn't you let me know?"

"I tried. I spoke with Lilith but she blew me off. She said you were working and couldn't be disturbed. She and Carlton are already on the outs. I didn't want to make waves."

"Do you know why there's this dissension between them?"

"Carlton didn't say much. Just that she had finally slipped and shown her true colors."

"Joan, did he tell you where he was off to?"

A soft sob came through the receiver. "He spoke with a Joseph Cloud in the states. Their conversation had Carlton all fired up. Something about a journal and how he was going to find out the truth."

"Dear God," Duncan said in a whisper. "Blind. I've been

blind." He raised his voice. "Joan, don't worry. We'll hear something soon. Now try and get some rest." Duncan's hand trembled as he put the receiver down.

"Duncan, what's wrong? Can I help?"

When Duncan answered it was obvious that he was fighting for control. "The man in Joseph's cabin might be my son, Carlton. He was obsessed with proving my innocence. His fiancée said he'd gone to the states to see Joseph."

"Duncan, I'm sorry. Truly sorry."

Duncan got up from the chair. "I'd better speak with Lilith. Simon, if you will, please call Mike O'Connor. Tell him I'm coming home to clear up the mess I left behind. If it isn't asking too much, call New Orleans."

Simon glanced at his watch. In the states it was not yet dawn. He picked up the telephone and dialed the number for Hawk House where Luke was house-sitting and taking care of the dogs. The phone rang for some time before a disoriented voice answered. "Yeah, what is it?"

"Luke, this is Simon."

"Simon, what the hell?" Luke said as he fumbled for his watch. "It's the middle of the damn night." His voice became more alert. "Is something wrong? You and Clara all right?"

"We're fine. Luke, first thing in the morning call the Chief. Tell him the man found dead in Joseph's cabin may be Carlton Hawk . . . Carlton Devlin. He's Duncan Hawk and Lilith Devlin's son."

"Jesus! Is Duncan alive?"

"Yes. He's coming home. Tell the Chief I'm almost certain I know who killed Libby–and it wasn't Duncan."

"Simon, what about David and Adam?"

"They'll have questions I'm not prepared to answer. Could you bring them up to speed?"

"I'll take care of it," Luke offered. "Let me know the flight. I'll pick you up–Syracuse, New York. Whichever is easiest."

"I'll let you know, thanks."

Duncan strode into the room. His despair was overridden by

a barely controlled fury with anger replacing grief as a means of staying sane. "Lilith is gone," he said. "She isn't in her room. Went without a word, not a note–gone." He spun and glared at Simon. "Say it. Say what you're thinking. Tell me what a fool I've been."

Simon spoke softly. "Duncan, I don't know what you mean."

"Think of Clara's words from the knowing. 'Destroyed my life, took my life. Now I take yours.' I saw your expression. You knew they meant something to me."

"Yes," Simon calmly answered. "But I wasn't certain who would have spoken them."

"Clara's first words were different. Initially, I thought of Corrine Pillard or rather Melrose. Andre Belmont was first and foremost, a de Pillard and Corrine's grandfather. Libby may well have told Corrine what was in the journal. It all fit. Even the words–if you tell about him, about me, I'll kill you. More importantly, Corrine had a serious problem with drugs. Libby had been trying to convince her that she needed help. Corrine wouldn't have wanted her addiction made public nor for the world to know her grandfather was a smuggler, a dealer in illegal arms. Marcus was running for the senate. In those days, scandal destroyed political careers."

"What made you dismiss Corrine?"

"Remember Clara talked about shadows flowing, disappearing, appearing. There seemed to be two distinct conversations going on. Different words, a different person? A woman falling, a shadow pacing, blood. You took my life, now I take yours. This doesn't fit Corrine, but . . . but . . ."

Simon said the words Duncan was finding it so hard to speak. "But it does Lilith."

"I wasn't sure. Couldn't be sure–but Lilith is gone. Why, God damn it, why would she have killed Libby?" Realization washed expression from Duncan's face and he suddenly looked years older.

"Duncan, was Lilith here when Joseph was murdered?"

"You think she also killed Joseph." He stared into space. "I've lived with her, loved her, and never suspected, never would have believed she was capable of. such murderous rage, cold-blooded murder?" Duncan stared at Lilith's portrait. "I should have paid more attention to what Carlton was trying to tell me."

"May I ask what that was?"

"Not long ago, he told me that I'd never known who his mother really was, never seen her dark side. How could I believe . . . God, she saved my life."

"And her own."

"I never once questioned where she was earlier that night."

"How did you leave Devlin's Island?"

"On Joseph's sloop. He took us up the Rideau into Canada." Duncan shook his head in confusion. "You do understand that this was what I was told? To this day, I have no memory of that time."

"It was a traumatic experience. How did you come to be in Ireland?"

"Lilith somehow got me an Irish passport. I'm now known as Duncan Devlin, a very distant cousin of the Devlin's, and Lilith's husband."

"You mentioned Canada. From there to where?"

"Switzerland to a private clinic–three years of nothingness. I began to sculpt in clay, did wood carvings. In time with therapy, I came out the other side."

"Was that when you came here?"

"Yes, this has been my home. My sculptures became known and I've earned a good living from them. Lilith has always handled the business end, the gallery show–any event that requires a public appearance. The mystique of my absence is apparently good for business."

Simon looked toward the life size rendering of a hawk in flight. "When I saw that, I knew you were alive. It's a wonderful piece."

"Thank you. Sculpting has been the sustaining force in my life."

"Duncan, why did the ring strike such a cord?"

"Carlton has always been interested in the knowing. In fact it's the only common ground he and his mother had. A couple of years ago, she mentioned the ring and its significance."

"Which is?"

"As I mentioned, it symbolizes the never ending circle of life. The woman is representative of all the women of the knowing. The man, the men who were destined to serve and protect them. One evening Lilith mentioned the ring. She said she'd once had one. It had been given to her by her father, Roger via Moria Devlin to celebrate the birth of her first child. She claimed she'd lost it in the sea."

"Do you think it was ring that was found under the floor boards in Libby's studio?"

"Who else? The ring had once been in Belmont's possession and passed on to Lilith through her great aunt, Moria Devlin, who was Belmont's wife. Lilith's lost ring is how the other ring came about."

"How so?"

"I thought a replacement would make a great Christmas gift for her, and I knew Carlton would enjoy wearing a replica of the knowing. I asked her to draw the design for me. She did better than that. She showed me an engraving in an old book. I forged two rings in silver. One for Lilith. One for Carlton. Lilith was thrilled . . . anything of the knowing gave her pleasure."

"When Lilith spoke of the knowing, it was with a kind of awe," Simon mentioned. "When Clara was telling Lilith what she believes the knowing to be, Lilith suddenly seemed afraid."

"Lilith's spent a great deal of both time and money in its pursuit."

"Why would she do that?"

"When Lilith was younger, the knowing was a powerful force. As she aged, its strength has diminished. Now it's almost lost. She has this . . . this obsessive need to get it back, to understand it."

"Do you think I might see her research?"

"Of course, but why?"

"For Clara. It may help her."

"Lilith keeps the files in the library. I'll get them."

Upstairs, Clara lay curled in sleep. Within her mind came a presence, a voice drawing her into wakefulness. Moonlight illuminated a tapestry of Renaissance figures. They appeared to be dancing to music only they could hear.

In the stillness, the air seemed to whisper. The knowing came like an echo out of time bringing a warning. There was danger in staying in this house–danger and death.

Clara swung her legs over the side of the bed and quickly dressed in black sweat pants, turtleneck, and oversized black sweater. Not knowing why, but certain she should, she pulled on a pair of heavy hiking boots.

Duncan came back into the great room. He carried a stained leather bound book and a thick yellow legal pad. "Everything else is gone," he wearily said. "These were on the corner of a stand. She must have been in a real hurry to overlook these. There's no longer any need to speculate. Lilith won't be back."

"You're wrong, Duncan." Clara set hers and Simon's overnight bags by the door. "Either she'll be back or she'll send someone, but she won't leave us alive. We've got to leave right away."

Daltry came to the door. "Madame is right. There's light of two cars making the turn from the main road. Best leave now."

"The sea's behind us and only the one road out," Duncan calmly stated.

"If I may, Sir," Daltry put in. "Take the footpath down to the sea. The way over the cliff is difficult but can be done. I'll stall the boys."

Simon opened a suitcase and pulled on a heavy navy-blue sweater. He kicked off his loafers and put on hiking boots. "She may have someone watching the house," he said as he shrugged into a down jacket. He handed Clara a dark hooded parka.

Daltry grinned. "That would be me, Sir. She told me to keep you here until the others came. But it's been a long time since I felt any loyalty to her. Still, I'll live longer if she doesn't suspect my defection. A bruise or two would help."

Simon stepped forward and delivered two quick blows to Daltry's face. "Better than a bullet in the back."

"Right you are, Sir." Daltry stepped into the closet. "Lock it. Will be good cover."

Simon nodded with a grim smile of thanks. "Duncan, grab your passport. I've got mine and Clara's."

Duncan shoved the leather bound book and Lilith's notebook into a back pack. "I'll pick up my passport on our way out the back."

Once outside, Simon and Clara followed closely in Duncan's footsteps. They moved silently from shadow to shadow. As they passed the stables, the horses stamped restlessly in their stalls.

"Stay close, the tracks narrow," Duncan warned. He paused in a grove of gnarled trees whose twisted branches hid them from slight and spoke softly. "Follow in single file. There's pitons in the face of the cliff for hand-holds. About halfway down, the path has broken off. I set pitons at foot level, hand holds above. Step along them to where the path begins again. Be damn careful. It's tricky and sure to be slippery."

Duncan moved to the cliff's edge. He sat down, turned to his stomach, and cautiously lowered his body until his boots touched the narrow shelf. Clara imitated his movement and felt Duncan's hand on her ankle. He guided her to a safe stance. She shuffled toward him and he directed her hand to a piton. "Simon," Clara softly called. "Your turn."

Soon Simon stood next to them and they began to traverse down the slick rock face. The gusting wind whipped and howled as if ordered to push them from the rock and into the waters far below. Clara raised her head and listened to a voice in the wind. With a secret smile, she slid her foot to the next piton. "Piece of cake."

Once off the face of the cliff, Simon gave Clara a warm hug. "Okay?"

"Just fine?"

The three of them crouched at the base of the cliff and listened. Nothing could be heard but the mournful sound of the wind. Duncan touched Simon's sleeve. "Simon, come with me. I could use a hand. Clara, you too."

They followed Duncan down the long dock to the weathered grey boat house. Clara went to the window and stared up at the cliff. "That's a long way down."

"How in hell do you normally get down here?" Simon asked.

"A steel stairway. It bolts together in sections. Every fall we take it in. Even when it's in use, the bottom section is pulled up far enough to be unaccessible."

"Why?"

"Lilith doesn't like surprises. When she took the bank from her father, he threatened her life. Here, grab this wheel and help me turn it. Turn toward the water. This time of year the damn thing freezes up."

The two men put all their strength into freeing the mechanism which would lower the boat into the water. Finally they felt the gears give, catch, and move again. A final turn and the boat slowly began to lower.

"Take it easy," Duncan warned. "I don't want the winch to slip."

In minutes the boat floated restlessly on the water. Duncan freed the lines. "Tanks are topped off. Lilith always wanted the boat at ready."

"Bless her slimy little soul," Simon muttered under his breath.

Clara held up a hand for silence. From the top of the cliff came flickering lights, distant voices drawing closer. Duncan motioned Clara and Simon toward the back of the boat house. They slipped further inside its dank darkness. From a back window they watched the cliff.

Voices shouted back and forth, their words carried by the wind. "Don't bother along the cliff. There's no way down."

A second voice joined the first. "Where could they have got to? Daltry, you lying piece of dog shit, where they be?"

Silence, then a shriek followed by loud raucous laughter. "Sure and there's a way down. Daltry got there quick enough."

"Those bastards," Duncan spat into the darkness.

Hot tears flowed down Clara's cheeks. Simon gathered her into his arms but she resisted his comfort. "I've got to see if he might be alive."

Duncan caught her arm. "That's a long fall onto rock. Let me check."

"He saved our lives–I have to see."

"Start the engines," Simon suggested. "I'll go with Clara."

They stayed low along the dark dock. About fifty yards down the beach a dark shape lay sprawled on the rocks. Clara ran across the black stone to Daltry's side. Blood ribboned from the side of his mouth. His open eyes were glazed. Clara gently stroked his cheek. "Daltry, it's Clara. Can you hear me?"

His hand moved and Clara clasped it between hers. He coughed and tried to speak. His lips shaped a soundless, "Go with God."

Simon bent down and passed his hand over his eyes to close them. "Come on, Clara. He's beyond our help."

Inside Devlin Manor the telephone rang. Patrick Kelly reluctantly picked up the receiver. "Devlins."

Lilith heard the tension in his voice and knew he had failed. "What happened?"

"Sorry. We were too late. The Hawks have flown the coop. Your husband with them. Daltry's dead."

"The book and the notebook?"

"Not there." Lilith's voice was filled with rage. "Failure. Total failure. Are the Mercedes and the Volvo still there?"

Kelly sighed. "They are. Even Daltry's old wreck is still out back by the stable."

"They went by sea," Lilith snapped.

A hint of annoyance crept into Kelly's tone. "And how did they get down the cliff? They may be Hawks but I don't believe they can fly."

Lilith's tone was ice. "My husband is an amateur mountain climber. He climbs that cliff for practice. You can do no good there," she spat. "Use Daltry's truck, run him and it off the cliff.

Make it look like an accident. Take the Volvo back to The Dove and leave it in the parking lot."

"Anything more?"

"Make certain all the airports are covered. They'll be leaving the country."

"Daltry is at the bottom of the cliff. Isn't that accident enough?"

"No. He'd have no reason to be out there. Do as I say."

A cold thread of fear crept down Kelly's spine. To retrieve Daltry's body from the beach meant a cold wet trip by sea. But there was no question of not obeying. "As you say," he said in resignation.

With a snap, Lilith terminated their conversation. She stared unseeingly out the limo's window. Spillage from the past had overflowed into the present. It must be prevented from polluting her future. The worst of it was Duncan. Duncan was lost to her. Poor payment for all the years she had loved. Loved him even though she knew Libby had never been forgotten. Their son–no Duncan's son–was another moralistic Hawk. He, too, was a danger to her. All she had was the knowing.

Lilith had always believed that only the strongest survived and the strongest of the strong ruled. From her research, it seemed that over time the knowing had weakened. Perhaps when those with the knowing had mixed with a negative gene pool. If Clara Hawk was right, then the knowing could be commanded–if only one knew how. Clara Hawk's knowing was strong, the strongest she had ever seen.

Lilith sighed. Libby's, too, had been strong. That was why she had to die. She was of the Killarney line and as such a female child of hers would likely hold the mysteries. Just as Lilith had believed a child of hers and Duncan's would. But fate had played a cruel joke by allowing them only one child, a son–a useless male.

Lilith closed her eyes and thought of Clara Dunn Eaton Hawk–also a spawn of the Killarneys. It may well be that she held the mysteries. No matter. They all had to die, even Duncan. But then for her, he might as well be dead. Unfortunate, but necessary. She analytically examined her options. No matter what the Hawks suspected, nothing could be proven. Duncan might be cleared of Libby's murder but even so, no charges could ever be brought against her.

With Duncan out of her life, she could devote all her time to her search for the knowing's archives. Lilith smiled–and she wouldn't have to seek alone. She had the Duke and his resources at her beck and call.

And the book, she would have it back.

New York State

Simon glanced out the car window and watched the Hudson River slide by. They'd only been gone a few short weeks and already the snow was gone. The smell of spring was in the air.

Luke grinned at Simon. "You look like hell."

Simon rubbed his unshaven face. "Come on, tell me what you really think."

"I think from what I've heard thus far, you're damn lucky to be alive. A run through the Irish sea to some God forsaken village dock. A rented plane to London. London to New York via the more traditional airways. At least you're awake. Your companions are out like a light."

"Duncan is running on empty. I don't know how he's kept it together. Clara, she's just plain old fashioned pooped. Me. What I want most is a hot shower and a change of clothes. I've been three days in these. By the way, the limo is a nice touch. Whose idea was it?"

"Thank Clara's dad. John said Duncan should arrive home in style. He and Lydia will rally around this weekend. Oh, let me run this by you. I've made a suite available for Duncan. He might not be ready for Hawk House."

"Good thinking. How about the New Orleans contingent?"

"Judith came with Adam and David. She's at Hawk House making certain there aren't any nasty dust balls lurking about. Perfect, the woman said. Everything has to be perfect."

"How about you and my sister?"

Luke shrugged. "We both need time. She's got the bank. Me, I've got The Haven and the schools."

"Time will tell. It's probably best to take it slow."

"My, my, aren't you the master of the understatement. I take it your advice doesn't fall under the living by example philosophy."

"Not exactly. To change the subject–did Nicole and Duncan Joseph make the trip?"

"Nope. Duncan Joseph has an appointment for shots. Nicole and the baby will join David the end of the week."

Simon rubbed his temples. "Beef up security. This is a long ways from over."

"Already taken care of," Luke assured him. ""Are we sure Libby and Joseph's killer is Lilith Devlin?"

Simon nodded. "Proving it may be a different story. Luke, how are my father and grandfather doing?"

"They haven't said much–happiness goes without saying. I think maybe some resentment, a little anger, relief. Look, I told the Chief we'd let him know when we get back. He said to give Duncan time to settle in but not to take too long. In actuality, Duncan's still a fugitive. The Chief wants to clear him as quickly as possible before the media kicks in."

Simon felt Clara shiver in her sleep. He pulled a car robe up around her shoulders. "Luke, if you don't mind. I'm going to catch some sleep."

Luke tossed him another wool throw. "Rest is wise."

They were turning off the main highway onto the secondary road toward the St. Lawrence and The Haven when Clara came awake. She kissed Simon's forehead. "Okay, rise and shine."

Simon lifted his head from her shoulder and yawned. "Rise and shine. I've never known what that meant."

Duncan opened his eyes and glanced out of the window. "Almost there," he softly said as if to himself. Years of exile and what was waiting for him at its end?

Simon glanced at Duncan. "Duncan, Dad and Grandfather are at The Haven. Do you want to go there first?"

Duncan shook his head. "Not until I know whether or not Carlton is alive."

"Let's take care of it now," Luke said as he opened his cellular phone and punched in the number for the village police station. The conversation was brief. "The Chief had the body moved to LeBlanc's Funeral Home. He'll be waiting for us." He compassionately touched Duncan's shoulder. "The body was badly burned. This could be rough."

"Not as rough as not knowing," Duncan sadly said.

Le Blanc's Funeral Home was the lower floor of a large white Victorian house. A circular drive rounded its front where a canopy enabled mourners to avoid the rain and snow. Mike O'Connor in his off duty outfit of jeans and flannel work shirt peered out the window. "They're here."

Aupre Le Blanc opened the double wide door into the viewing room. "I'll let them in and disappear. If you need me, I'll be in my office."

"Thanks, Aupre."

Duncan was the first up the sidewalk. When he came through the door, he saw Michael O'Connor waiting just as he had every summer for so many years. "Mike."

The Chief came forward, his eyes glistening. He pulled Duncan into his arms in a hug. "Duncan, welcome home. What in hell took you so long?" he growled.

"I'm beginning to think sheer stupidity. Mike, let's get this over with."

Clara, Simon, and Luke filed into the viewing room behind Duncan and the Chief. The unadorned oak casket brought home death's reality. The body was clothed in a grey suit. One side of the face was badly charred, the other unmarked.

Duncan gripped the edge of the casket and stared down.

"Thank God. It isn't Carlton. It isn't Carlton."

Clara took his arm. "Let's go out in the other room."

Duncan fell back onto a Chippendale couch. "I don't know what to feel. I'm so damn glad it isn't Carlton and at the same time . . . damn" He brushed tears from the corners of his eyes. "I know him. His name is Drake Standhope. He's a friend of Carlton's. They were at Oxford together. Christ, what was he doing involved in this nightmare? And where's Carlton?"

Clara watched Duncan with concern. He was awash with pain, an anguish so overwhelming he could drown in it. "Duncan, if Carlton was injured where would he go? Does he know anyone here?"

Duncan wearily shook his head. "All he knows is what he's heard from Lilith and me. Hawk House, The Haven, Devlin Island . . ." He raised his head. "Devlin Island's land side dock. There's an old carriage house that I mentioned. It has an apartment above it."

Luke opened the front door. "It's a good ten miles. Let's beat feet."

"Right behind you," the Chief said.

The trip to the carriage house passed in silence. Duncan stared at the passing scenery as if seeing everything for the first time. And in a manner of speaking he was. Since he'd been in exile, the area had grown and now new housing developments stood where there had only been woods.

Luke spoke into the intercom. "Take the next left."

The carriage house set back from the road on the banks of the St. Lawrence River. Years of neglect had taken their toll. The ramshackle structure of weathered barn board had lost many of its windows leaving only skeletal frames. Shingles were missing from large sections of the roof.

Duncan, Simon, and Luke cautiously circled the building. On the far side toward the river, they found an Arctic Cat snow machine partially covered with a tarp. The Chief pulled in behind the limousine and parked. He got out of his rusted Ford pick-up and walked over to where Clara was looking at the base of the front doors.

She pointed at fresh marks in the wood. "These old doors have recently been opened. Looks like someone chipped the ice away and took chunks out of the bottom."

"Yep. There's drag marks in the ground where the door was pulled open." The chief walked to the corner of the carriage house and called, "Over here. Let's get these doors open."

Simon gripped the metal handle on one of the doors and pulled hard. The door only gave a few inches.

"Lift up a bit," Luke advised. "Upper hinge is broken. It's dragging against the ground."

Simon lifted up on the handle and the door swung open. Parked in the dark gloom was a mud-splashed Land Rover. The Chief flicked on the flash light he had brought with him. A stack of old tires lay against the wall. Dead leaves crackled underfoot.

Duncan pointed at the ceiling at the rear of the building. "The caretaker's apartment is upstairs. If memory serves me, the stairs fold up right about here. Mike, bring the light. Let's see if we can find the pull cord."

The Chief shined the light at the ceiling. "Outline, no cord." He moved the light. "Here's the ring where it was tied."

Simon looked on the floor and picked up a dried strand of frayed rope. "Here's what's left of it. Clara, come on in here."

"Simon, I'm right behind you."

"Sorry." He interlaced his fingers making a cup of his hands. "Put your foot in here. I'll raise you so you can reach the hook."

Clara stepped into Simon's hand and he lifted her up until she could reach the protruding metal. "Got it. Take me down."

Simon squatted, lowering both Clara and the stairs as they folded down out of the ceiling. Through the opening they could see a sky light encrusted with years of neglect. Clara stepped on the bottom step. "I'm lightest. Let me take a look. These stairs don't seem very sturdy."

The wooden steps creaked under Clara's weight but held. At the top, she glanced around the living area–big overstuffed couch and stairs, their fabric faded to a dusty rose by years of exposure to sunlight. From behind a closed door, Clara heard a scraping sound, as if something was being dragged. "Someone's up here," she warned.

Simon followed by Duncan quickly climbed up through the opening with Luke close behind. The chief appeared at their side, his gun out of its holster. "I always have to cover your ass," he told Duncan with a smile.

"Some things haven't changed, my friend."

Simon silently moved toward the room. Just as he reached the door it swung inward. A man leaned against the frame. Duncan came out of the shadows. "Carlton."

"Dad, I thought I heard your voice, but I thought I was dreaming. How in . . ." he tried to take a step toward Duncan and collapsed into Simon's arms. Simon picked him up as though he was weightless and laid him on the couch.

The Chief did a quick survey of the room. On the counter was a loaf of moldy bread, a six pack of soda, and an open liter of bottled spring water. Apples and oranges spilled out of an open bag. There were several unopened tins of dried meat.

Luke came up behind the Chief. He poked one of the oranges. "Doesn't look like he's been eating to well."

The Chief grinned. "The Haven it ain't."

Clara kneeled by the couch. "His pulse is weak and he's cold and clammy. He could be going into shock. We'd better get him to the hospital."

Carlton groaned and opened his eyes. "No hospital. I'm okay. Give me a minute and I'll be fine."

Duncan gently brushed the hair off his son's forehead. "Carlton, what in hell were you and Drake doing here?"

Carlton pulled himself up to a sitting position causing fresh blood to seep through the cloth wrapped around his shoulder. "Drake's dead, isn't he?"

Duncan nodded. "He is. I'm sorry."

"I tried to help him . . ."

Clara touched Duncan's shoulder. "Duncan, we can figure all of this out later. Right now Carlton needs care. We'll take him to

Hawk House."

Carlton forced a smile. "Finally, Hawk House."

Clara smiled down at him. "To be sure."

Hawk House

Clara came downstairs carrying a basket of bloody bandages. "Carlton is sleeping. The knife wound seems clean, no infection. Chief, thanks for getting Doc to make a house call."

"He was glad to do it."

"Simon, Carlton said thanks for helping him into the shower."

"No shower in God knows how long–poor guy was desperate."

Clara glanced around and frowned. "Where's Duncan and Luke?"

"Luke took Duncan to The Haven. Right now Hawk House is too much for him–and he wanted to let Drake Stanhope's parents know of his death. I don't envy him that one."

Clara sighed. "I'm sure Duncan felt it was his responsibility. Chief, legally–where is he?"

The Chief handed Clara a cold bottle of water. "There isn't now and never has been any physical evidence. His explanation clears up the arguments. Doc verifies what he said. I had Duncan sign a release for his medical records from the Swiss clinic. Once that's verified, I'd say he was out of the woods. Clara, honey, you look whipped."

Clara took a thirsty swallow of the water and brushed her still damp hair back from her face. "My own shower felt wonderful. I feel a whole lot better. I've got to say that is was some honeymoon my husband took me on."

"You must admit," Simon jokingly censored. "It was never boring."

"It was many things, but you're right, boring wasn't one of them." Clara sat down on the floor pillows to play with Dog and the puppies. The Irish wolfhounds tumbled around her. Rhett climbed on her lap and licked her face. She pushed him off. "Stop that you clown." And tickled his stomach.

Not to be outdone, Scarlett nudged Clara's arm insisting on her fair share of attention. With a low growl, Dog called an end to the puppies antics and they reluctantly settled down next to Clara. She snuggled closer to the fire and closed her eyes.

"Clara," the Chief said. "Can you hang in a little longer?"

"Sure," she said without opening her eyes. "What's up?"

The Chief pulled a foot stool near the hearth. "While you were getting Carlton settled in, Simon and I had a talk with Duncan. Given what Duncan has told us. We can conclude that Lilith was responsible for both Libby and Joseph's deaths."

Clara's eyes narrowed. "Responsible for? Come on, Mike, tell it like it is. The bitch slaughtered Libby and slit Joseph's throat."

The Chief glanced at Simon. "Is she always this direct? Never mind, stupid question. You're right, Clara. She is a killer but there's absolutely no proof linking her to a damn thing. Not Libby's murder, certainly not Joseph's."

Clara sat up and glared at the two men. "I'm telling you. It was she."

"We know, miss sweetness and light, we know," Simon said. "She murdered Joseph. But it's a safe bet, given her IRA connections, that when she entered the country, she was using a false passport. We'll find no record of her entrance either here or in Canada."

The Chief grunted his agreement. "Tricky bitch. So Clara, here's the thing. We have to trap her, force into a situation whereby we can hope she'll make a misstep."

"Don't hope for a confession–that is unless, she's planning on slitting your throat immediately afterwards. Just how do you expect to entice her into this . . . trap?"

"The knowing," Simon answered.

"Yep," the Chief agreed. "Duncan told me Lilith's obsessed

with it–bit round the bend. She's convinced that if she can find a way to control the knowing, she could virtually run the world–at least her world."

Simon handed Clara a leather bound book and a notebook. "Duncan said to tell you that you're now in possession of a book, Lilith will want back. She believes it's the key to the knowing."

Puzzled, Clara traced the design in the leather cover. "Book of the knowing–now isn't this something?" Clara leafed through the pages. "It's written in old English, some French." She peered at some notations in the margin. "This looks like . . . I can't really say, Sanskrit, Chinese."

"According to Duncan," Simon said. "Lilith is paying a team of grad students to research its contents, translate the phrases you mentioned. There are obscure locations mentioned where she is convinced she'll find other written records that will open up the secrets of the knowing."

Clara put the book aside. "She wants it back?"

"That's an affirmative," the Chief said. "From what Duncan told us, a big affirmative."

"Let me get this clear," Clara said. "Lilith believes this book is proof that the women of the knowing secreted written records. She thinks this book will lead her to them." Clara snapped her fingers. "Whereby she'll have all of the power of the knowing at her fingertips."

"So she believes," Simon answered. "We, on the other hand, plan to thwart her efforts. "We're planning to regroup here tomorrow evening for dinner and a planning session."

Clara tilted her head and looked at him. "And who's cooking?"

Simon laughed. "I can tell from your tone. It's not going to be you."

"As the Chief said–that's an affirmative."

Using his fingertips, the Chief gave the top of his beer can a drum roll. "Presenting for the first time in the kitchen at Hawk House the gourmet chefery . . ."

"Chefery?" Clara whispered to Simon.

"Yes, indeed, the chefery," the Chief repeated. "Of Judith Hawk and Luke Dunn performing their famous Cajun concerto of food for the famished."

Clara giggled. "I can't wait."

The Chief stood and stretched. "I can. Something tells me this food's going to be . . . what was it Judith said?"

"Smokin'" Clara and Simon answered in unison.

"Smokin'" the Chief shook his head. "My stomach may never forgive me. Rachel is visiting her sister in Canada. Poor woman, she doesn't know what she's missing. Tomorrow, six o'clock. See ya."

Simon nudged the dogs aside and lay down on the floor pillows next to Clara. He turned her face to his and kissed her eyes, her temples, her ears. His tongue teased her lips.

With a groan, she reached up and captured his mouth with hers. "Three days without you–too long, much to long."

The Haven was a dark silhouette against the moonlit sky. Duncan Hawk hesitated at the entrance. His father and brother were waiting for him. Waiting and expecting an explanation for all the years of silence.

Luke held open the heavy brass door. "They're upstairs. D Suite."

Duncan nodded and crossed the familiar lobby. The comfortable chairs and couches were the same, yet logic told him they must have been upholstered. If so, it was with the same fabric he remembered. Rather than take the elevator, he slowly climbed the curving stairway, silently cursing himself for being a coward. It made no sense to postpone the inevitable.

In front of the foyer door to D Suite, Duncan knocked and stepped into the present. At his entrance, Adam and David came to their feet. Duncan's face was expressionless but the huskiness of his voice betrayed deep emotion. "Dad, David I'm sorry. I can't tell you–."

Adam impatiently held up a hand to silence him. "Please, Duncan, let me say what I must. When Luke Dunn called to tell us you were alive and coming home, I was elated. Moments later, I was furious. More angry than I've ever been. All those years, not a letter, not a phone call. Didn't you trust us? Why did you cut yourself out of our lives? Damn it, your mother died asking for you. Help me to understand."

David wanted to clasp his brother in his arms, but first the gap between his disappearnace and his return had to be bridged. "No recriminations," he said. "Just talk to us. We've already lost too many years."

Duncan wearily slumped into an arm chair. Tears stood in his eyes. "After I found Libby . . . found her lying in a pool of her own blood. I think I must have lost my mind. Libby's death, the blood bath of Nam–somehow they were the same. Everything ran together into a colorless landscape of nothingness."

Adam saw how difficult it was for Duncan to speak of Libby's death. How he must have suffered. "How did you deal with it?"

"Three years of therapy in a Swiss clinic before I was capable of making decisions, of functioning in the world. By then Mother was dead, I was a wanted man–a fugitive. My first instinct was to come home. Find out who murdered Libby. Lilith convinced me to involve you, my family, would only put you at risk. There would be more scandal. A murder trial where it was probable, I'd be found guilty."

David frowned. "From what Luke told us, the arguments were easily explained, as is your disappearance. Why would you think you'd be convicted?"

"Lilith. She was my only source of information. The real killer was still out there and believed he was safe. What kind of danger might I be putting all of you in if I surfaced?" Duncan shook his head. "Nothing I say can justify those lost years. But please, I beg you–don't shut out my son. All of Carlton's life, he has wanted to know the Hawks and the Dunns."

David's voice was rough with emotion. "Dad said he was angry, as was I. What possible reason could there be for not letting us know you were alive–for not trusting us enough? God, Duncan. We didn't know if you were alive or dead. But please understand, we never stopped believing in you, in your inno-cence."

"Son," Adam said. "David and I talked for a long time before we saw how impossible the situation must have been for you. You had suffered tremendous loss and were alone."

"Done is done," David interjected. "Understand we never stopped hoping, nor did we ever stop loving. That your son is fam-ily is a given. Welcome home."

Hawk House surrounded Carlton like a living entity. He could feel the past with all of its joy, and its sorrow. He shifted on the stool and rested his arm on the kitchen counter.

Clara sensed that he was in some pain. "Are you feeling better?"

"Much. There must be something to the chicken soup theory."

"Twelve hours of sleep might have helped.'"

"Something did. I do feel better." He finished his eggs and reached for a blueberry muffin. "Breakfast is great. Thanks."

"How's the arm?"

Carlton raised the colorful sling that had been created from one of Clara's scarfs. "Perfect. I'm a regular fashion plate."

"You could start a trend," Clara said with a smile. "I do think, though, that you suffered a concussion. The symptoms appear to have passed, but don't ignore any persistent headaches or vision problems."

"I won't."

"I'm sorry about your friend. How did the two of you happen to be at Joseph's home."

"When Drake and I got to The Landing, we picked up a local paper. There was an article about Joseph's death . . . murder. Joseph was our reason for being here. He'd told me about the journal. Said he hadn't had a chance to read it but that you told him about it, described a ring that Ethan had mentioned. A ring fitting the description of one that was found in Libby's studio."

"Andre Belmont wore the ring. I understand he was married to Moria Devlin. She was the woman who passed the ring onto your mother."

"Yes. For me that was the final nail in her coffin," Carlton bitterly said. "When Joseph mentioned that you had described the ring Ethan had written of in the journal, I realized it was the same as the duplicate ring of the knowing that Dad made for my mother and me. In that instant, I knew Mother had lied when she told us she had lost the original in the sea." His eyes grew hard and cold. "I knew she had lost it in Libby's studio the night she killed her."

"And she murdered Joseph because she knew between the two of you, you would have nailed her hide to the wall." Clara frowned. "That would imply that she had somehow gotten wind of the journal."

"My money is on her. I know she's always kept tabs on what goes on in The Landing. If she found out about the journal, she'd have gotten her hands on a copy–bribery, theft. Nothing is beyond her."

"Why the carriage house instead of a hotel, The Haven? No one would have known you."

"Actually, the carriage house was intended to be a place to store the snow machines. Joseph said they were the best way to get into his place. But when I saw one of mothers' bully boys walk out of a restaurant, I decided to be invisible. She must have sent them to torch Joseph's cabin, maybe even to kill him."

Clara shook her head. "Whoever killed Joseph, and I believe it was Lilith, knew him. A stranger couldn't even have gotten close. As for the fire, there was bad blood between Joseph and the two who did it. These are not standup guys. If someone hired them, they'd have said so."

"If that's the case, Mother sent him for another reason."

"Simon's suite was broken into–plastique in the keyboard or some such. I know little about things that explode."

"Could have been. Blowing things up is an IRA specialty. Would seem at Joseph's, Drake and I were in the wrong place at the wrong time."

"Why did you go there?"

"We figured Joseph might have made some notes, something,

anything. The door to his place wasn't even locked. Just a yellow tape across the frame. Once inside, we divided the room between us. The book shelves seemed most likely. Then, out of nowhere, there were two men. Drake went down. I rushed to help him and got a blade in the shoulder. I twisted the knife from the bastard's hand, but the second one clubbed me from behind. When I came to the cabin was in flames."

"It's lucky you was on the floor or the smoke . . ."

"Yeah, I'd have been a goner. I crawled to Drake, tried to pull him out, but I couldn't. The one arm was useless. That must have been when my ring slipped off. As it was, I barely managed to make the door before the roof caved in."

Clara saw raw emotion in his eyes. "Don't blame yourself. There was nothing you could have done that would have mattered. Drake was dead before the fire. It was the blow to his head that killed him."

Carlton forced a smile. "Thanks, Clara, but the how doesn't matter. He was here because of me."

"I take it you rode a sled back to the carriage house."

"The ride back is hazy. I kept falling off the damn thing. I was dizzy and my head hurt like hell."

"Yep, concussion." Clara confirmed. "Just like Doc said. You got back to the carriage house and?"

"Drake was an outdoors man. He insisted our supplies include a first aid kit." Carlton's eyes were distant. "Funny, I made fun of him when he insisted on it. Told him he'd never need it . . . he didn't. I did. I managed to clean and pack the knife wound."

"Why not a doctor?"

"Mothers' henchman–if he learned I was in the area, she would have known she'd been found out. I was afraid of whom she might harm next. I'm sorry, sorry . . . I don't know, sorry for all of us. For all the people she's harmed."

Clara poured herself a cup of coffee. "Carlton, if I'm over-stepping, please say so. But would you mind telling me more about your mother?"

"In what context? Mother, wife, IRA facilitator?" he bitterly asked.

"Wherever you'd like to begin."

"My mother and I have never been close. To nurture wasn't part of her makeup. When I was growing up there was always two—no make that three overriding factors in my life. My mother's obsession with the knowing and Ireland, and Dad's deep abiding sadness." Carlton glanced at Clara and looked away. "My mother hated me. She blamed me for the loss of her knowing. She desperately wanted another child, a girl. In her scheme of things, I was worse than worthless."

"Because the knowing comes through mothers to daughters . . . or so it seems," Clara said.

"Yes, but strangely enough, the knowing was the only thing we could talk about." Carlton's face grew tight with remembered suffering. "She used her knowing to cause pain."

"Pain—physical, emotional?"

"Both. When I was five, maybe six years old, I suppose I was testing the boundaries."

"All kids do."

"But all kids don't live with my mother. She'd speak once. If I didn't immediately stop whatever it was I was doing, I'd feel pain. Like a fist grabbing my heart. She'd be across the room but even as young as I was, I knew she was causing it. That it was from the force inside her."

"What kind of a monster is she?" Clara muttered.

"Clara, the knowing. What do you think it is?"

Clara realized her answer was somehow vital to Carlton. That he needed a validation of his own feelings. "Based solely on my own experience—I think the knowing was once a culture, a living philosophy. The women were once able to direct the force but one of their own betrayed them . . ." Her breath caught in her throat. She had no idea why she had said the women were betrayed, but once said, she was certain it was true. She forced herself to continue. "From dreams or what I call knowings, I've seen men who were . . . I suppose they would be called the women's protectors."

222

Carlton nodded. "When you read the book, you'll see how right you are. Do you think there's a way to tap into the source . . . the energy?"

"Michelangelo said the sculpture was inside the marble and all he had to do was chip away at it until it came out. That's kind of been my approach to the knowing. I chip away with meditation, martial arts, yoga–and hope it will eventually come out. That eventually I'll perceive it's true essence."

"Do you think the knowing is both good and evil?"

"Joseph Cloud could have explained far better than I. I wish you could have known him."

"I feel as though I do. I knew of him through Dad and in recent months, he and I often talked on the telephone."

"Joseph was the most spiritual person I've ever known. Had it not been for him, I probably wouldn't have survived the knowing. He told me that within all of us there are both good or light, and evil or darkness. One cannot exist without the other. We each must choose our own path. It follows that the same exists within the knowing."

"Clara, do you think that men can experience the knowing or some form of it?"

"With any degree of certainty . . ." She thoughtfully paused. "Let me put it this way–Simon has perceived things from out of my knowings. Did you with your mother?"

"I use to think so but I'm not certain. She has to be stopped,"he harshly said.

"She will be. To change the subject, I understand from your Dad that a lady in London was very happy to hear from you."

For the first time a true smile lit Carlton's face. And Clara could see something of all the Hawks in his eyes.

"Joan is the absolute best," Carlton said. "She understands my need to be a Hawk, to wash the Devlin blood out of my veins." He ruefully smiled. "Sorry, didn't mean to get on a soapbox."

Clara patted his hand. "When I look at you, I see only Hawk. Lilith was just a biological donor."

Yawning, Simon came up to the counter. "Whoo, I did sleep.

223

Morning, Carlton." He grabbed Clara and kissed her. "And a good morning to my blushing bride."

"Unhand me. You brute. It's my food you're angling for."

"Man does not live by bread alone," he joked. "But I could use breakfast."

Clara poured him a glass of orange juice. "Fresh blueberry muffins. What else would you like?"

"Coffee–and a muffin. That's plenty. I need a good workout." He patted his stomach. "Don't want to stuff myself."

"Been there. Done that. Well, at least an hour of Tai Chi. I was planning on a real session after I took care of the troops ."

Simon glanced around. "I knew something was missing. Where are the beasts?"

"Outside, morning constitutional. I'll bring them in after our workout."

Simon raised an eyebrow. "Our workout?"

"Where I will kick your butt."

"What's this," Carlton asked. "World class wrestling? Can I watch?"

Simon broke his muffin in two. "We are world class wrestlers, but I don't see you as a voyeur. Now a demonstration of Tai Chi or Kung Fu–that you may observe." And in an aside to Carlton, whispered, "I promise to go easy on the little woman." He took a bite of his muffin. "Delicious. As for you, Carlton. When you're not running around proving your father's innocence, what do you do?"

"Devlin Bank–I went to work there right after getting my MBA. Partially to annoy my mother but primarily to find out what she was up to."

Simon reached for a second muffin. "Did you?"

"In a manner of speaking. I can pin point accounts used by the IRA to disperse funds but I can't connect them to her." A broad grin spilt his face. "But she's in for a surprise. My great-grandfather, Harry left me a block of stock that my mother con-trolled until my thirtieth birthday. I recently sold it all to a board member who wants my mother out. It gives him the leverage to make a run at her."

Simon chuckled. "She isn't going to like that."

"Nope, but I do. So I'm out of the bank . . . and out of a job."

"What now?" Clara asked.

Humor left Carlton's face and he stared into space. His mother was a dull, empty ache where there should have been love. All he'd ever wanted was to connect with his heritage. To be a Hawk. He shook his head as if awakening from a dream. "Beyond marrying Joan–I haven't got a clue. Turn about is fair play. Simon, I know you're a writer. I've read all your books–great stuff. It's Clara whose the mystery."

"I keep busy with Lundquist/Dunn Schools." She saw his puzzled expression and said, "Let me give you the kiss verison."

"Kiss?"

"Keep it simple stupid–an abridged version. The schools are alternative education for society's rejects. Kids from dysfunctional families, kids trying to get out or stay out of the gangs. We give them a shot at becoming as it was."

"Sounds like quite an undertaking. How does one fund such a project?"

"Ah, the banker talking."

Simon looked at Clara over the rim of his coffee cup. "I've been wondering myself. Where did the seed money come from?"

"I raided the trust my grandfather, Martin set up for me. Ditto, Luke. Gunnar used his personal funds. I also set up a sustaining trust where the money from my paintings is automatically deposited."

Simon set his cup down and in a deceptively soft tone said, "Paintings?"

Carlton coughed to prevent a laugh from escaping. Clara looked like a deer caught in the headlights.

"My darling, wife. You never cease to amaze. These, ah, paintings. Might they be seen?"

Clara pushed away from the counter. "As if I have a choice." She took a key from a drawer and unlocked a recessed door that was around the corner from the door to the basement. She ushered Simon and Carlton into her studio.

Paintings were everywhere. Some hanging, some were stacked against the white walls. Simon walked in one direction. Carlton in the other. They slowly circled the room. Simon paused in front of a canvas. The river viewed through Clara's eyes. It had strength and an illumination so real it felt as if you could step into the frame and sail its waters. The next was a portrait of darkly handsome man standing on a dock with a sloop in the background.

Clara saw Simon looking at it. "That's Joseph. I'm going to give it to John Cloud as a remembrance of Joseph—not that he needs a painting to remember him."

Carlton stood entranced before a large landscape. Its focus was a massive stone house that was atop a cliff below which was the rushing sea. A man stood in the shadows staring up at a long narrow window where a woman's shape was perceived through sheer curtains. "Clara, could you come over here?"

"What is it?"

"When did you paint this?"

"Several months ago. Why?"

Simon joined them and looked at the oil painting. It sent a chill up his spine, a feeling that was akin to fear. The man's destiny was to be played out in the room behind the curtained window.

Carlton's face was pale. Clara touched his arm. "Carlton, what's wrong?"

"I'm fine. It's just that you've painted Devlin manor as it was two hundred years ago." His finger touched one wing. "All of this wing was gutted out in a fire and later torn down. A fire started by Rory Devlin's wife in a rage over her husband's obsession with Claire Killarney." He outlined the tall, wide windows in the front. "These windows were made larger to let in the light. How . . . how would you have known what Devlin Manor looked like two hundred years ago?"

Simon shook off his foreboding. Yet the feeling that all that the Hawks were, all that the Dunns were somehow stemmed from Liam and Clarie. "Did this come out of a knowing?"

"Yes. I've seen this house many times." Clara's eyes misted. "And a man, Liam."

"Liam was Rory's cousin," Carlton said.

Clara turned the painting back toward the wall. "Rory killed Liam and Claire's suicide followed. Lilith filled in the blanks for me. I suspect she rather enjoyed doing so."

Simon put his arm around Clara. "Let's put the knowing aside. There are marvelous. Why would you want to hide talent as great as this?""

"I'm no critic," Carlton said. "But these are tremendously compelling."

"Please, both of you. I'd rather you didn't mention these to anyone. Only Joseph, Luke, Gunnar and now the two of you know."

Simon pointed to the bottom of one of the paintings and read, "Ida." He glanced at Clara. "This is you?"

"That's me–I do art."

"How is it your family hasn't found you out?"

"I sell, but not in the galleries my parents frequent. Gunnar. He's the director of the schools," Clara said for Carlton's benefit. "A friend of his is an art dealer in SoHo. He hooked me up. I get a pretty good price and all I make goes directly into the trust."

"Why can't anyone know," Simon insistently asked.

"It's hard too explain–partly because of Aunt Libby. She was just beginning to be recognized as an artist when her chance was taken away. I don't want to cloud her accomplishments. But it's mostly for a selfish reason. I don't want to become part of the art world and all that entails."

Carlton sighed. "You have my promise. I do understand your desire for privacy, but not the rest. The paintings . . . I think Libby would feel like they are a continuation of her work. It's almost as if the two of you have a shared destiny."

Simon nodded his agreement. "From everything I've heard about Libby, I think she'd be pleased. But I'll keep your secret. Now woman, about that workout. Time's awastin'. Carlton, we'll change and meet you in the dojo."

"Where might that be?"

"Doors to the left of the stairs. You blend in so well, I forget you've only just got here," Simon told him.

In the dojo, Carlton seated himself on a bench along the side wall. Above him, through the sky-light, he could see the blue of the sky. He cushioned his shoulder with a towel against the wall and waited for Clara and Simon. He was beginning to feel comfortable with his new found family.

Clara treated him as though he'd always been family, and Simon had accepted him without question. A warm glow of acceptance banished the cold of his mother's rejection. Finally, a place where he could belong. One more hurdle, his grandfather and uncle–he wondered if he would be able to measure up to Hawk standards.

Clara and Simon, dressed in the traditional white cotton gi, came into the room. They bowed formally to Carlton and to each other and began to move in graceful unison through the forms of Tai Chi. A dance to the music of the universe. Their concentration was centered in the slow flowing postures. One into the other like waves onto a white sand beach.

Carlton was lulled into relaxation by the powerful symmetry of their skill. When they bowed to each other ending the session, he could not have said how much time had passed. He knew only that there had been something magical, otherworldly in their togetherness.

Simon glanced at Carlton. "Now we get serious."

Clara faced Simon in the center of the sun-streaked mat. She circled forcing him to react to her, to counter her strategy. Simon moved in low and fast going for her knees but Clara used a basic neutralization and countered with a converse attack.

Carlton found himself enthralled by their quickness and expertise. Although Simon was much larger than Clara, he was none the less light on his feet, tremendously strong, and frighteningly fast. But Clara was always a heartbeat ahead.

Clara smiled, a secret smile as she let her internal energy flow and expand. She loved this wonderful combination of freedom and control. Clara countered Simon's every move as if she knew where he would strike.

Simon's expression was grim and thoughtful. There was something out of the norm. He aggressively attacked giving her no respite, forcing her to constantly defend. Yet no matter his strategy, Clara was unfailingly a microsecond ahead.

Clara began to recognize a pattern in his attack sequence. She waited using one neutralizing technique after another. No longer attempting to counter attack. The extra time let her ready herself for the break in the flow of his attack. She deflected the first assault, moved past his second, and knowing where the third would come slid into the gap just as it began to open. She caught him off balance and took him down to the mat. The edge of her hand was at his throat.

Simon smiled and rolled to his feet. He bowed formally in acknowledgment of her victory. Carlton handed them each a towel. "Awesome. No other way to describe it."

Simon wiped the sweat from his face. "What did you see?"

Carlton took his time before answering. Simon's tone made it obvious that the question hadn't been asked in jest. "Total concentration, focus–a centering of self. Both of you have to be black belts. I know something of the martial arts, but you two would surely kick my ass."

"No. What did you see?" Simon persisted. "How did Clara win?"

Carlton looked perplexed. "She's fast, she always seemed to be ahead, to know–"

"Exactly. Clara knew where I would strike."

"Know being the operative word," Carlton said.

Clara put her hands on her hips. "Bull! It's me. I am strong. I am woman. I am good. I told you I was going to kick your butt."

Simon picked her off her feet and kissed her to silence. "Clara, that win wasn't based in the intrinsic energy of the martial arts. This was something entirely different, beyond my understanding of an intuitive sixth sense."

"Where are you going with this?" Clara asked.

"This foreknowledge came from the knowing. I'd bet my life on it."

Carlton grinned. "They were once warrior women. You'll see when you read the book."

Clara tossed her towel into a wicker basket by the bench. "And here I thought I was just good."

"Oh, you're good. Very, very good," Simon assured her. "You'd be good without the knowing."

"Clara, doesn't the knowing frighten you?" Carlton asked.

"Not anymore. I've learned how to live with it. If I should suddenly lose it, I'd probably feel abandoned–lost."

"Its loss has driven my mother to acts of despicable desperation."

"Perhaps it's because she always preferred the dark side." Clara glanced at Simon. "I think I'll catch a shower and do a little reading."

"Would your reading material relate to our conversation?"

"See, I'm not so different. You've got it, too."

Clara quickly showered and retreated to the balcony alcove. She glanced out the window and saw the sunlight dancing across the river and noted that the trees that were just beginning to bud. She thought of Joseph and of how he had revealed the river's mysterious spirit to her. How she wished he was alive, to know Simon, to be a part of the future.

She pushed away the sadness and picked up the leather bound book and curled into the wing-back chair. In moments, she was transported back into the early days of the knowing. She found that in some aspects it was a historical account of the knowing with its beginnings in Tibet. In other ways, it was a clarification of things she had experienced but previously had no way of understanding.

So deep was Clara's concentration that to get her attention, Simon leaned down and kissed her cheek Startled, she looked up. "How's it going," he asked.

"It's fascinating. Slow going because of sentence structure and the handwriting is cramped. On some of the pages the ink has faded, but it's worth the trouble. I'm learning so much about the knowing, and beginning to understand so much about myself."

"That's wonderful. When you finish, I'd like to read it. But I'm afraid you'll have to put your reading on hold. It's nearly time for our guests to arrive."

Clara rubbed her eyes and looked out the window. Already the sun was low over the water. "I guess I really got wrapped up in the book. I had no idea it was so late."

"I only bothered you because I thought you might want to change out of your sweats. Oh, I let Carlton read Ethan's journal."

"Good. He needs to feel as though he's a Hawk. And from everything I've seen thus far, he passes muster."

"Agreed. He and I set the table. The wine is chilled and there's a fire in the fireplace. Judith and Luke are in the kitchen cooking up a storm. We got spices flying everywhere. Your crazy cousin had crawfish flow in overnight from New Orleans."

"Chefery in motion–speaking of which, I'd better get moving."

From the bottom of the staircase came a banging. Simon looked over the railing and saw Luke pounding a wooden spoon against the bottom of a pot. "Get with it, you two. Your guests are arriving."

Clara dashed for the bedroom. "I'll be quick."

Simon went downstairs and joined Luke and the Chief in greeting Duncan, David, and Adam. Carlton nervously waited by the fireplace. Adam and David shook off their top coats and immediately went to him.

Adam took Carlton's shoulders and looked into his face. This young man was blood of his blood. His eyes were the distinctive Hawk yellow/green. He was a reflection of his father, of Simon. Nothing of his mother was apparent. His spirit came from the Hawks. "I'm sure you've figured out that I am your grandfather."

Adam's smile brought a smile to Carlton's face. Adam continued to welcome his grandson. "Carlton, we can't get back the lost years, but we have the future. Time to get to know each other–a future to share with each other."

David's eyes shown with pleasure and he playfully pushed

Adam aside and pulled Carlton into an embrace. "I'm your Uncle David. That you are loved is a given. There are no words to tell you how welcome you are."

Carlton's face flushed with happiness. "Thank you. You can't begin to know what this means to me. All my life, I've wanted to know my family, to be a Hawk."

David laughed out loud. "This has already been a banner year for me. My son came home and brought a wonderful woman into our lives. My wife gave birth to a beautiful baby boy. My brother whom I've missed more than I can say is back in our lives. Now I have a nephew. I am a man truly blessed."

Judith and Luke began to serve glasses of champagne. "I know the need for something to toast with when I hear it," Luke told them.

When everyone had a glass, the Chief raised his. "To the Hawks and the Dunns."

All glasses rose. "The Hawks and the Dunns."

Adam pointedly glanced at Clara who was coming down the stairs. "To the incredible, Clara. Whose wisdom brought my son and grandson home."

Clara accepted a glass of champagne from Luke. "To family and friends. There is no greater blessing."

The Chief sipped his champagne and beamed. He felt as if he had slipped back in time and found the future.

Judith motioned for Luke to join her in the kitchen. She put a chef's hat on his head and one on her own. "Call the crew. We're good to go."

Luke again banged the bottom of a pan. "Yawl come sit a spell. We're readyin' to offer up the crawfish."

As they walked to the table, Clara whispered to Simon. "What happened to e'toufee?"

"You got me."

When they reached the dining area, they found the table and chairs had been moved to one side. In the center of the room was a long picnic table with benches along its sides. It was covered with layers of newspaper. There was no evidence of silverware or plates. Only stacks of men's bandannas in bright red and blue which tonight would serves as napkins. Wine buckets were filled with bottles of ice cold beer. Cajun music provided an authentic note of festivity.

Simon grinned. "The last time I saw this room it was china and crystaled to death. Looks like we're entertaining a change of venue."

Judith and Luke dumped the first batch of salt potatoes, sweet corn, and crawfish in the middle of the table. "Don't be shy," Luke advised. "Dig in. Beer in the coolers. More crawfish cookin'."

Judith set baskets of hot crispy French bread on the table. "We'll keep the crawfish a-comin'. Beyond that, you're on your own."

Clara sat down between Simon and David. "Little did I know that my sweats were the perfect dinner attire."

Luke raised his beer. "This is in honor of Carlton Hawk. Y'awl got to instinctively love Cajun. Come from both sides of the family. Meanin' y'awl can't tell where the Hawks end and the Dunns begin."

Carlton took a thirsty swallow of his beer. Duncan nudged his arm and demonstrated how to eat the crawfish. Soon there were piles of shells in front of everyone.

Duncan held an ear of sweet corn in his fingers. "Sweet corn is great," he mumbled between bites. "Where'd you get it?"

Luke reached for a slice of bread. "The Haven's freezer. It's from our gardens. Not bad for a frozen product."

Clara glanced around the table. This was how Hawk House was intended too be–filled with family and friends. She saw that the pile of shells in front of the Chief was as large as anyone's.

As he reached for more crawfish, Clara heard him mutter. "I be smokin'"

Adam Hawk wiped his hands on the cloth bandanna. "I think I've had my fill."

Carlton reached for yet another pile of crawfish. "Just a few more."

David laughed aloud. "Typical Hawk. In my memory, there's never been one who didn't love Cajun."

Laughing and talking, the well-fed group drifted back into the great room. Clara began to help Judith clear the table but she waved her off. "Luke and I have it under control. Go take care of business."

Duncan lingered behind. "Luke, Judith, thanks so much. It's wonderful to see Hawk House filled with family and old friends. To say nothing of the best damn crawfish feed I've ever had."

Simon waited until everyone was seated and did a quick summation of what was believed to be Lilith Deviln's role in Libby and Joseph's deaths. "The clincher was the ring found under the floor boards, the ring that was described in Ethan's journal. In all probability, it was the ring given to Lilith by Moria Devlin, the wife of Andre Belmont/Pillard. The ring lost by Lilith the night she murdered Libby." Simon glanced at the Chief. "Care to take over?"

The Chief leaned forward. "As we know, the ring and Clara's knowing doesn't constitute proof. We need something concrete. Lilith's motive is clear but we need to place her at the scene or find some physical evidence–say the murder weapon. Carlton, we don't mean to put you on the spot but is there anything else you call tell us?"

Carlton's tone was controlled. "As Dad knows. My mother and I have been at odds for much of my life. Certainly from the time I could think for myself. Let me begin with Devlin Bank. She swore that the bank was free of any involvement with the Irish Republican Army. She lied. I tracked the accounts that she showed particular interest in. IRA business as usual–even more so than when my grandfather, Roger ran the show."

The Chief frowned. "Northern Ireland has made great strides toward peace. What does Lilith perceive her role to be?"

"She wants to play a role in governing Ireland. Consequently, her past can't become public knowledge. Not so much the IRA connection but the deaths that can be layed at her doorstep–deaths that have nothing to do with Ireland."

"Murder of two people by her own hand would certainly tarnish her lady bountiful image," Clara said under her breath.

Adam leaned toward her and said in an aside. "You really

despise her, don't you?"

"I do. For all she's done and all she's likely to do if she isn't stopped."

Carlton glanced at his father. "I really can't prove this, but I've always believed she had backing–someone with influence and power."

"Any suggestions as to how she can be stopped?" The Chief questioned.

"Her only weakness is her obsession with the knowing," Duncan tersely said. "She's insulated herself from everything else."

"Dad's right," Carlton said. "To tie her to anything illegal is well nigh impossible."

Duncan glanced at Clara. "You have the one possession she'll do anything to have back."

"The book," Clara answered.

"Yes, my dear, and I'm afraid that puts you in the line of fire."

"What my mother wants, she gets," Carlton said. "She'll send her minions to get the book."

Clara shook her head. "They won't find it. Ethan's journal was hidden for more than thirty years."

Simon harshly laughed. "As usual, Clara, you show no concern for your own safety–and you should. She is dangerous."

"Simon's right," Carlton said. "As I mentioned, I've always believed Mother isn't in this alone–especially in those things related to the knowing. I don't know who he is–but he's out there." He glanced at his father. "Sorry, Dad. It might be important."

"No apology necessary. If I'd taken your assertions more seriously, this entire mess may have been averted. I couldn't have saved Libby but perhaps Joseph would still be alive."

"Dad, you can't be faulted. I was there. She made certain that you never saw her dark side."

"Fact of the matter is," the Chief bitterly snapped. "Lilith is going to get away with murder."

Clara enigmatically smiled. "There's the law, and then there's justice."

On River Road, Corrine Pillard Melrose drove the luxurious Lincoln with a lightness of spirit which had long been missing from her life. The simple act of speaking the truth had freed her from the burden she had carried. Entrapped in the web of memory, she drove the familiar road faster than normal. Oliver was a wonderful man, the very best of husbands. She loved him with all her heart. But Libby, Joseph, and Duncan were encapsulated in a time when friendship, and love had lost their meaning. Her drug dependency had become all there was, all that mattered.

Yet in spite of everything, those three people had been steadfast in their commitment to get her the help she needed. They had never let her down. Now Libby and Joseph were dead. Nothing she could do would change that. But Duncan was alive–alive and here in The Landing. Perhaps now she could in some way make restitution–not for those acts of commission, but for those of omission. She would see Duncan and tell him all she knew of Libby's death. Help him to clear his name. At long last she would be free of the past.

The air in the car seemed stuffy and close. Corrine lowered the window on the driver's side. The soft spring breeze blew her hair and for a moment she was seventeen again, sailing the river. Her eyes filled with tears of memory. All the good had ended when Libby died and Duncan disappeared. But now the Hawks were back. How good it would be to see Duncan. She laughed softly to herself. Duncan–her first love. If only Joseph was here to share the moment. If only they could all be together just one more time.

As she approached Pillard Island, she slowed and glanced out the side window. From this distance she couldn't see the distinctive pink of its rock. Today, traffic was slight but soon the tourists would begin their annual summer migration to the islands and it would be bumper to bumper.

Corrine touched the gas pedal and the Lincoln picked up speed. Up ahead, she saw a dark blue minivan taking a curve faster than was safe. It swerved across the double white line and into her lane. Where to go . . . how? In desperation, she spun the wheel to the right. The heavy car skidded past the front of the van and down the incline at the side of the road. The front of the car careened off a rock ledge and rolled over.

At Hawk House the telephone rang. Simon answered and listened for a moment. He handed the phone to Clara. "Clyde Meridian. He needs to talk to you."

Clara took the phone. "Clyde . . . what? Slow down. I can't understand you. Yes, Duncan is here. Please come. I'll be waiting for you."

Simon saw the color drain from Clara's face. "What's happened?"

"Corrine Melrose was in an accident on River Road. She died about a half hour ago. Duncan, she was on her way to talk to you. Her daughter, Luci, insists that she has to tell you what Corrine told her this morning."

Duncan's expression was one of shock and something more–something that made Clara afraid. "Killed in an accident. How very convenient."

"Dad," Carlton put in. "One of Mother's henchmen is here in The Landing or at least he was. I thought he might have been sent here to burn the cabin, but Clara said since the men who did it are a known quantity, it wasn't likely. But the bastard has to be here for a reason."

"In so far as we know, Corrine's death was an accident," the Chief grimly stated. "But it can't hurt to check this guy out. Carlton, what can you tell me about him?"

"His name is Kip–Kip McCoy. He's of medium height. Blonde hair in a brush cut–one of his eyes is slightly crossed."

"Excuse me," the Chief said. "I want to move on this." He opened his cell phone and speed dialed the police station and passed on the information.

Duncan stared into the past. "I remember Corrine as a beautiful young woman. She had such a lust for life."

Tears slowly ran down Clara's cheeks. "Oliver is in Canada. Clyde is going to drop Luci here, and drive up to Toronto to tell Oliver and drive him back."

"Oliver, Clyde?" Duncan asked.

"I'm sorry, I didn't think," Clara said. "Oliver is Corrine's husband. Clyde is her son-in-law. Luci and Clyde should be here soon. I'd better make some coffee."

Simon followed Clara into the kitchen. "You all right?"

"Seems like you ask me that a lot," she said as she reached for a cannister of coffee.

"Life happens. How's Luci doing?"

"Clyde said she's destroyed. She and Corrine were close." Clara measured coffee into the filter. "Corrine was always kind to me. The only time she was ever anything but gracious was the night of our engagement party."

Simon leaned on the counter. "Yeah, her behavior was very different from that of the elegant charming woman I'd met at Sailors."

Luke and Judith finished putting the table and chairs back in place. Luke tossed the last of the silverware into the dishwasher. "Clara, I think it's best if Judith and I clear out. Luci doesn't need a crowd for what she has to say."

"Why not take Carlton with you. He's been wanting to see The Haven."

"Sounds good," Luke agreed. "I'll go get him."

"Clara," Judith said. "I'll say goodbye now. I've an early flight in the morning."

Clara hugged her. "We'll miss you. Come back soon."

Judith's eyes were sad. "Not for a while."

"You and Luke, a problem?"

"Timing, distance–Luke is betwixt and between the schools and The Haven. I've the bank."

"Judith, some things are meant to be. I've a feeling about you two."

Judith forced a smile. "The knowing?"

Before Clara could answer, Luke, Carlton, and Adam came into the kitchen. Adam gave Clara a hug. "Thank you for everything. I 'm going back to The Haven. The poor child doesn't need an audience. I'll see you tomorrow."

"Car just pulled in," Luke said. "We'll slip out the back way."

"Judith, we'll talk soon," Clara said as she went to greet her friends. She opened the front door. "Luci, Clyde, I'm so sorry."

Clyde brought Luci into the room as if she were a fragile piece of china. "Will you watch out for her until I get back with Oliver?" He asked. "I've called Susan and Holly. They'll be over later. I asked them to give Luci time to speak with Duncan."

"Don't worry. Luci can spend the night here. We'll take care of her. You go on."

Luci came into Clara's arms. "Oh, Clara, she's gone. I can't believe it. This morning when I left her she was so happy, so alive . . ."

"Come on, Luc. Let's go and sit down." Clara guided her to the couch.

"I'm Duncan Hawk," Duncan said as he sat down next to her. "I'm very sorry about your mother."

Luci looked at him through her tears. "Mother was right. You and Simon could be twins. She told me you were her first love. She never forgot."

"Nor did I. I was looking forward to seeing her again. Are you sure you feel up to talking to me?"

"Yes . . . yes, it was important to her. Important enough that just before she died she asked for you." Luci clenched her hands in her lap. "This is all so unreal, strange. It's like it's happening to someone else."

Duncan took her hand in his. "This can wait."

"No. I have to tell you. Early this morning, Mom called and asked me to come over. She said Dad had left for Toronto and she wanted to speak with me in confidence. When I got to Mother's, she'd been crying. I won't go into details but we first discussed her drug problem and recovery. What Mom wanted you to know was that she didn't murder Libby, but she did lie to the police."

"I would never think your mother was capable of murder," Duncan quietly assured her. "What was it she felt she had to lie about?"

"Mom told the police that the last time she saw Libby was at lunch the day before she was killed. The truth was that the night

Libby was murdered, Mom had been at the studio. They had a terrible fight over Mom's grandfather. Mom said her and Libby had been best friends and that she had told Libby about him, and how he had once used the name Belmont to smuggle booze. So when Libby read Ethan's journal, she knew exactly who Andre Belmont was."

Luci looked at Clara. "Mom said old Andre raped the first Clara."

Clara nodded. "Yes, according to Ethan's journal, he did."

"What a despicable animal he must have been. Anyway, that day, the day Libby was murdered, Mom had been doing drugs–coke, acid, smoking. God, I still can't believe it. It's so unlike her . . . wasn't like her." Luci's voice grew wooden and distant. "That night, Libby confronted Mom about her drug usage. Libby said Mom got either help or she would tell Uncle Harmon and Uncle Marcus. Mom said she lost it. Threw vases, pulled the phone off the walls–even slashed some paintings."

Clara closed her eyes. The knowing of Libby's death took clear form. Duncan had been right. There had been two different persons in the studio.

"But Libby was alive when Mom left," Luci attempted a weak smile. "Furious but alive. Duncan, it was Mom who tore Hawk House apart. She wanted the journal. Somehow she got it into her head that Libby was going to use it against her. She was afraid if old Andre's past or her drug problem got out it would hurt Uncle Marcus' political career. Mom said she watched you leave and went in by way of the back door."

"I thought it was locked," Duncan murmured, and with a grin said, "Locked it may well have been, but Corrine knew where the key was. Libby always kept an extra one taped to the bottom of the planter."

"There's more. That night when Mom stormed out of the studio, she ran head on into a woman."

"Did she know who it was?" Simon asked.

Luci shook her head. "No. Mom said she was so out of it, she didn't even remember the woman until days later. Not long after

Libby's death, Mom had a major breakdown. My uncle's got her into treatment in a clinic in France. But it was months before she got a handle on things." Luci looked toward Simon. "When you came here–you triggered all the old guilt and regret. She started to drink a lot. She was nasty and difficult to be around but Dad and I didn't have a clue as to why."

Duncan glanced at Simon. "Corrine wouldn't have known Lilith. The year Lilith was here in The Landing. Corrine and Libby were in Europe with Sylvia."

Luci nodded. "I remember Mom talking about what a good time they had. Duncan, yesterday when she heard you'd come home, she was determined to tell you the truth. No matter how bad it made her look."

"It takes a lot of courage to do what she intended," Duncan said. "I wish I could thank her."

Luci started to cry and through her tears said, "Art Lawler saw the accident. A guy in a minivan forced her off the road. Didn't even look back, just kept right on driving."

The Chief said in an aside to Simon, "Looks like Carlton was on the money. I'm going to talk to Art. Maybe I can get a fix on the vehicle."

"Lilith is running scared."

"Why kill Corrine? According to Duncan, she wouldn't have known who Lilith was," the Chief speculated.

"Lilith would have made it her business to find out who it was that she ran into that night. There was no need to act on it–that is until Duncan returned to The Landing. Corrine talks to Duncan. He puts two and two together. It's all unraveling."

"So it would seem."

"Think of her victims. Libby, Joseph, now Corrine. In Ireland Clara and I saw a man tossed off a cliff because he turned against the bitch. She's killed often enough not to be concerned it there's a few more deaths on her side of the ledger."

"Your point?"

"We've got to take Lilith out of the game."

"Got a plan?"

241

Clara heard the Chief's question. She patted Luci's hand. "I'll be right back."

Simon smiled as Clara approached. "We're talking about Lilith."

"I heard."

"Yeah," the chief put in. "We're agreed that she has to be dealt with but haven't a clue as to how."

"Any thoughts?" Simon asked.

Clara's grim expression matched her tone. "As a matter of fact, I do."

"And," Simon prompted.

"And you don't want to know."

After everyone had left, Simon took the dogs for a run. He and Clara were to join the family at The Haven for a nightcap. Luci had insisted that she go to her parent's home to be there for her father when he arrived from Toronto. Holly and Susan had promised to stay with her, and to call if Clara was needed. Corrine's death had been a shock to everyone. It had also made clear that Lilith's tentacles were long.

Clara looked out the bed room window and watched Simon romp with the dogs. She turned from the window and sat down of a bench in front of the Queen Anne's vanity. Her thoughts circled from Corrine, to Libby, to Joseph.

With every fiber of her being, she believed that the knowing was the root cause of all that had happened. Beginning with Andre Belmont's presence at the Dunn dinner table. No, it had begun far, far longer ago than that.

The knowing. Omnipresent and becoming stronger. Clara knew she had to control it . . . or it might well control her. She picked up her hair brush and glanced into the mirror. She saw not only her own face but flashes of other faces fading into the background. The air grew still seeming to shiver with anticipation.

Out of the silence came the knowing.

The plaintive sound of the pipes filled her mind. In the darkness was the murmer of voices as the women of the knowing filed into the cave, gathering together for the final time.

Light from the torches brushed the walls of the cave. Kaila, the eldest of the sisterhood, stood on an elevated slab of dark stone. She saw in the shadows only twenty women–twenty remaining out of more than two hundred. Her voice trembled with the effort of keeping the tears at bay. Tears for the dead–tears for the end of the knowing.

Kaila raised her arms for quiet and the women fell silent. Kaila looked at each of them and began to speak. "Yes, it is true. We were betrayed by one of our own, but we are all to blame. Our balance has been lost because we allowed emotion to take over. The consequences of what we think cannot be escaped. Any more than we can prevent day following night.

"Everything we think exists in the universal consciousness. Each thought starts a chain of events which continues on into eternity. To restore the rhythm of life, we must change our thought patterns. We of the knowing are entrusted with the mysteries and as such we must keep them alive."

A voice broke in. "All of us have its power."

"Yes," Kalia answered. "But before we had the sisterhood to teach us how to deal with its force. Now, to keep the flame alive, you must mask your abilities."

A second voice. "We are few. Most of our protectors are dead. How are we to survive?"

Kaila's tone was disparaging. "From necessity, we have become skilled warriors. To be weak and dependent is a luxury we are denied."

And yet another voice. "The knowing is a manifestation of divine intelligence. If we must live apart, it will become bastardized."

"This I cannot deny," Kalia admitted. "But the time of seclusion from the world has passed. I wish it were possible to solely embrace the wisdom of the knowing, but it is not. Those who desire our destruction have become many."

Although Kalia spoke quietly all listened. "Once when we were many, we were taught to fully use all we'd been given. No longer.

Each successive generation will lose more of the knowledge. Those who possess the knowing will search alone, stumbling in the darkness. Many will die before their time."

Kaila thought of the future and shivered. "Without a mentor it is almost impossible to learn to control the power. The path of those who follow will be fraught with hardship, but there is nothing to be done. Those who possess the knowing will for a time walk in darkness. Eventually, they will seek the absolute inside themselves and learn from out of their own memories. For others, the knowing will burn itself out and be lost to them forever. We cannot change what has gone before. We can only persevere and survive so that others may follow."

A man spoke. "What of us? Are we to blame for what happened? Did we, by the breaking of our vows, bring this to pass?"

"No. The knowing is evolving as is your role in our protection. It falls to you and those women remaining to keep the flame alive." Kaila gestured to one of the women and she brought Kaila a deerskin pouch. She opened it and dumped out the finely crafted silver rings. "These have been fashioned to provide future generations with the means of identifying each other—and as a reminder of whom we are. Each of you take one and make your goodbyes. Never forget that one of us will always be here in the mountains."

The wail of the pipes cried their unshed tears.

Clara took a deep breath and opened her eyes. The knowing was growing stronger and coming more frequently. But with each knowing, she better understood it, and herself. She heard a door open and Simon call, "Clara. Dogs are fed, watered, and down for the count. You ready?"

Clara came to the balcony rail. "Simon, why don't you go ahead. I really want to finish reading the book."

"You sure? I hate to leave you here alone."

"Alone—you've got to be kidding. I've got Scarlet. I've got Rhett. And I've got the one and only Dog."

"Right you are. Don't open the door to strangers."

Clara turned on the Tiffany lamp and found her place in the

book. She quickly became engrossed in the cramped script. When she reached the final page, she regretfully closed the leather cover. She had learned so much—some familiar from out of her own knowings. Places described but without a frame of reference that would enable them to be found.

Still, the combination of tonight's knowing and the book had answered many of her questions. Now she understood why her knowing grew in strength, while Lilith's had all but disappeared. She couldn't help but wonder if Corrine Pillard Melrose had been afflicted with the knowing—hence the drugs and mental break-down.

Chances were that Moria Devlin had to some degree possessed the knowing. Her lineage would account for Corrine. Lilith's had obviously been stronger—from the Devlins via Moria. From the Killarney side through Madeline. In Lilith's case the dark side was obviously victorious.

The sound of the front door opening startled her but since the dogs didn't react, it had to be Simon. She stayed curled in her chair and waited for him to come upstairs.

"Hey, I thought you'd be in bed."

She held up the book. "Just finished. How are things at The Haven?"

"Solemn. Conversation kept drifting back to Corrine's death. The funeral mass is at St. Marks day after tomorrow. Viewing is tomorrow evening at Le Blanc's Funeral Home."

"Have Harmon and Marcus and their families arrived?"

Simon nodded. "They're staying at The Haven. Harmon and Marcus both look like they've aged ten years. Damn, death makes you feel so helpless."

"Corrine died trying to do the right thing," Clara said.

"Yes, she did. Oh, Carlton stayed at The Haven. He's going to share Duncan's suite. Right how they need to support each other. Both think Lilith is responsible for Corrine's death."

Clara turned off the Tiffany lamp. "The blame isn't theirs. I don't know about you but I'm not ready for bed. How about an Irish coffee? "

"Sounds like a plan. In fact, I'll even make the coffee."

"You got it. I think I'm going to put the book in a safe place."

"Better safe than sorry," Simon agreed.

Downstairs, Simon went into the kitchen to make the coffee. Clara, using the light from the fire to see, pulled the peg next to the bookcase and laid the book of the knowing on the stone ledge next to Ethan's journal. It seemed fitting. She tossed small logs into the fire and turned on the lights.

"Clara," Simon called from the kitchen. "Nicole and Duncan Joseph will be here tomorrow. They're flying into Kennedy and driving up from the city with your Mom and Dad."

"Ah, ha! I get to meet your first love."

"First lust" he said as he poured a dollop of brandy into the coffee and spooned a generous covering of whipped cream on top. "My first and only love is you."

"You silver-tongued devil you."

Simon handed Clara her coffee and they nestled together on the couch. Clara sipped the coffee. "Tastes great."

"I'm just a multi-talented fellow." He kissed her temple. "Want to talk about the book?"

"No. I don't think so. I'd rather you read it first. That way we'll both be on the same page."

Simon stared into the fire. "Judith was a no show tonight, too. What's up with her and Luke?"

"I think they're taking a couple of steps back. Logistics . . . maybe too much too soon."

Simon took her hand and kissed the palm. "Not everyone has our adventurous spirit." He leaned back against the couch cushions. "Remember I told you that I let Carlton read Ethan's journal?"

"Hu huh."

"He's come up with an interesting hypothesis as to why Andre Belmont was at the Dunn dinner table."

"How so," Clara sleepily said.

"That what Belmont was really after was the knowing. Maybe the ring had been worn to provoke a response from Kathleen."

Clara's answer was a tired sigh. Simon took the cup from her hand. "Time for bed."

Early the next morning, Clara awoke to an empty bed. She tossed the covers aside and showered, and dressed in old jeans and a sweater. She found Simon seated at the kitchen counter deeply engrossed in the book of the knowing. "Good morning, husband of mine."

Simon waggled his fingers in a hello.

"I can see you're busy. I'm going to work out."

He nodded without looking up. "I'll be right here."

Smiling, Clara went on into the dojo. Sunlight streamed in through the skylight. Puffy, white clouds stood out against the blue sky. She gave in to her spring fever and slipped out the back door to the terrace. At its edge, she sat down on the stone wall. The sun struck the river turning its water a ghostly pink. The river and Joseph–she never thought of one without thinking of the other.

She breathed in the fresh spring air. All around her new life was bursting into bloom. There were buds on the Lilac trees and daffodils were pushing up through the earth. A rabbit scurried into a hedge row chasing a flock of sparrows into the air. Off in the distance, she thought that she could almost hear the hum of the insects, and the songs of the nesting birds soaring high above the reeds of the great marsh.

Beneath her bare feet, the sun warmed stone of the terrace felt like satin. She began the slow, graceful, flowing movements of Tai Chi. Images flashed in her mind. Faces came and faded. Trees and mountains and cliffs formed and disappeared.

She abandoned her workout and hurried into the studio. Picking up a stick of charcoal, she opened a sketch book. Her hand sped across the pristine white surface. She filled one page after another until her hand began to cramp. With a sigh, she dropped the charcoal onto the shelf of the drawing board and flexed her hand. When she looked up from the board, Simon was watching her from the doorway.

"About time," he said. "Do you know how long you've been at it?"

Clara rolled her neck stretching away her tension. "Not a clue. But this series is going to be my best." She moved away from the drawing board. "Take a look. I'd like your opinion."

Simon slowly flipped through the pages and went back to take a second look. A man leaned against a fireplace mantel and smiled at a woman lying against the pillows of a four-poster bed. The walls of the room were only suggested. As if the couple's existence was dependant solely on each other.

The next were less defined. The suggestion of mountains, deep ravines, distant hills–and on a high plateau a barely fleshed in structure that could have been many things. In the corner was a circle with a man on one side, enjoined by a woman on the other–the same concept as the silver ring.

Without asking the significance of the sketch, Simon turned to the next. This was of a man wearing a kilt and holding a broad sword at ready. He was standing at the edge of a cliff and watching riders on horses charging out of a cut in the mountain. "Is this all or will there be more in the series?"

Clara stared at the final sketch. "I'm not sure–possibly more."

Simon pointed to the man in the kilt. ""Wouldn't you say Scotland?"

"One of us will always be in the mountains," Clara said under her breath.

"What did you say?"

"Yes, Scotland."

Devlin Island, St. Lawrence River

Lilith Devlin raged through the island cottage. It was apparent that the house had been searched. On the kitchen table was a bag with the familiar golden arches. Styrofoam cups with dredges of coffee sat in the sink. Whoever it was, they wanted her to know they had been there. They were thumbing their nose at her.

Once her initial anger was under control, she found she was amused. She wished she could have witnessed their disappointment. There was nothing to be found, no physical evidence to link her to Libby or Joseph's murder.

It was a shame Joseph had to die. In his time, he'd been a marvelous lover. If not for the ring, . . . the damn ring. Had it not been for Carlton coming to The Landing to see Joseph, she may have chanced that Belmont's ring would have had no significance to Joseph.

During the summer of her affair with Joseph, the ring hadn't been in her possession. But Carlton knew she'd received the ring from Moria Devlin and that she had lost it. Together, he and Joseph would have followed the trail to her doorstep.

As for Corrine Pillard Melrose—running into her leaving Libby's studio had been unfortunate. How gracious it had been of Libby to mention Corrine's name and offer an excuse for her friends violent behavior. Otherwise finding out who Corrine was might have proved difficult.

Corrine only became a problem when Duncan returned to The Landing. She might conceivably have told Duncan she'd seen a woman that night–a woman, the ring, and the damn journal that had set everything in motion. The pieces would fall into place. Corrine's death had been a necessary precaution.

Lilith tossed the transcript of the journal into the fireplace and added kindling. The dry wood blazed turning the pages into a pile of ash. Those fools at Dunn House Publishing should have known an Irish lass with the brogue of the old sod still on her tongue could not be trusted.

"Kelly," she called. "Did you check out Hawk House?"

Patrick Kelly strolled up toward the house from the dock. "I did. I saw the woman on the terrace. No sign of her husband."

"Any easy access?"

"Hawk House is well known. Tourists often ask of it. I cozied up to a local contractor. The glass in the house—bullet proof. Its doors are solid oak. The tunnel you mentioned is blocked off with a steel door. There's no access, easy or otherwise."

"I must have the book."

Kelly shrugged. "You don't know with any certainty that the book is in Clara Hawk's possession. Much less that it's hidden in Hawk House."

Dark fury filled Lilith's eyes. "She has it and I want it back. It's the key to the knowing."

Kelly watched her pace back and forth across the cottage floor—a sleek, predatory beast of prey with a smoldering sexiness. In spite of himself, his groin tightened.

Lilith felt his eyes and turned to face him. His lust was a palatable thing. For the first time, she appraised him as a man. He was boyishly handsome, and young with a hard muscled body. "Kelly," she whispered as she unbuttoned her blouse. "Come here. Come here and fuck me."

Hours later Lilith awoke from a deep sated sleep and stretched in satisfaction. Mindless sex—no fuss, no muss, far better than love. Her love for Duncan had kept her entrapped, forcing her to play the role of perfect, devoted wife, perfect, loving mother. Where was the perfect devoted husband? When she and Duncan had made love she had always wondered if he thought of Libby. He'd never forgotten the bitch. Never let her be dead. She had always been second choice.

Love had turned out to be nothing more than giving the other person a better weapon. It was no wonder she and the Duke had become lovers. Between them there was no pretense of love. Only sex and the shared desire to possess all the secrets of the knowing.

Her son, her loving son who had become her nemesis. Who would sacrifice her to clear his father's name. Carlton had fought her from the cradle. Even worse, there was no love in him for Ireland. He believed the peace accord was a good thing. A good thing! Only a fool would believe the IRA would ever disarm. No matter, she would not allow either her husband or her son to stand in the way of her destiny.

Kelly groaned and turned in his sleep. She reached over and took his flaccid penis into her hand and gently squeezed. An answering surge brought a smile to her face. Her grip tightened. This time she wanted it hard and fast.

Hawk House

Simon put the phone down just as Clara came into the room. "Anything important?"

"The Chief. His surveillance team called in. Lilith is on the island. She has one man with her. That doesn't mean there aren't more in the area." Simon's brow furrowed. "I don't like this."

"This house is a veritable fortress. The Chief's men are watching her every move."

"Forgive my lack of confidence, but they're not faster than a speeding bullet." Simon tersely said. "I'd rather give her the damn book and send her on her merry way, than have anything happen to you."

Clara didn't bother to argue. It was a losing battle. "Did the Chief learn anything on the van that forced Corrine off the road?"

"Not yet. He figures it was stolen and that the driver was likely to have been the guy Carlton saw. Chances are he has already beat feet out of the area. The van will turn up abandoned in Syracuse, Watertown–across the border in Canada."

"Can Art identify the driver?"

"The Chief said that Art gave a good description of the van but the man was a blurr–hat pulled low, sun glasses."

"Figures," Clara commented. "We haven't had any luck yet."

"That's why, my darling wife, you must exercise some caution." Simon shrugged into his suit jacket. "Ready?"

"Just let me get my handbag."

Once in the Jeep, Clara adjusted the beaded, vintage shawl over the long, black silk dress.

Simon smiled at her. "Did I mention that you look very beautiful?"

"You didn't, but I take my compliments where I can find them. And you look very handsome." Clara glanced out of the window. "Simon, you've passed the turn to The Haven."

"We're early. Let's just drive for a while. I want to talk to you."

Clara settled back in the seat. "Go for it, big fella."

"Lilith is dangerous and she wants the book back. Can we at least agree on that much?"

"Simon, my love, you're overstating the obvious. We've been over this so often I've a groove worn in my brain–Lilith dangerous, book back, Lilith dangerous, book back."

He reached over and put his hand across her moth. "Okay, I get it. Let me run this by you. I think there is a second danger."

"Which is?"

"The knowing itself." He glanced at Clara. "Correct me if I'm wrong but isn't your knowing growing stronger and coming with greater frequency?"

"It is," she said simply.

"According to the book the knowing can be dangerous."

"I didn't need the book to know that."

"What I'm making reference to is the fact that without a mentor to teach how the knowing is controlled it can lead to violence and madness. Misused, the knowing can do great damage. The way I see it is that you sought the pure source inside yourself. Lilith had no proper foundation for its use–no meditation, no martial arts. As it result, Lilith's knowing became weak and insignificant."

Clara nodded. "Many don't even remember having possessed

it. I think Corrine is a case in point."

"After reading the book, I see where you're coming from." You instinctively or with the foreknowledge of the knowing sought the path you might conceivably have taken if the proper training had been available. You learned how to control the knowing without losing its source." Simon pulled into a parking area. "Clara, I've asked you before but now that you've read the book, has your perception of what the knowing is changed?"

"Based on the book–I'd say it was once an esoteric discipline." She paused and thoughtfully added, "but after the women were betrayed by one of their own, the few who remained had to live apart from the others. Consequently, through the generations more and more of the knowing was lost."

"In essence, what you're saying is that the empowerment remains but with no means of utilizing it."

"Basically, yes."

"What do you make of the mention of all elements flowing like a river as one."

Clara thought for a moment. "Right now we are surrounded by nature–earth, wind, water, fire. These are the elements of nature, components of the universal order."

"And?"

"The language in the book is unclear. My interpretation of it is that these were pathways. Door or portals to the culmination of all knowledge–the universal mind."

Simon drummed his fingers on the steering wheel. "You told me Carlton said that Lilith used to punish him–hurt him when she wasn't anywhere near him."

"Yes. The answer is yes, I think the energy can be used in such a way."

"There's a dark side?"

"A rather star-warish assumption, but I'd say so."

Simon frowned. "Lilith is also aware that your knowing is growing stronger while hers is waning. That she wants the book is a given. More important, I think she wants you dead."

"I wouldn't worry about Lilith," Clara said with assurance.

"She'll destroy herself."

"One can only hope." Simon put the Jeep into gear. "We'd better get to the party."

Clara watched the river. "Joseph used to talk of being entranced by the splendor of living life in harmony with the rhythm of the universe. I'd like to think I'm learning how to do this. Wisdom, the realization of the power of the knowing–my entire life has been a spiritual quest. Even the schools is an extension of where the knowing has taken me."

When Simon didn't comment, Clara glanced at him. "I see by the set of your jaw that I haven't assuaged your conviction that there's more to this than Lilith."

Without taking his eyes from the road, Simon reached over and patted her hand. "Right on, Sherlock."

The Hawk and Dunn families were again gathered in The Haven's private dining room–a welcome home for Duncan. A welcome into the family for his son, Carlton. This was the evening Carlton had looked forward to all his life, but his emotions were in turmoil. Tonight, what he thought of as his sort of knowing carried a warning. Along with the air of festivity there was a calm. A feeling that they were all in the eye of a storm whose main force was yet to be experienced.

David Hawk carried his infant son in his arms. The sleeping child was blissfully unaware of the showering of ohs and ahs taking place around him. The baby's nurse watched from the sidelines, anxious to claim her young charge and retreat to their suite. She was overwhelmed by The Haven's opulent luxury and unsure of how to behave with the very rich, who insisted on treating her as an equal.

Nicole Hawk stood at her husband's side. Her slim figure was encased in a silver grey gown that shimmered in the candlelight. David lowered his head and whispered. "You look positively gorgeous," he proudly told her.

"Thank you, so do you." Nicole glanced around the room and saw Simon and the woman who had to be Clara come into the room. She nervously moved closer to David and took his arm.

David chuckled. "Don't worry, Nicole. Clara doesn't bite . . . but I have heard she can kick the by Jesus out of anyone she doesn't like."

"Thanks, darling. I feel much reassured."

Simon and Clara slowly made their way through the crowd, pausing along the way to greet family. Simon spotted Nicole and his father and walked toward them, drawing Clara with him. "Nicole, glad you made it. Clara, this is Nicole. Nicole, my wife Clara."

"Nicole, it's a pleasure to finally meet you," Clara said with a welcoming smile. "I hope your trip was pleasant."

Nicole returned her smile. "It was, especially the time with your parents. I'm glad to meet you."

Simon wondered what the two women was thinking, but realized it was probably best that he didn't know. He smiled down at his infant brother and held out his arms. "May I?"

"Of course," David said. He carefully handed the baby over into his brother's care. "Watch his head."

"He's quite a guy. Look at the size of those hands."

Duncan Joseph languidly stretched and opened his eyes and with a gurgle, gripped Simon's thumb. Clara's breath caught in her throat. Watching Simon with the baby brought deep overwhelming emptiness. "Please excuse me for a moment." She slipped out of the room and leaned against the hallway wall. The sadness and longing were unlike anything she's ever experienced. She understood what Libby must have felt . . . or perhaps what she was feeling was Libby.

Nicole followed her into the hall. "You looked like you had seen a ghost. Are you all right?"

Clara weakly smiled. "I'm fine, really."

"Judith told me you have this knowing, this ability to see things, know things that other don't. Was it that? Is something wrong with my baby?"

"Oh, no, not at all. He's perfect."

Nicole accepted Clara's reassurance. "It's strange though,

when Judith mentioned this knowing it brought to mind my grandmother. She had this uncanny ability to know when things were going to happen. I used to think she could read my mind."

Clara smiled. "Every woman has the knowing . . . at least to some degree. Most would call it women's intuition. My Dad calls it our bewitchment." Beyond Nicole's shoulder, Clara saw Lilith Devlin and Patrick Kelly enter the lobby. "Nicole, please go and tell Simon that Lilith is here."

Nicole looked confused but without protest complied. Clara hurried into the lobby to confront Lilith. "What are you doing here?"

"I want my book," Lilith spat.

Clara contemptuously stared into her eyes. "How does it feel to want?"

Patrick Kelly warily watched their exchange. Something about Clara Hawk made him certain that having her as an adversary was a mistake. Lilith was playing a dangerous game.

Simon came to Clara's side. "What have we here? Ireland's answer to Bonnie and Clyde?"

"Save the witticisms. Your wife has a book that belongs to me. I want it returned."

"Or what?" Clara asked. "You'll call the police."

Simon simply ignored Lilith. "Our young Lothario, what does he want?"

"I'm just a simple tourist enjoying your lovely country," Kelly quipped. In spite of himself, he felt shame at his role in Lilith's latest scheme.

Lilith spoke softly to Clara. "Beauty is fleeting. Would be a shame to see yours destroyed."

Clara's eyes narrowed. A chill wind seemed to blow and she saw the monastery in flames, blood staining the courtyard. And a woman, the traitorous bitch who had betrayed her own.

Simon sensed that Clara had slipped into the knowing and put his arm around her waist. He could feel her simmering rage. "Clara, not now. Let it go."

Lilith drew back in fear. Something in Clara's eyes told her that is she made a single misstep, she would die.

Clara's body relaxed into Simon's. "She brought about the end of the knowing. She was a killer then, and she's a killer now."

Behind Clara and Simon, a supporting group of all the Hawks and Dunns had formed. Duncan and Carlton came to stand beside them.

Lilith spread her arms wide. "My husband and my son–what a lovely welcome."

Duncan looked at her as he would at a stranger. "You slaughtered Libby. Killed Joseph. Ordered Daltry's death and the deaths of God knows how many others. You reek of the grave."

Carlton stared at his mother. "Those people must be avenged."

"Vengeance is mine sayth the Lord," Lilith sarcastically said.

Clara laughed–a genuine laugh of pure enjoyment. "No. Vengeance in your case will come through me. I'm who you would be if only you could–but you can't. Not now, not ever."

"Return the book and I'll happily leave."

"Your precious book. You need it very badly, while I have no use for it. I hold the mysteries. You lose . . . centuries later. You lose." Clara stepped closer to Lilith and lowered her voice to a whisper. "Listen closely. Listen for their laughter in the howling winds, in the surge of the sea. Look for their faces in the clouds, and out of the flames of a blazing fire. Listen, for their laughter will haunt your dreams and walk with you in the daylight hours."

Lilith's face was starkly white with fear. She looked from her husband to her son. Hawk eyes, cold and hard, stared back. Her voice came in a harsh croak. "It isn't over."

"Sure and it is," Simon mocked. "At least for you."

Adam Hawk plucked a long stemmed rose from a porcelain vase and tossed it at Lilith's feet. "To commemorate the ending of our nightmare and the death of your dreams."

Simon nodded toward Kelly. "Take your lackey and run, run as far and as fast as you can."

"But I wouldn't run to Ireland," Duncan advised. "Daltry's death and all the others must be accounted for."

Lilith didn't protest the accusation, nor claim innocence.

Instead, she said, "Nothing can be proven–not here, not there."

Patrick Kelly took Lilith's elbow. "We should be going."

Lilith backed away. Her head pounded and she glanced from side to side to find the source of the laughter. Kelly guided her toward the front entrance. Her eyes were wild. "Make it stop. Can't be. Make it stop."

"Lilith, what are you asking? Make what stop?" Kelly asked in confusion.

"The laughter. Make it stop."

Clara watched Lilith and Kelly go out the front door. Her expression was openly pleased. "Shall we have dinner?"

David walked with Nicole. "Clara's quite a woman, isn't she?"

"I can see it's best to stay on her good side," Nicole answered.

Carlton quietly spoke to Duncan. "Did I get a family or what? Grandfather and the rose. . ." The humor went from his tone. "Hard to believe her blood runs in my veins."

Lydia Dunn Eaton put her arm around her daughter's waist. "I'm sorry your grandmother missed this."

Clara kissed her mother's cheek. "Hi, Mom. Sorry I didn't get a chance to say hello before. Speaking of Grandmother, how come she isn't with you?"

"She's knee deep in plans for your and Simon's reception. Your Uncle Carson is hosting. He's paying penance for having missed the wedding. They seem to be organized but keep mumbling about wishing Luke was there."

"Oh, Mom, I'd forgotten all about it."

Simon suppressed a grin. "Remember, Clara. Soul of propriety."

John Eaton joined them. "My irrepressible daughter–don't make promises you're not certain you can keep," he warned with a loving smile.

"Why, John," Lydia defensively said. "Clara will certainly be at her own reception."

"Her attendance isn't in doubt. It's the soul of propriety I question."

Lydia ignored her husbands joking disparagement.

"Everyone from here is invited. Simon, your friends will be coming–Stephen, Pepe, Elise and Jacques. Is there anyone else you'd like to invite?"

"Can't think of a single soul."

Clara and Lydia walked ahead of the men discussing the plans for the reception. John Eaton waited until they were out of earshot. "Simon, this Devlin woman. Do you feel she's a serious danger to the family?"

Simon knew that when John spoke of family he meant both the Dunns and the Hawks. "I do. And nothing will convince me that she's acting alone."

John Eaton frowned. "A group with like ideology?"

"Maybe. All I'm certain of is that the knowing is the key to events beginning, not as we've believed with Ethan's journal, but generations before."

"I can't disagree. When I was researching old records, others had been following the same trail."

"That helps to validate my own conclusions. But at the moment, Lilith Devlin is our most pressing concern."

John Eaton's eyes were cold. "She must be stopped."

Clara, waiting in the doorway of the dining room for Simon, overheard her father's comment. She linked her arm with his. "I would guess you two were speaking of Lilith?"

"Yes, my darling daughter. We were."

"Not to worry," Clara airily said. "Believe me. Lilith has ceased to be a problem."

Devlin Island

The St. Lawrence River flowed black and cold. Its waves lapped against the wood dock bringing with it the sound of laughter. Lilith shivered and pulled the blanket over her bare shoulders. At her side, Patrick Kelly slept his sated sleep, deep and dreamless.

Lilith stared at the ceiling. She was afraid to sleep. Afraid to allow her mind to be quiet, for in the stillness would be the laughter. She tossed the covers aside and got up and poured herself a brandy. She wanted to leave this place and go home to Ireland.

Her life bore the horrifying imprint of violence. The knowing had begun early, filling her with meaningless flashes of faces, places, and a raging desire for power. As she grew older, the knowing translated into sensuality to become yet another weapon in her arsenal. The knowing enabled her to use her mind and body to achieve her ends. It gave her insight into which men could be used and manipulated. If their desire was strong enough, she could convince them of anything, to do anything. All accept Duncan.

With the thought of Duncan came the memory of Libby. And out of the memory came the laughter exploding in her mind without surcease. She flung the brandy snifter against the wall. Libby Dunn's death had been necessary. Now Clara Hawk stood between her and the knowing. Her death was necessary. Her death would stop the laughter.

Hawk House

Simon sat by the fire and waited for Clara to finish with her shower. The evening had been wonderful but he was unable to put Lilith's presence from his thoughts. What would her next move be?

Clara came out of the bathroom brushing her wet hair. The shell pink dressing gown gave a translucent look to the ivory of her skin. Her face lit up with delight. "A fire and a bottle of wine. How romantic."

"Don't get your hopes up. This isn't a seduction."

She came to him and leaned down to kiss him. She smelled of sunlight and flowers. His arms reached for her but laughing she moved away. "Hoisted on your own petard, big fella."

"Dirty pool, Clara," he said with a chuckle.

She poured two glasses of wine and sat down in the chair opposite him. "What is it you want to talk about? Are you hiding me away somewhere or is it your plan to hire a platoon of marines to guard me day and night?"

"What say we take a tour of your schools? I'd like to see them up close and personal."

"Transparent, very transparent. Fess up, you want me to disappear until Lilith is no longer a threat." She got up from her chair and took a brochure from the drawer of her bedside table and dropped it into his lap.

"What's this?"

"An alterative–a woman's wilderness group and a walking tour through the Scottish highlands."

"Because you think the knowing's archives might be secreted somewhere in the countryside?" he asked, only half joking.

"Smart ass. But yes, I do think Scotland plays a role. I want to take a look. See if the knowing shows me anything new."

"Not a bad idea." He began to read the information. The tour would begin the Monday after the reception at Carson's estate. Clara would be out of touch for ten days . . . out of touch and safe. Time he could use to search for whoever pulled Lilith's strings. "Sounds good."

Clara leaned back and looked into his face. "Uh huh, too easy. You're up to something. I can see you're still in the old I gotta protect Clara mode."

"Me, protect you? How dare I even suggest? Never, you are invincible. You are . . ."

Clara stopped his words with a kiss. ""Seducing you. So shut up."

Northern Ireland

Devlin Manor was hidden in heavy fog. The angry sea rhythmically slapped against the base of the cliff. Lilith dropped the curtain back over the window. There was nothing to be seen. Only the ghosts of people no longer present. She lit a match and touched it to the kindling in the fireplace. She watched as the fire took hold and put on some larger wood.

Patrick Kelly came into the room. Lilith saw that he was dressed in a dark grey business suit and a black top coat. "My, my, aren't we looking like the erudite theologian."

"That's who I once was. As you well know."

In the open doorway was a suitcase. Lilith frowned. "Going somewhere?"

He nodded. "I'm headed to Dublin to report to Terrance O'Neil."

"He's Sinn Fein. Who in hell made that decision?"

"I did. I'll no longer dance to your tune. The killing is out of control. I'll not be a party to it."

"Since when has killing troubled you?" she said snootily.

"Since you ordered old Daltry's death for no reason other than to vent your spleen. It had nothing to do with the freeing of Ireland. It was personal. Just like the woman you had Kip run off the road. And the poor sod whose throat you slit in The Landing. Now you want the death of Clara Hawk. She has nothing to do with Ireland. It's on your head."

Lilith laughed and patted his cheek. "Let's put this moralistic nonsense aside. Killing is killing."

"I've killed for Ireland," Kelly admitted. "To take what is rightfully ours. To give our children their birthright. But I've never killed out of malice. Even so, I wake in the night and wish it were different."

"I've not killed for Ireland?"

"Once, no more. Now it's personal—you and the damn knowing."

Lilith slapped him in the face. Kelly's lips thinned and she saw anger in his eyes. She felt a cold thread of fear crawl her spine and stepped away from him.

Surprisingly, Kelly chuckled. "The laughter must be loud today." He cupped his ear with his hand. "Yes, there it is. Sure and the laughter rides the wake of your defeat. What was it the lovely Clara said? The laughter is in the wind and the waves. A wonderfully droll way to die–madness from out of the very thing you cherish above all else."

Lilith turned her back to him. "Get out," she whispered. "Get out."

The door closed punctuating her aloneness. She poured a large brandy and taking the bottle with her sat down by the fire. Eventually her role as paymaster for the IRA would come out. Ireland, like the knowing, was lost to her. With a shaking hand, she took a swallow of brandy and another and another and poured a second snifter.

Her mind was filled with mocking laughter. Voices of those long dead. She picked up the telephone and punched in a number. "Be there, Adiran, be there," she whispered into the silence.

On the third ring the phone was answered.

"Adiran?"

"Who is calling?"

"Lilith Devlin."

"Lilith, this is Jacques. I'm sorry. I didn't recognize your voice. Hold on, I think father just came in."

Lilith reached for the brandy snifter. Her hand trembled and the brandy splattered the marble table top. Golden drops pooled together into staring eyes. With a sob, she swept the table bare.

"Lilith?"

"Adiran, I need your help," she said in desperation. "The laughter, eyes everywhere . . . staring. Voices in the night. Help me."

"Calm down, my dear. Tell me what's wrong."

"It's the Hawk woman. Her knowing is strong, too strong. I can't fight it. She's destroying me. I want her dead ."

"Hawk. There's no Hawk lineage."

"Dunn, through the Dunns from the Killarneys. Clara Dunn

Eaton Hawk. She's Sylvia Mitchell's granddaughter."

"Would she be inclined to aid in our mission?"

"Never," Lilith snarled. "She wants it all for herself. She must die."

Adiran Severin impatiently sighed. "Lilith, you have the resources to deal with this matter yourself."

"I can not. She's cursed me, used her power to destroy me. You must help me. She put the laughter in my mind. The eyes watch. They see everything."

Lilith began to babble. "Laughter in the wind, the water, faces in the fire. Help me."

"Lilith," Adiran snapped. "You're either drunk or mad. You need help. Get some."

The phone clicked in her ear with finality. Adiran Severin tapped the arm of his chair. His son, Jacques looked up from the computer screen. "Problem?"

"Lilith. She's behaving irrationally. She wants a woman killed." Adiran harshly laughed. "Fate seems to be stepping in. Do you recall the kidnaping and murder of a Mitchell Media executive?"

"In Japan. I recall it well. Carson Mitchell has been hot on the scent ever since."

"Yes, and poking his nose into the arms trade. He's becoming a nuisance."

"Rumor has it. His demise is planned."

Adiran nodded. "At a soiree honoring his niece. One Clara Dunn Eaton Hawk. Lilith's nemesis."

Jacques raised an eyebrow. "And?"

"I'll have to think about it." Adiran poured himself a cognac. He stared contemplatively into the topaz liquid. His family archives contained detailed records of the women of the knowing and of their demise.

Always the women of the knowing had thwarted his family. In the late fifteen hundreds, the women and their protectors fled from the wrath of the Holy Roman Catholic Church. They disappeared from Basque to surface in Scotland where the Catholic

Church had been rendered impotent. They believed the Highlands would give them sanctuary.

But the women had underestimated the church's tenacity and its fear of their power. The Bishop of Paris desired them destroyed and had so commanded. The Duke of Cristobal, in accordance with the church's degree, had assembled a force and followed them to the Scottish Highlands. It was here that they were betrayed by one of their own.

Most of the women and their protectors had been slaughtered. Those who survived were scattered to the four winds, and no longer considered to be of any consequence. Adiran reflectively sipped his cognac. Yet in the end, his ancestor had been defeated. Defeated by his desire for the women's knowledge and the power it would give him. He had died, poisoned by his nemesis–a woman of the knowing.

Adiran allowed himself to remember the young Lilith. She had been beautiful, passionate. One of the most sensual women he had known–and just as willing to betray the knowing as her ancestor had been. A shame she had been unable to fulfill her early promise. In her case, the knowing had been her betrayer.

Adiran was not given to self delusion. At one time, Lilith had been very important to him. With her, he had come as close to love and loving as he ever had. Perhaps he owed her this much. If Clara Hawk's death would give her peace . . . so be it.

Carson Mitchell was already on the terrorist agenda. One needed only to expand the mission. He thoughtfully drummed his fingers on the arm of the chair. It might be best to include the husband–eliminate the possibility of reprisal.

Devlin Manor, Ireland

Lilith stood in front of the blazing fire and tossed in everything she possessed that related to the knowing. Years of research, personal notes, books, computer disks–all went up in flame.

As the fire burned low shadows gathered around her. She sat down in a high-backed chair next to a table where a glass of port wine had replaced the brandy. In her hand was a small vial. She pulled the stopper free and sprinkled the white powder into the wine.

For a moment the poison was suspended like miniature snow flakes on the surface of the blood red liquid. She swirled the wine and it disappeared. The laughter was everywhere–contemptuous, menacing, unceasing laughter. She stared into the fire and it grew distant, supplanted by faces staring from out of the flames. Gone, all gone. Ireland, the knowing–even Adiran had turned away. Mad, he had said. You are mad. The laughter grew louder. It filled the spaces in her mind becoming a pain behind her eyes.

Lilith picked up the glass. Hidden in its depth was the means of counteracting her failure in this life. She would escape from the staring eyes, from the never-ending laughter. She would die and thereby win. For in her next life she would again have the knowing. This time she and the knowing would be as one. The power would be hers.

Her throat muscles worked as she swallowed. She carefully set the crystal wine glass down and rested her head against the back of her chair and closed her eyes. The laughter grew distant, fading into the silence of death.

St Lawrence River Valley

Simon ran along the river road. Early morning traffic was

light but later in the day it would be every vehicle for itself. The season was gearing up and would soon be in full swing. As he rounded the curve, he saw Hawk House. The sun struck the stained-glass fan window and the hawk with its outspread wings seemed to fly into flame.

He turned down the long drive and was immediately accosted by the Irish wolfhounds and Dog. They chased around him in wide circles and rolled in the tall grass of the field. At the front entrance, he unlocked the door and called the dogs in. The telephone was ringing but he waited for the answering machine to pick up. Clara was running errands and he wasn't in the mood for conversation.

After the machine's beep, he heard, "This is Patrick Kelly. It's imperative that I speak with you concerning Lilith Devlin. I can be reached at–"

Simon picked up the receiver. "Kelly. It's Simon Hawk. What is it?" he brusquely snapped.

"Mr. Hawk, last night Lilith Devlin died by her own hand. I've not been able to locate her husband nor her son. I thought you might know where they can be reached."

Simon's mouth went dry with surprise. "How?"

"She took a massive dose of sleeping powder in conjunction with some kind of poison and alcohol. Was toxic. Mr. Hawk, I'd like you to . . . I want–"

"Spit it out, Kelly. What do you want to say?"

"I'd like you and your wife to know I had no part in the death of your friends, nor in Daltry's. Daltry was my friend and mentor. The bloody politics has turned Ireland into a living hell. From here on, I'll be working with Sinn Fein. Helping to make certain the peaceful compromise holds. The killing must end."

Simon was surprised at the sincerity in his voice. More surprised to discover he believed him. "Are you aware of something Lilith would have referred to as the knowing?"

"Yes," Kelly said in clipped tone.

"Do you know of anyone Lilith worked with or contacted concerning it?"

"Sorry. She was closed mouthed about it. I only saw the end product–death. Mr. Hawk, I'll see what I can find out. Please understand. I do this not in justification, but because it's the right thing to do."

Simon's tone softened. "Kelly, before the IRA. Who were you? What did you do?"

"Would you believe I fancied myself a scholar–a doctor of theology?"

Before Simon could answer, he heard a click and the connection was broken.

Simon rested against the headboard of the bed. It had been an eternally long day. Lilith's death had immediately wrought change. Carlton and Duncan were on their way to Devlin Manor with a promise to search through Lilith's personal papers for anything relating to the knowing.

Strangely, as much as Lilith had deserved her fate, there was an element of sadness. Her destiny and the knowing had been irreversibly intertwined into a bond which had ultimately brought about her death.

Clara got into bed and rested her head on his chest. "Simon, can we talk for a minute?"

He kissed the top of her head. "What is it?"

"Somehow we've never discussed having children."

"No, I guess we haven't. Are you asking if I want children?"

"Do you?" she said softly.

"When the time is right, very much. You?"

"I've always imagined a family, children, but more as a fantasy than actuality. The other night when I saw you with Duncan Joseph, I wanted nothing more than for us to have a child."

"You or was it Libby?" he quietly asked.

Clara got up from the bed and quickly dressed in old sweats. Hot tears of anger propelled her downstairs. Simon pulled on a pair of jeans and followed. "Clara, I'm sorry."

"Don't be. You have a right to your opinion. Just as I have a right to be angry. If you don't mind, I'd like to be alone."

"Can't we talk this through?"

"Not now."

"Clara, I didn't . . ."

"Yes, you did. The knowing is my reality. I live with it and believe me I can tell the difference between what I am and what it is. Obviously, you can't."

Simon could see from the set of her shoulders, the cold frozen expression of her face, that it would be best to give her time to cool down. Defeated, he turned and went back upstairs.

Clara's body was tense with anger and disappointment. Simon's response had touched a nerve. But how could she blame him, she had dropped her sudden need for a child into his lap without giving any thought to how it might seem to him. She went into the dojo and after stretching and warm up exercises, she began the slow, flowing movements of Tai Chi.

Abruptly, she broke off the movement and sat down on the bench. What was it the woman in the knowing had said? The rhythm of life had been lost and must be restored. Restored by changing our thought patterns. How, how would one accomplish this? Perhaps, she thought, by directing the energy of one of the pathways.

She stepped back onto the mat and again began the movements of Tai Chi. She focused her mind on first finding her center. Gradually, the slow, flowing movements drew her into the eloquent silence of self. As the motion changed, she selected water as the pathway which seemed to match the flow of the katas. But she found this caused her to lose her own balance.

She worked her way back to her center and anticipated the kata, forming in her mind the pathway suggested by the movement. Water flowing, running, a current streaming forth, changing, becoming. There was an almost imperceptible shifting in energy and she was one with the water, was the water.

Upstairs, Simon lay awake. The air around him seemed to stir with life. He waited and the energy seemed to grow and expand. A sharp, piercing scream of pure anguish pulled him from the bed.

Simon found Clara curled in a fetal position with the dogs anxiously milling around her. He kneeled and brushed her damp hair away from her face. "Clara, I'm here. It's all right. Come on baby, open your eyes. Everything's all right. You're safe."

Clara's arms came up and he gathered her against his chest and carried her to the couch. "Clara. What happened?"

"I was so angry. I just wanted to work through it." She took a deep breath. "The knowing–I touched its pure source. I know how it's done."

"Can you describe what happened?"

Clara walked him through it. "I pictured water, the river, rain, a swiftly flowing current." She took a deep breath. "Suddenly I was one with the water. The energy was frighteningly strong. Yet I knew I could direct it, change it. I was terrified."

"Just before you screamed, I felt something–a shift in the air. Some sort of atmospheric change."

"Yes, there was. That's when I panicked. It was as though I was paralyzed."

"Clara, this won't go away. You've opened too many doors. To survive, to have a life . . . to have children," he added, recalling their earlier argument. "I think you have to discover all the . . . what was it you told Lilith? The mysteries?"

Clara nodded. "But I don't know as I have them. I just wanted to upset her. According to the book, the mysteries are all the knowledge of the knowing–a culmination."

"We're already fairly certain that the knowing is a psychic discipline. One older, more powerful than any of the known martial arts." Simon sighed wearily. "Even so it's possible, especially after what happened to you tonight, that the martial arts can be a vehicle. A way to reach the essence of the knowing. When you touched this source did it give rise to psychic energy?"

"Yes, in a manner of speaking," Clara answered. "In this instance becoming one with the water . . ." Her voice trailed off.

"Go on, Clara," Simon encouraged.

"Once I was one with the water, I knew I could transform thought into action and create energy." Clara sat up and wiped tears from her eyes. "The knowing isn't just power. It's a discipline. The energy or force plus the discipline equal the knowing. Power/discipline–like two sides of the same coin."

"How so?"

"One is incomplete without the other. The force itself is one side–the discipline the other. I'm certain that once the knowing was fully integrated." Clara shivered with fear–fear of where this would take her.

Simon held her close until the trembling ceased.

Clara sighed. "I've never been more frightened. But I did learn that when something new of the knowing is revealed. So is the means to control it."

Simon stared into space. Clara's future was irrevocably linked to that of the knowing. His concern lay not with the knowing but with whether or not he'd be able to keep her safe.

Clara closed her eyes and relaxed against Simon's body. Her mind drifted, and she entered the stillness of all time. Mist, like a sheer curtain in front of a window, obscured her vision but a breeze came blowing it in languorous swirls–first revealing then concealing the crags and valleys below.

She saw jagged mountain peaks. A hawk lazily circling the ground searching for prey, its wing feathers spread like a woman's fan. Far above, etched sharply against the blue sky was the flame blackened walls of the monastery.

Simon watched Clara and decided to attempt to enjoin with her in the knowing. He breathed deeply, gradually entering into a deep meditative state. He opened himself to Clara's energy. There came the smell of smoke, and he could hear the wail of bagpipes. A sword was in his hand.

"Simon, open your eyes," Clara pleaded. "Please open your eyes."

Simon, responding to a voice he had always known, reluctantly left the landscape of the knowing. "Clara."

"Damn you. What did you do? You scared me to death."

"Turn-a-bout is fair play. Wipe that look of concern from your face. I'm fine."

"I want to know what you . . ."

"Not now," he said firmly. "I need time to think it through. We'll talk about it in the morning."

Simon sat in front of the blank computer screen. His latest book was on the shelves and on the Times best seller list. He was well into the next book but today the words wouldn't come. Last night was stuck in his mind. What had happened had most definitely not been a dream. The knowing was distinctively different. Its images replayed in his thoughts. Bagpipes and the shrieks of the dying as arrows struck their targets. Men engaged in hand to hand combat. Horses hooves drumming against the stone of a courtyard. He had felt a sword in his hand. A battle, but what battle? It was frustrating to not be able to put the pieces of the puzzle together.

He and Clara had yet to discuss his experience. She had left early on her shop 'til you drop excursion with Susan Fowler. But in typical Clara fashion, she had left a note reminding him that they still needed to talk.

The telephone beeped and he absently punched the talk button. "Simon Hawk."

"Hello, Simon, Carson Mitchell."

"Carson. I'll bet you want to speak with my blushing bride."

Carson laughed. "Clara, blushing–boggles the mind. The information I have can be relayed to you just as well as to her."

"Shoot."

"The invitations to your reception are in the mail, but with a change of venue. We, as in Stephen and me, have moved it to my place near D.C. Clara knows it."

"What happened?"

"My mother and sister kept adding names until we overflowed my mother's house and in the words of Sylvia Dunn Mitchell–a hotel ballroom simply will not do."

"You know, Carson. It's been my observation that the women in your family are very strong minded."

"Not a shrinking violet among them."

"I also hear you're quite strong minded yourself."

"There's been worse said," Carson answered. "I take it you've heard something definitive which prompted the evaluation."

"Pepe Hawkins is an old friend. We worked together."

"Ah, the fog lifts. He's a good man."

"Says the same about you but he's a little concerned about where your investigation into terrorism is going. Care to enlighten me?"

"You're family. Why not? About a year ago one of my people in Tokyo was kidnaped. Americans seem to make the best targets."

"Ransom demand?"

"Exorbitant. Against state's advice, I paid. I knew it was a crap shot, but it was also the only possibility we had of getting Graham back alive."

Simon was fairly certain of the outcome. Terrorists never played by any rules but theirs.

"I lost the gamble. They dumped him in front of our Tokyo bureau. His tongue had been cut out, fingers sliced off. A note was hammered into his chest–silence is golden."

"Red Army?"

"Maybe–Graham was poking into terrorist activity's world wide. He'd rattled a lot of cages."

"A warning to cease and desist?"

"So your friend Pepe thinks."

"But you haven't backed off?"

"I didn't get where I am by burying my head in the sand."

"I hope you've at least beefed up security."

"I have. Pepe has convinced me that it would be wise to curtail overseas travel. I'm doing that . . . at least for the time being."

"No wonder Pepe's worried."

"Say, Simon. You swam in that pool. Anything I can use?"

"Sorry. I've been out of the loop way to long."

"Understood. See you soon."

Simon put the phone down. Carson had stuck his toe into some very hot water. He'd be best served by paying attention to Pepe. The blank screen stared stared balefully back at him. He put the computer on standby and wandered to the window. Out on the river, a large tanker flying the Canadian oak leaf made its cumbersome way east toward the Massena locks and the Atlantic Ocean.

Clara's face was reflected in the window just as Simon felt her arm snake around his waist. She had become so much a part of him that he could not imagine life without her. "Hey, shopping done?"

Clara stuck her foot out. "Like my new shoes?"

Simon looked down and saw that she was wearing Timberline hiking boots. "Whoa. You are a fashion plate."

"That I am. Got to break them in."

"Trip still on?"

"Sure. Lilith may be dead but the knowing is alive and well." She stared up at him. "As you well know."

Simon shook his head. "You are tenacious. Let's put this to rest once and for all. I smelled smoke, heard bagpipes. I held a broadsword . . ." His expression grew blank. "I was wearing a kilt. I didn't remember that until just now. Maybe your trip to Scotland is right on the money."

"Once the door is opened, it can't be closed. You'll keep getting flashes of it–fragments, bits and pieces." She grinned and playfully punched his arm. "Welcome to the club. Can't say you haven't been warned."

"I do believe I get the picture."

"Speaking of picture. I'm going to work on the painting for Nicole and David. How about you–book?"

"Let me put it this way. There are no words of wisdom gracing the computer screen." He glanced down at her boots. "So clump off to the studio. I'll see if I can get my creative juices flowing in the kitchen."

Clara purposely stomped across the hardwood floor. "This is me, clumping off."

In the kitchen, Simon stood at the stove and tasted the spaghetti sauce. He added a pinch of oregano and ground in fresh pepper. With the blade of a knife, he crushed a large clove of garlic and tossed it into the now simmering sauce. He tasted again and added a hint of hot sauce.

"Simon," Clara called from the doorway of her studio. "Could you come and take a look at this?"

"Minute babe." Simon turned the flame low under the cooper pot.

He found Clara in front of an easel staring at a partially completed canvas. In its center was a colorful clown juggling three balls. Duncan Joseph Hawk was scripted on the center ball. The time and date of his birth were on another. The third had his birth weight and length.

Simon looked over her shoulder. "A most unusual birth announcement. It's destined to become a family heirloom. Dad and Nicole will love it. I'm glad you're going to let the family in on your talent."

"You and the newest Hawk, as in Carlton, didn't give me much of an option. But what you said did have a certain kind of logic. So I'm coming out of the closet." She frowned and pointed at the background. "Basketball, baseball and bat, skates, soccer ball, trucks, boats, books–something is missing."

"There're all there."

"What I mean is what else does little boys play with?"

"How about a puppy?"

Clara nodded. "That'll work."

The telephone beeped and Simon picked up the paint-splattered receiver. "Hawk House."

A distinctively Irish voice said, "Carlton Hawk for Simon Hawk."

"This is he."

"Hello, Simon," Carlton said. "How are things along the St. Lawrence?"

"Blooming–flowers, trees, tourists. How are you and Duncan doing?"

"Dad is at Devlin Manor. I'm here at the bank. Dad thought you'd want an update."

"He's already been through Lilith's personal papers?"

Carlton's laugh was harsh with bitterness. "A fox to the end. There were no personal papers to go through. She'd burned everything."

Simon glanced at Clara and raised an eyebrow. "Not surprising."

"On the other hand, I have found something–an account of my mother's with irregular but sizable deposits. All the expenditures were to further her interest in the knowing. A small percentage went to research assistants–a larger portion to auction houses, dealers in rare books, manuscripts, antiquities."

"We know she was obsessed with the knowing. What's strange about it?"

"In terms of what the money was used for–nothing. It's the account itself, and where the deposits came from. The money wasn't transferred from any of her other accounts. I cross referenced everything."

"Were you able to track where they did come from?"

"To be sure. Was a challenge but I've a friend who is a genius at just such a thing. He worked backwards. Here's the sequence–Devlin Bank back to the Cayman Island. From there to a bank in Switzerland where we find everyone's most popular banking regs–onto a bank in Luxemburg. Luxemburg to Liberia to Beirut. Final destination–right back to the issuing bank in the Caymans."

"Whose account?"

"Numbered."

"Then we're nowhere."

"Not exactly," Carlton said with satisfaction. "Issuing bank is private–as in a family owned investment bank."

"Anyone we know?"

"Severin, Adiran Severin also known in financial circles as the Duke–make that very well known in financial circles. He's a power with more money than God. Runs an international conglomerate but keeps a low profile."

"I know the name, but in a different context," Simon put in. "Arms dealing–a small Severin company at the tail end of their very large kite. That is small in terms of the conglomerate, but large in terms of international arms dealing. The company should have been investigated but it never did get beyond the suspicion stage."

"Arms dealing," Carlton repeated. "Does give one pause."

"Why? We know your mother was up to her eyebrows in the IRA."

"That's certainly true. To get back to the account–a guy I've done a lot of business with is an upper level executive at the Severin bank. He was a tremendous help, albeit unwittingly."

"How so?"

"I had a hunch and ran with it. I told him of my mother's death. Said I wanted to return the last deposit to the account holder, and to notify him of her death. I said I wasn't sure which Severin to contact. He volunteered to handle it for me."

"A Severin by inference–nice work." Simon thoughtfully paced. "Carlton, why would a man like Severin be pursuing or have any interest in the knowing?"

Carlton was silent for a moment before saying, "Power, Simon. The knowing is power. I don't think any of us have any real idea of its potential. Maybe Severin does."

"How reassuring."

"At least we know who's been the man pulling the strings."

"There's that. Are you and Duncan going to make the big reception?"

"Indeed. And Joan will be along."

"Clara and I are looking forward to meeting her. Our best to Duncan–and thanks for all your work. It's appreciated. See you in a couple of weeks."

As Simon put the receiver down, Clara asked, "Severin?"

"Funds were funneled from him to an account of Lilith's that was used exclusively to further her interest in the knowing."

Clara put her pallet down. "The man in the shadows?"

"A strong possibility. We'll see."

"Simon, do you still think there's a reason for concern?"

"Not really. Just a nagging doubt that it isn't over."

277

Clara tilted her head. "There's a hissing sound coming from the kitchen."

Simon dashed from the studio. "Damn, water's boiling over."

Clara stared at the empty space where her husband had been standing. Simon was beginning to experience the knowing. She wondered where would it take him. For the moment his knowings were in conjunction with hers–but there was no guarantee they would continue to be. It was possible that yet another facet of the knowing was making an appearance. She couldn't shake this feeling that events were forming around them. Events over which they could not exercise any control.

Mitchell Estate, Chesapeake Bay

Crystal vases of white and yellow roses graced every room of the huge sprawling mansion. On the off chance of rain the long balcony overlooking the bay had been tented. Tables were set for the more than three hundred guests from New York City, Washington, D.C., The Landing, London, Paris, New Orleans, Boston. Even a few from the west coast.

Clara and Simon stood in the entrance foyer to greet their guests. Clara had vetoed the formal receiving line and kept it casual. She pushed away her feeling of trepidation–chalk it up to nerves over the party. This sort of event really wasn't her style. But in the back of her mind was a nagging fear–fear that before the day was done disaster would overtake the Hawks and the Dunns. There was nothing she could do to change what was to be. The knowing kept its truth hidden. It was useless to her, useless.

Most of the Dunn family was assembled by the massive stone fireplace with Sylvia Dunn Mitchell very much the matriarch. The Hawks had not as yet arrived. They had called from their car to say that an accident on the belt way had slowed traffic to a crawl.

Simon bent down and whispered in Clara's ear. "Remember, sole of propriety."

"Absolutely and without edification, I will so be," Clara vowed with a forced smile. "How about you? You were the one who made the promise."

Simon crossed his heart. "Trust me."

"I do," Clara said softly. "With my life."

Carson Mitchell handed them flutes of champagne. "You look thirsty."

Clara reached up to kiss his cheek. "Uncle Carson, this is absolutely perfect. Thank you so much."

"No need to overdo it, my dear," Carson growled. "I know this isn't your kind of thing, but it means a lot to your parents."

Simon sipped his champagne. "That's why we're all here."

From across the room, Luci Meridian, Susan Fowler, and Holly Lawrence waved to Clara. "Excuse me for a moment," she said to Simon and Carson.

As she walked toward the trio, a wave of energy stopped her in her tracks. She was suddenly lightheaded with fear. In her minds eye, she saw flame and heard screams. But there was no form, no clear picture of what was being foretold. Only that danger, violent death was imminent. Her head pounded with unreasoning terror and she spun on her heel to find her Uncle.

Carson saw his mother motion and point to Simon. He patted Simon's arm. "You are being summoned. I have to check with the caterer. I hope the Hawks get here soon."

Clara found Carson standing by the French doors to the balcony. At that instant, she knew *both* her and Carson were targets and the perpetrators didn't care how many people had to die to achieve their ends.

An explosive roar like thunder presaging a storm blasted through brick and mortar. Flames licked out of the black hole that moments before had been the mansion's seaward wall. The outside wall where Sylvia Dunn Mitchell and several other guests had been standing had disappeared. Flames grew in intensity and shot upward through the roof. Black smoke rolled out of the shattered windows.

The shock of the blast had driven Simon to his knees but the marble staircase had withstood the explosion and protected him from the worst of it. Stunned, Simon got to his feet, his eyes tearing from the haze of smoke. Coughing, he pushed through the debris. He had to find Clara.

Clara was flung backward through the window. Her head struck the rail of the balcony and she crumpled to the marble floor. Carson lay a few feet away. Shards of glass from the French doors had sliced his face open. Blood pooled around his head and gushed out of a deep chest wound.

Dazed, Clara tried to regain her footing but found she couldn't stand. She crawled toward her uncle. Don't die, she silently begged. Don't die.

John Eaton, who had gone to call the Hawks to see when they might arrive, missed the brunt of the blast. He raced to where he had last seen his wife and found Lydia pinned beneath a section of the collapsed wall.

Frantically, he pulled bricks and lathe off her chest and freed her upper body, but her legs were still entangled in what appeared to be the rubble of a book case. By the time he had managed to free her, his hands were red with blood.

Lydia groaned and coughed and feebly pointed to the fireplace shell. "Mother, help her."

John could see that Sylvia's head was crushed and knew she was beyond help. "Let me get you outside and I'll come back for her."

Outside on the estate grounds, Luke Dunn and Pepe Hawkins strolled back from the garage after having viewed Carson Mitchell's classic Bentley. The shock wave from the blast took them off their feet. Pepe Hawkins rolled and regained his footing. "The trees," he shouted at Luke.

Luke got to his feet and in a crouched run made for a grove of weeping willow trees. Pepe raced after him and the two men dove over low shrubs and into the relative safety of the trees whose long, feathery branches provided some concealment.

Pepe looked toward the mansion. Fire shot from the seaward windows, smoke billowed through the roof. As he watched, a section of wall collapsed sending flames shooting out. "I warned him," Pepe muttered. "I warned him. God damn it . . ."

Pepe turned to look for Luke and found him hunched over gagging. At his feet, one of the security team stared sightlessly at the sky. His head had been nearly severed from his neck.

"Get over it," Pepe harshly said. "There's nothing to be done for him. People need our help." He bent down to pick up the downed man's pistol. Out of the corner of his eye, he saw movement. In one motion, he shoved Luke aside and fired twice at a terrorist who had entered his field of vision. The rounds hit the man in the face and snapped his head back.

Pepe wasted no time in confiscating the man's M16. "Luke, catch." He held onto the M16 and tossed Luke the pistol. "Follow me and keep a sharp eye."

The two men stayed low and using the hedges for cover made for the steps to the balcony. Simon saw Pepe and Luke appear out of the smoke. He pointed to where John Eaton was fanatically working to free those trapped under the collapsed wall. "Help John. There's more people under there."

Simon pushed his way toward the shattered frame of the bay window where he had last seen Clara.

She saw him and called out, "Simon. Uncle Carson, he's bleeding. Help him. Don't let him die."

Simon swung his leg over the window frame and climbed out onto the balcony. Suddenly his way was blocked by a man wearing large sun glasses with silver lenses that concealed much of his face. Simon's mind registered the automatic weapon in the man's hand at the moment its bullets stitched a pattern from his shoulder to his waist.

Clara screamed and staggered to her feet. The roar of a second blast tossed her over the baluster and into the grey-green sea. The man with the sunglasses strolled over to the edge of the balcony and sprayed the water with automatic weapon fire. He was so entranced with his mission of death that he never heard the shot from Pepe's M16 that killed him.

Luke rushed to Simon while Pepe bent over Carson and tried to staunch the blood flowing from his chest. Groans and screams filled Luke's mind. No one was alive by the fireplace. Roof caving in . . . Clara. God, and Sylvia–his parents. He couldn't see them anywhere.

Pepe had the presence of mind to remember Carson mentioning that his Bell Long Ranger helicopter was on standby to take General Tremont to Andrews Air force Base. "Let's get them to the chopper."

When Clara struck the water, she immediately felt the pull of a strong rip tide and instinctively let it carry her along. She moved her arms and legs to stay afloat and fought against her rising panic. Debris from the balcony floated around her. A round plywood top from a caterer's table scraped against her shoulder. A wooden bench struck her from behind. She grabbed at one of its legs and managed to loop an arm around the seat and held on with all her remaining strength. The rip tide took her further along the shore.

A sloop came out of the darkness, its lights raking the ocean's surface. Clara called out but her words were lost in the whistle of the wind. The fast running sea swept her away from the estate. It could have been hours or minutes before the incoming tide caught her and drove the bench toward the shore. It scraped over the rocky bottom and she lost her grip. Her body, trembling from exposure, lay half in half out of the water.

Clara knew if she were to live she had to move, to find shelter. She pushed herself up onto her hands and knees and crawled toward the beach. Once out of the water, she rested on the damp sand. Her mind circled in confusion unable to understand how it was that she had come to be here in this place.

Through the low, hanging fog, she could make out the outline of a house. She got to her feet and swaying with the effort, stumbled toward the slope. The pain in her head caused her vision to blur and made it hard to concentrate. The rain grew heavier driving the cold deeper into her body. She reached the stone steps, and leaning heavily on the wrought iron railing, climbed up the incline.

By the time she reached the deck encircling the cedar and glass house, her strength was at an end. She weakly pounded against the rain splattered sliding glass door. There was no answer, no sign of life. A wave of dizziness caused her to stagger and she fell against the wall. She held onto it and made her way around to a side door. She sank down onto a bench and her foot hit a clay pot of dead geraniums. Using the pot as a hammer, she smashed one of the window panes and reached in and turned the lock.

A telephone hung on the wall next to the stainless steel refrigerator. She lifted the receiver. No dial tone. It didn't matter. She had no one to call. Why couldn't she remember? Her body trembled violently and the receiver dropped from nerveless fingers.

Cold, she was so cold—insupportable cold becoming one with the pain bursting in her head. If only she could get warm, she'd be able to remember. She limped into the next room. Its walls were a blur seeming to shift in and out. Beamed ceilings undulated like snakes. Windows peering like eyes into the fog.

Through an open door, she saw a bed and unsteadily made her way to it. Without further thought, she stripped off the shreds of her gown and crawled under the heavy down quilt. Its warmth lulled her into a deep sleep.

Clara slept through the night and into the next day. When she came awake, it was late afternoon. Fear held her in its grip—she was afraid but knew not of what or whom. She tried to sit up and the motion brought vision blurring pain and nausea. She saw the bathroom and lunged toward the toilet, vomiting until there was only emptiness. Gripping the edge of the pedestal sink, she tried to pull herself upright. The white porcelain seemed to become liquid and the room's dimension faded into nothingness. The knowing came surrounding her with its awesome power.

Resting against pillows propped against the bed's massive carved headboard, Adia stared out at the rolling hills. The trees were just beginning to green and the bright yellow of the daffodils lined the garden walk. She had survived the cold, harsh winter to see one more spring. Soon her own transformation from this life to the next would take place. She thought of it as her own rebirth. Soon–it would be soon. Her life force was readying itself for the journey. She closed her eyes and drifted into sleep.

When Adia awoke, Maggy, her charge of more than twenty years was sitting by her bedside holding her hand. Maggy was her beautiful, magical child, the daughter of her heart. From under Adia's lowered lids, she watched Maggy and wished she could spare her the pain of loss. In her short life, she had already known far too much tragedy–the death of both of her parents.

Maggy's father, Liam Devlin murdered by his cousin, Rory. Claire, Maggy's mother, choosing to die rather than become Rory's possession. Adia closed her eyes and saw Claire's face. Maggy was so like her. The same cloud of red gold hair and the luminous green eyes, green as the leaves of summer . . . and also from her mother, the knowing. Maggy's blessing and her curse, for Maggy wished with all her heart that it was not a part of her being.

Adia gently squeezed Maggy's hand. "No tears, child. We've had a glorious life together."

Maggy forced a smile. Her grief was a dull, empty ache. Adia was her only family. It was Adia who had taught her all she knew of the knowing, but not enough to have it gone. Adia who had given her love–unconditional love. With Adia's death, she would be alone.

As if reading Maggy's mind, Adia tightened her grip on Maggy's hand. "You won't be alone child. You have Ian."

Maggy slowly shook her head. "He protects me because he must. There is no love in him for me."

Adia knew Ian's love for Maggy was so great that he feared the danger inherent in the knowing. He knew Maggy's parents had died because of it. What was first and foremost in Ian's mind was keeping Maggy safe and his fear that he might not be able to. "Time will show you his true heart." Adia gasped and closed her eyes steeling herself for the pain to come. A wave of agony swept through her body. She let her breath out in tentative notches testing to see if the pain was receding.

Maggy lifted Adia's head and held a clay flagon of laudanum to her lips. "Will ease the pain."

Adia breathed a little easier but death was near. "Maggy . . . Maggy."

"I'm right here. I'll not leave you."

Adia's voice came in fragments as the drug began to cloud her mind. "Remember . . . the mountains. Saddle of the wind . . . when it's time . . . go there, go."

"When, when must I go?"

Adia pulled Maggy closer. "May not be this lifetime." Adia coughed and her hand slowly slipped from Maggy's. ""Love you, child," she whispered. "Saddle of the wind . . . you'll know. Knowing will tell you. Swear . . ."

Maggy bent and kissed Adia's forehead. "I will that. Rest now."

Adia's eyes closed and she sighed. "Love you . . ." and her loving spirit surrounded Maggy for a final time. Then she was gone to become one with the universal order from whence she had come.

"And I you," Maggy whispered as tears of despair streaked her face.

The knowing slipped away. Dazed and disoriented, Clara forced her eyes open and reached for the door frame. She tried to get up but pain kept her on her knees. Through the pain came irrational fear. A demanding voice overrode the stabbing thrusts of pain in her head. Go to the mountains . . . to the saddle of the wind. The voice faded and pain drove her back into blackness.

Walter Reid Hospital, Washington, D.C.

The room was in shadow with only slashes of sunlight trickling in through the closed blinds. Simon Hawk lay motionless on the pristine white sheets of the hospital bed. His upper body was bare except for the wide bandages wrapping his chest. A blue cotton blanket and sheet was pulled up to his waist.

David Hawk sat in a generic mustard colored arm chair by his son's bedside. He counted the drops of the slow drip of fluid running from a hanging bag through a tube and into Simon's vein. That Simon was still alive was nothing short of a miracle.

If Carson Mitchell's private helicopter hadn't been available to transport the injured, it was unlikely Simon or Carson himself would have survived long enough to make it to the hospital.

David rubbed his forehead. Simon and Carson had been lucky. Luckier than Sylvia who had been crushed beneath a section of the wall. Luckier than six out of eight of the security team who were mercilessly killed. Luckier than fifty of the guests who died crushed under the collapsing ceiling and outer walls. Fifty-seven people dead. Fifty-eight if you counted Clara, but no one in the family was ready as yet to give up on the possibility that she might be alive.

Many others had been seriously injured but were recovering. Lydia had sustained two broken legs, but her physical injuries would heal far quicker than the emotional ones. She had lost her mother and in all probability, her daughter. Carson–alive, but he had lost one eye. Fortunately, Lucas and Gabriele Dunn were uninjured. Elise and Jean-Claude had been on the balcony and received cuts from flying glass but overall were fine. Clara's friends, Holly Lawrence, Susan Fowler, and Luci Meridian survived. But Susan Fowler's face was badly scared by flying glass and would require plastic surgery.

God played strange games. Were it not for the accident on the belt way. It was likely the Hawks would have been in the thick of it. David rubbed his forehead. It didn't seem possible it was only a few days since the attack at the Mitchell estate. But much to long for Simon to remain unconsciousness.

David whispered into the sterile silence. "Don't give up, son. Fight. You've never been a quitter. Damn it, keep fighting."

Judith Hawk reluctantly entered the hospital room. White walls, white ceiling, white bed underscoring the presence of illness and death. She touched David's shoulder. "Dad, my turn. You go on back to the hotel and get some rest. I'll call if there's any change."

David stood and stared down at his son. "Judith, hold his hand. Talk to him. Let him know you're here."

"I will Dad. I promise."

Judith took her father's place in the bedside chair. Talk to him . . . about what? How would anyone be able to tell him that Clara was dead. She swallowed back tears. Clara was gone–Elise and Jean-Claude had been on the balcony and saw Clara go into the sea. Both Pepe and Luke had seen the gunmen spray the area with gun fire. When Pepe killed the terrorist, Jean-Claude had dived into the waters and searched for Clara but to no avail–and that day there had been a rip tide.

Judith took Simon's hand in hers and said the first thing that came to mind. "John Cloud is taking care of Scarlet, Rhett, and Dog. We all know Clara wouldn't want them in a kennel. Dad and Nicole and Duncan Joseph are staying at the Watergate. So is Grandfather. Luke will be in later . . ."

Her voice trailed off and realizing her silence, she began again. "Luke is such a fine man. It's me, I'm such a coward. Not brave like you and Clara. Luke and me–maybe it's just a physical attraction, a flight of fancy. More likely the problem is timing. I've got the bank. Luke, he's tied to The Haven and the schools."

Judith's voice broke and tears ran down her face. "Oh, Simon. Please, please don't give up. We all love you. I need you. Please don't die."

Simon's fingers moved. "Clara?" he asked in a voice rusty with pain.

"Simon, thank God. I'll be right back. I've got to get the doctor." Judith escaped from the room, from the necessity of telling Simon that Clara was dead.

By the time Doctor Lowenthal had completed his examination, Simon had slipped into a deep sleep. Judith stopped him in the hall. "How is he?"

"Weak. But all in all, he's doing well. In all probability he'll sleep through the night. I'd advise you to go back to your hotel and do the same."

"No, I'll stay with him. We don't want him left alone."

"I don't think there's any reason for concern. A police officer is stationed outside his and Mr. Mitchell's door, and anyone entering this wing is checked by hospital security. To say nothing of the antiterrorist team that's lurking about. He's well protected."

"I know. But someone has to be here to tell him about Clara."

"Clara is his wife?"

"Yes, the authorities believe she drowned. The Coast Guard have changed their mission from search and rescue to recovery. Doctor, should my brother be told that Clara is dead?"

"I'd advise giving him the simple facts. The concern, the anxiety of not knowing could be more detrimental than the truth. I'll leave instructions for sedation."

Sometime in the night, Luke Dunn took Judith's place at Simon's side. Luke stared at the man who had so quickly become his friend and an integral part of his life, just as Clara had always been. But Clara was dead. Clara is dead, he silently repeated to himself, but the words had no meaning.

Luke restlessly paced the narrow space between the bed and the window. Hospital rooms always seemed like prison cells. He pushed back the beige striped drapes and looked out at the city. At this time of night traffic was sparse. Solitary vehicles, their headlights tunneling through the city streets, appeared and disappeared.

Against the grey skyline, the buildings looked like blocks stacked one atop the other with only scattered frames of light in their concrete walls. With a sigh, Luke sat down by the bed.

"Okay, here's my problem. Your sister said I had to talk to you. As you well know, I'm a stimulating conversationalist but right now, I'm kind of at a loss for words."

He put his hand on Simon's forearm. "But then you are a captive audience. Let's see. Carlton and Joan are at The Haven. They love the place and are thinking about living in The Landing and running the show. Mom and Dad are back at the Riverwalk house and they're going to show Carlton and Joan the ropes. A trial run, so to speak. That frees me up to take care of Clara's schools . . . Clara's schools. Funny, both Gunner and I think of them that way. Speaking of Gunner, he's postponing retirement until I can take up the slack."

Thoughts of Clara brought tears to Luke's eyes. He knew if Simon woke up he'd have to tell him that Clara was dead–how was it possible that she was dead? He forced himself to pick up the thread of the one-sided conversation. "I'm sure Judith must have mentioned that we're kind of taking a time out. I don't know, maybe a case of too much too soon. Don't get me wrong. Judith is great. It's just circumstance. Things didn't fall into place for us like they did for you and Clara. Who can say, maybe down the road, we'll take a second look."

Simon's arm twitched and he groaned and opened his eyes. When he tried to move his legs, pain came keeping him immobile. He carefully turned his head and saw Luke sitting at the side of the bed. "Luke?"

Luke forced a smile. "Hey man, about time. I'm really sick of talking to myself."

"Luke, Clara?" Simon begged. The simple effort of speaking beaded his face with perspiration.

"Simon. There's a button by your right hand. Push it. It's to help with the pain."

"No. Clara, please?"

Luke's grief broke free and tears wet his face. "I'm sorry," he said brokenly. "She's gone."

A harsh cry of anguish tore from Simon's throat. "No, nooo."

Luke pushed the call button and in moments the night nurse

came into the room. Everyone working this wing knew of the bombing at the Mitchell estate and of the subsequent deaths–and that Clara Hawk was believed dead. The nurse injected a sedative directly into a vein. "He'll sleep now," she compassionately said. "You might try it yourself."

Luke nodded his thanks and resumed his bedside vigil. Sleep was only a temporary escape. How would Simon deal the incomprehensible loss of the woman he loved? Luke leaned back in the arm chair and rested his head against the faux leather. As he drifted into sleep, he saw Clara's face and muttered, "I'll watch out for him, cuz." And for a time, he was at peace.

By the time Simon's sedation wore off and pain drew him from sleep, dawn was lighting the sky. He focused on Clara. Between them was a bond that time and distance could not diminish. He could see her in his thoughts. Feel her reaching out to him. It wasn't imagination nor desperate hope, but a spiritual link. An even greater bond than if they were chained together. No matter if everyone thought it was impossible for Clara to be alive, they were wrong.

With closed eyes, he searched beyond the physical pain of his injuries seeking the inner light that was Clara. Faintly, out of the darkness came a flickering of light–weak and far away, but as convincing as if she stood beside him. Clara was alive.

Chesapeake Bay

A cab drove down the brick paved drive and parked. Maude Wakefield steeped out and into a not at all clear future. She handed the cabby his fare and a generous tip and turned to take a first look at the house which would now be her home.

The property fronting on Chesapeake Bay had unexpectedly come on the market. Maude's sister, Anne and her husband, Tom heard through the local grapevine that the prime real estate was on the block to settle the owner's estate. They had called Maude at her London flat and said they thought it was just what she was looking for. They warned that she would have to act fast. Maude had purchased it based solely on their say so and a video tape.

Now Maude was back in the states but her life was still without a focus. When she had resigned her position as director of the Behavioral Medicine Research Center at John Hopkins, she had been running from a life made barren by the death of her husband, Max. Maxwell Wakefield. Fun loving, wonderful Max who had opted to leave life at a time of his choosing, rather than suffer the indignities and diminishment of self which would come as a result of an inoperable brain tumor. London had been her refuge but now it was time to pick up the pieces of her career and begin again.

Medicine was and had always been her choice, but this time around it wouldn't be a high profile position that was more administrative than patient oriented.

Maude wandered around the grounds and onto the back deck. She liked the long, low lines of the cedar and glass house and how it conformed to the contours of the bluff. She leaned against the rail and watched the silver waves slap against the shore.

A cool breeze blew across the water. Maude shivered and retraced her steps to the heavy glass and wrought iron front door and stepped into her new home. She flipped on the lights and smiled at the large welcome home sign that was propped on an easel set in the middle of the foyer.

The note, penned in her sister's bold hand, read: Welcome home. Electricity is on. Telephone will be on Monday in the am. Can you believe no security system? ProTect Security can do next week–up to you. Fridge is stocked. A few well-chosen bottles of wine on kitchen counter. Soap, shampoo, etc. in master bathroom. You'd better love the furniture. See you as soon as we get back from Egypt. Love.

Maude glanced around the foyer–pale marble floor, recessed shelves, cream textured walls. She pushed open the double doors and stepped into the living room where she was greeted with a breath taking view of the water.

The room was sparsely furnished with only a few items–soft, buttery suede in brown for the long couch and arm chairs, and an antique rosewood partner's desk. The gleaming hardwood floors had been left bare. Anne had said she would select only the necessities and leave the personal touches to her.

Maude looked at her watch. Early evening here, but her body was on London time. For her it was the middle of the night. As she walked past the glass door to the deck, she caught a glimpse of herself. A cap of dark brown hair framing a pixie face. She thought that she was thin, too thin. Perhaps now that she was home, she'd gain back some of the weight she's lost. Time was a healer and it was past time for her to get on with her life. She went on into the bedroom and fumbled for the unfamiliar light switch. Her breath caught in her throat.

A woman's seemingly lifeless body lay near the bathroom door. There were cuts on her back and on her feet and legs. A gash in her forehead was red and angry looking. Dark purple/black bruises were beginning to yellow against the white of her skin.

For a moment, Maude was frightened but quickly realized this woman was certainly defenseless. She kneeled and took her pulse. Surprisingly, it was strong and steady. At Maude's touch, Clara groaned and her eyes flew open–eyes that were filled with pure, unreasoning terror.

Maude's tone was warm and reassuring. "It's all right. I only want to help. I'll get you to a hospital."

"No, please. No hospital," Clara said without understanding why. A man's face drifted in front of her eyes. "No hospital. He'll find me."

"Let's see how badly you're injured, then we'll decide. If I help, do you think you can stand?"

Clara nodded and allowed Maude to help her to her feet and

into the bedroom. Clara weakly sank down on the bed.

"So far so good," Maude said. "Why don't you lie down? Those cuts need cleaning. I'll be right back." She went into the bathroom and in the medicine cabinet found hydrogen peroxide and a small first aid kit. She dampened a clean towel with warm water and returned to Clara's bedside.

"I'm going to clean the head wound first. This will sting a little," Maude warned as she leaned over Clara and gently wiped away the dried blood. Using sterile cotton, she cleaned the cut with peroxide. It wasn't as deep as it had appeared, but she didn't like the looks of the swelling around the wound site.

Clara winced but didn't protest as Maude systematically cleaned the cuts on her feet and legs.

"Roll to your side," Maude requested. "Let me get those on your back."

Movement brought a wave of nausea and sharp shooting pain that drove away thought, keeping memory at bay. If only the pain would stop, she'd be able to remember.

Maude pulled a sheet over Clara's body. "All finished."

"Thank you," Clara murmured.

"Tell me, have you experienced any double vision?"

"No, not really–some blurring."

"Bad headache?" Maude persisted.

"Yes."

"Hard to think, to concentrate?"

Clara nodded.

Maude held up two fingers. "How many fingers do you see?"

"Two."

"Do you know where you are?"

"No."

"Do you know how you came to be here?"

"No." With each successive question, Clara grew more frightened. What was wrong? What had happened to her?

Maude recognized Clara's confusion and suspected what her answer to the next question would be. "What is your name? Who are you?"

Clara's eyes went blank. " Don't know. Oh, why don't I know?"

Maude compassionately took Clara's hand in hers. "You've taken quite a blow to the head. This kind of trauma can cause memory loss."

"I don't understand. Why don't I know who I am?"

Maude reassuringly smiled. "Give yourself time and you will. Since I do know who I am, I'll fill you in. My name is Maude Wakefield. This is my house. I've just returned from an extended time in England. I'm a doctor, my specialty is Behavioral Medicine."

"No hospital,"" Clara insisted.

"I understand. Let me explain–as a medical doctor, I can examine you and access the extent of your injuries."

"You, no hospital," Clara said without hesitation.

Maude knew her medical bag would be on the closet shelf where she had asked Anne to put it. With a tiny flashlight, Maude examined Clara's eyes. Her pulse was strong and steady, heart–ditto. Using a small rubber hammer, she checked the response in Clara's knees and Achilles tendons. She gently pressed the area around the head wound. "Your physical injuries don't appear to be serious. But if your memory doesn't return soon, the problem will have to be addressed."

"Thank you," Clara said. "Thank you."

Maude patted her hand. "You'll be fine. Now let's see what I can find for you to wear." Maude opened a dresser drawer. "Underwear, socks, not quite it. Most of my things were shipped ahead of time. I just have to find where my sister put them," she muttered. In the second drawer, Maude found a pair of navy sweats. "They'll work for now."

Clara slowly sat up and swung her legs over the edge of the mattress. She took the clothes from Maude's outstretched hand. "Thank you . . . again."

"You need nourishment. I'll fix us some soup."

Clara nodded and pulled the sweat shirt over her head and tugged the pants on. The movement brought nausea but the pain in her head seemed to have eased and was less debilitating.

In the kitchen, Maude checked the refrigerator and found a container of her sister's specialty–homemade chicken soup. She ladled enough for two generous servings into a pan. While the soup warmed, she sliced a mini loaf of French bread and thought of the battered woman in the bedroom. Obviously she was afraid of something or someone, but there was nothing cowardly in her demeanor. Maude sensed that under the delicate facade was great strength of character.

Clara limped into the kitchen. "May I help?"

Maude warmly smiled, pleased to see she was able to move around without dizziness. "Under control. Please sit down. As yet I've no table so the breakfast bar will have to do."

Clara held onto the edge of the inlaid tile counter and seated herself on a high-backed upholstered stool. Maude took a bottle of water from the refrigerator and poured Clara a tall glass. "You should have something to drink. You might be a bit dehydrated."

Clara sipped the cold water. The smell of the warming soup brought hunger. She couldn't remember when she had last eaten.

As Maude set the counter with red linen place mats and silverware, she surreptitiously watched Clara. Her memory loss was certainly a concern. Especially since there was no way to know what she was afraid of or who. "Since for the moment, you don't have a name. What would you like me to call you?"

Clara forced a small smile. "You pick."

"Okay, how about . . ." Maude thought for a moment. There was something about her that called up memories of a young Katherine Hepburn. "How about Kate?"

"Kate is fine."

Maude set a basket of warm bread on the counter and ladled the soup into white ceramic mugs. "Try and eat," she suggested as she sat down across from Clara.

Clara smiled a thank you and picked up the soup spoon. The soup was delicious–generous chunks of chicken in a rich broth. Clara managed to eat almost half of the serving. "This is really very good, but I can't finish."

"Back to bed then. You need rest as much as you need nourishment." As Clara stood up, Maude saw the color drain from her face. "I can see that you're still in pain but given the head injury. I'd rather not medicate."

"It's better than it was. I'll be fine. Maude, I know I sound like a broken record, but thanks."

Maude pointed to the door. "Bed, go." She finished her own soup and cleaned up the remains of the meal. Over a cup of tea, Maude wondered who this woman was who had dropped into her life, and what had happend to her? Maude couldn't help but smile. Max would say she had stepped into it with both feet. But she knew if he was here, he would have done the same. A broad yawn escaped. Jet lag had kicked in with a vengeance.

On her way to bed, Maude checked on Clara and saw that she had fallen into a deep sleep. She pulled the quilt up over Clara's shoulders, quietly took a change of clothes from the closet, and went into a second bedroom. Its only furniture was an antique oak bed that Maude remembered from her parent's home. Her sister had always been generous to a fault.

In the morning, Clara opened her eyes to the slapping of ran against the window. She stretched and her muscles responded with only a hint of soreness. Her head no longer throbbed. There was still some pain but it was distant. Soon she would remember. She pushed her hair back from her face and found it was caked with blood. She swung her legs out of bed and went into the master bathroom.

The simple act of showering diminished her sense of disorientation. She knew she had done this many times. With closed eyes, she tried to picture another bathroom, one out of memory. Nothing came, only hazy darkness. Frustrated, she rinsed the shampoo out of her hair and shut off the water.

Maude heard Clara moving around and knocked on the door. "Come in."

Maude laid an armload of clothes on the bed. "I've found a few things that should fit."

Clara settled on a pair of jeans and a sweater. "I'm never going to be able to pay you back."

"My grandmother used to say what goes around comes around. Don't worry about it. You're looking better. Memory?"

"I am . . . somebody. I wish I could tell you who."

Maude smiled. "Well at the very least, we've learned you have a sense of humor."

Clara returned Maude's smile and followed her into the kitchen. She saw that the window she had broken had been temporarily repaired with a sheet of cardboard. "I'm sorry about the window."

Maude set a cup of coffee in front of her. "I thought it might have been you. What will it be–fruit, eggs?"

"Fruit." Clara's expression grew remote. "I know what fruit is. What an orange or a grapefruit is but I can't remember my own name."

"And it makes you angry, confused, lost, and?"

"Afraid. Somewhere way inside I'm terribly afraid . . . but I don't know of what or who. It's like someone is following me. I can't see who it is but I know this person wants me dead. Why would anyone want to kill me?"

Maude brought a bowl of apples, oranges, and grapes to the counter. "Last night I told you I was a doctor–behavioral medicine. I'm a little rusty when it comes to therapy but if you're willing, we can give it a shot. You'll be protected by client, therapist privilege."

"Just how do you plan to bill me," Clara said in a valiant effort to hide her fear.

"I'll take that as a yes." Maude put a mini recorder between them. "Do you mind if I tape the sessions?"

Clara shook her head. "It's okay."

Maude pushed play. "September eighteenth, eleven a.m. Kate, Session one. Now to begin–I'm going to ask questions. Try to answer without thought. Just say whatever pops into your mind. What is your name?"

Clara shook her head.

"Tell me any name that comes to mind."

"Liam," Clara answered.

"Liam," Maude repeated. "A man, someone you know?"

"No, from long, long ago." Clara's hands twisted in her lap. "How can I know a name from the past and know it's not from this past but from another time?"

"What makes you say another time?"

"Mountains, trees . . . I don't know. This man, he doesn't belong to the present. Why is it that I know things but don't know myself?"

"Something made you forget. In all likelihood it won't be for long, and you may not have forgotten everything. Your memory loss might well have been caused by the blow to your head or a different sort of trauma."

"Trauma, what do you mean?"

"Obviously something traumatic occurred for you to be so badly bruised, the cuts, the blow to your head. Memory loss in this situation isn't unusual. It's called anterograde amnesia. Almost without exception memory is back intact within a few days."

"Is this one of those good news, bad news scenarios?"

"In essence, yes. There's also a type known as retrograde. This can be of longer duration and should be evaluated by a professional. Someone who can help with the trauma situation and work with you to bring out the memories. We'll take it a step at a time."

"Not knowing who I . . ." Clara's voice trailed off and her eyes became fixed and empty. She heard the sound of chanting, the chime of temple bells, and a voice whispering. She blinked and repeated in a distant voice. "The mountains . . . saddle of the wind—must go there."

Maude sensed Clara's fear and confusion. It was possible she was repressing her life because she felt guilty for something she had done or felt responsible for. "Do you know where these mountains are?"

"No," Clara answered with despair. "Please help me."

"Of course I'll help you but we've talked long enough. Why don't you rest awhile?"

"Let me do the cleanup. I'll never get stronger if I spend all my time in bed."

Maude pushed away from the counter. Being useful might well be therapy in and of itself. "Okay, I've boxes to unpack."

Clara picked up their empty coffee cups. "As soon as I finish in here, I'll give you a hand."

Maude absently nodded. "Saddle of the wind. Wasn't that what you said?"

"Yes, why? Does it mean something to you?"

"Seems familiar but I can't say how. Maybe it'll come to me."

Clara picked up a sponge and began to wipe the counter. "Amnesia catching?" she said with wry humor.

"Funny, very funny," Maude answered and disappeared into the third bedroom that would ultimately become her study. Tapped and labeled boxes that had been taken out of storage were stacked in neat rows. Mostly books, some crystal and china, paintings, things collected on the trips she and Max had taken. They had been the very best of times and were not negated by his death.

Clara poked her head around the corner. "Wow. Where to begin?"

Maude pointed to the boxes labeled books. "Let's start with the books. I don't want you lifting the boxes. I can handle it."

"I can help. If I start to feel dizzy or lightheaded, I'll stop."

Maude could see that the woman she thought of as Kate was determined, "Okay, but we'll slide them to the shelves. They really are heavy."

By the time the boxes of books were moved near the book shelves at the room's end, both women were sweating. Maude stretched from side to side. "You hand me the books. I'll place."

Clara sat down on the floor and tore the tape from the first box. "Oops, mislabeled." She carefully unwrapped the bubble plastic to reveal a hand-carved flute.

Maude smiled in memory. "Burma, a little market in some small town. God, it was hot–a regular steam bath."

Clara didn't answer. She was holding a bronze statue of a perfectly proportioned woman. The slender figure seemed to glow with power and grace. Her face was stunning with a smile that suggested secrets.

Tear started in Maude's eyes. The bronze was Max's favorite. She had given it to him as an anniversary gift.

Clara ran her fingertips over its smooth, cool surface. "So ill," she whispered. "So much pain, couldn't go on. Water, to just drift away . . ." Her eyes blinked and she looked imploringly at Maude. "I'm sorry. I don't know where that came from."

Maude wiped away her tears. "My husband, Max collected bronzes." She took the piece from Clara's hands and cradled it against her chest. "This was his favorite. Max had an inoperable brain tumor. He was in a great deal of pain. One day he simply swam out into the ocean. His body was recovered the next day. How did you know?"

Clara's expression was bewildered. "I didn't know. When I touched the bronze . . . I don't know. It just happened."

Hawk House, St. Lawrence River Valley

Simon stared at the blank computer screen. The book was going nowhere, just as his life was going nowhere–static, without substance. In disgust, he pushed away from the oak desk and restlessly wandered through the house, ending up in the dodo. Sunlight fragmented through the skylight giving the blue/grey mats an opulent luster. He pulled off his sweatshirt. The angry red gun shot wounds were fading and would soon silver into small, virtually unnoticeable scars. If only the mind and emotions could heal as easily.

Anyone glancing at Simon would discern no change. But if one looked closely, they would see that his angular features were more defined, and in his eyes was deep, abiding anguish. He was one of the walking wounded. After the tragedy at the Mitchell estate, he had shut himself off from friends, from family. He was more alone now than he had ever been.

Simon worked out until his hair was damp with perspiration and sweat beaded his heavy, muscular chest. He slowed his movements and easily slipped from aikido into the intimate mind/body alliance of Tai Chi.

Using his key, Luke Dunn let himself into Hawk House. He stood for a moment and looked around the familiar room. The house was unchanged, yet without Clara everything else had. Scarlett, Rhett, and Dog came to him with tails wagging to be petted, but even they seemed to have lost their zest. It was as if they waited for Clara.

Luke reached into his pocket for the treats he carried for them. He saw that the doors to the dodo were open, but he was strangely reluctant to disturb Simon. To bear witness to his inconsolable grief and know that there was no way to relieve his torment. Three months, and all that kept Simon functioning was his unshakeable conviction that Clara was alive.

Out of the corner of his eye, Simon caught a glimpse of Luke standing in the doorway. "Luke." He picked up a towel from the bench, wiped the sweat from his torso and pulled on a faded sweat shirt. "What's up?"

"Lydia and John are at The Haven. They'd like you to join them for dinner."

"A telephone call would have done that."

Luke hesitated. "Can we sit down for a minute?"

"Sure." Simon went out into the living room and sat down in a chair by the fieldstone fireplace. His hand idly stroked Dog's head. "What seems to be the problem?"

"I thought I'd warn you, give you time to think about it."

Simon raised a questioning eyebrow. "Luke, get to the point."

"Lydia and John want to have a memorial service for Clara, but they won't do it without your consent."

"They're Clara's parents and I respect their need for closure, but no. As far as I'm concerned, no. If they wish, I won't object but I won't attend."

"I'm sure they'll understand. Simon, has Carson heard anything more on the bombing?"

"Several terrorist groups have taken credit–the Red Army, IRA splinter group, I forget who else. Could be one or all. I recently spoke with Pepe. He has a theory–one I hadn't considered."

Luke frowned. "How so? I thought it was a given that it was an act of retaliation against Mitchell Media's continuing investigation into terrorism."

Simon nodded. "Correct, in so far as it goes. Then why the assassin targeting individuals? Why the selective killing? Carson understandably, but why Clara, why me?"

"Ah, and Pepe doesn't believe in coincidence."

"Exactly. The operation was to well coordinated and executed. Pepe nailed two of them–one in the trees and the one on the balcony who fell into the water. Both bodies disappeared. They even carried their dead with them."

"The knowing . . . Lilith?"

"No, not Lilith. She was to small time to have planned an operation of that size. Keep in mind, by then she was dead. I've always felt there was someone in the shadows lending her a hand. Thanks to Carlton, I have an idea who it might be."

"Even so," Luke gruffly said. "It doesn't change things–terrorists, assassin. It doesn't change a damn thing."

Simon walked to the window and looked out at the river sparkling in the fall sunshine. A sloop tacked into the wind plowing through the grey/green waters. "Luke, tell me. When you think of Clara do you feel she's gone?"

"Simon, as much as I hate to point this out. Witnesses did see her go into the ocean. There was one hell of rip tide–that's simple fact."

"But she hadn't been shot. I know because just before the shots hit me, I heard her scream my name."

"Yes. But when Pepe took out the guy on the balcony, he was spraying the water with automatic weapons' fire. Simon, think about it. If she's alive, why hasn't she contacted us?"

"Yes," Simon conceded. "There is that." He glanced at Luke. "I feel her inside me. Have I ever told you that with the knowing,

I could sometimes sense what Clara was feeling. Even see some of the same images. Suppose I can trace the knowing to its roots. It's possible that I could learn to expand on this energy. Maybe, just maybe, it would help me to find Clara. Luke, you didn't answer me when I asked before. When you think of Clara do you feel she's gone?"

"Christ, Simon, I don't want her to be."

The telephone beeped and Simon waited for the answering machine to pick up. "Simon. Carson, I have . . ."

Simon punched talk. "I'm here, Carson. What is it?"

"I've been going through my mother's personal papers. In her safety deposit box I found a sealed envelope with Clara's name on it. Do you want me to send it to you?"

"No need. Just open it and read it to me."

Carson opened the envelope. "Sorry, Simon. Not much, just a telephone number. Looks like it would be the British Isles–England, Scotland, Ireland."

Simon pulled a pad toward him. "Let's have it." He scrawled the number. "I'll gamble if Sylvia wanted Clara to have it, it has something to do with the knowing."

"I'm inclined to agree. I only wish it was more," Carson said. "I feel so damn helpless."

"Hey, it's more than I've had. At least you don't think I'm crazy to keep searching for her."

"Clara was strong. Until her body is found, I'm going to keep right on hoping."

"Thanks, Carson. I'll let you know if it comes to anything."

"What did Carson find?" Luke asked.

Simon taped his pen on the note pad. "An envelope with Clara's name. He found it in Sylvia's safe deposit box."

"And?"

"A telephone number–just the number, no explanation."

Luke's expression was puzzled. "It wasn't like Sylvia to be cryptic."

"One way to find out." Simon punched in the number and listened as it clicked through the lines to finally reach an answering machine. Simon waited for the beep. "This is Simon Hawk. I received this number via Sylvia Dunn Mitchell who is now deceased. This number was intended for my wife, Clara Dunn Eaton Hawk who is missing and presumed dead."

A voice with a decided Scottish burr said, "Why did you call?"

"I believe that if Sylvia left this number for my wife, it has to do with something referred to in family as the knowing. I hope that through this knowing, I'll be able to find Clara."

"Come to Scotland."

A click terminated the conversation. Simon stared at the telephone. "A man said to come to Scotland."

Luke pushed out of the chair and began to pace. "So, Scotland. Want some company?"

Simon looked surprised. "You?"

"Yep. Your old sidekick, saddled up and ready to ride."

"How can you get away? What about The Haven, Clara's schools?"

"Carlton and Joan are doing fine and my parents are still around looking over their shoulders. Sam Maitland is there as backup. I just spent a week in New York with Gunnar–the schools are up to speed." Luke did a tap dance step. "So I'm foot loose and fancy free."

Simon smiled. It was the first genuine smile Luke had seen since Clara disappeared. Disappeared, he caught himself thinking. Damn if he hasn't got me believing she's alive.

"All right, Tonto. Sounds like a plan."

Luke raised his voice in feigned outrage. "Tonto! I suppose you're the Lone Ranger. Why is it you always get to play the lead? You're the native American, Tonto should be right up your alley."

"Heritage is immaterial–leadership abilities count." Simon's eyes darkened. "Let's hope whoever is at the end of that telephone number will be willing to help."

Luke snapped his fingers. "Not to worry. I'll dazzle whomever with my debonair charm. They will be putty in my hands. Did the gentleman say where in Scotland or are we winging it?"

"Winging it. When we get there, I'll give him another call."

Chesapeake Bay

Clara looked out at the ocean. This early in the day the water was calm and flat. She slowly came down the stone steps to the rocky shore and walked along the beach. Her bare feet left wet foot prints in the sand. This at least was a mark of her passing, proof that she was alive.

She walked out onto the dock and began the slow, fluid forms of Tai Chi. Where she had learned the discipline or when or who had taught it to her was lost, erased as was the rest of her life. She closed her eyes, and out of the darkness came the figure of a man moving with her. During these times she felt safe, her fear at bay. Yet no matter how hard she tried, the man remained a shadow on the face of her memory.

Maude had done everything in her power to help. There were days of blankness. Days Clara could not recall, conversations forgotten. Maude would patiently explain over and over that the anterograde amnesia which caused one to forget daily happenings would pass–and so it had. But her past remained lost in a blackness in which there was no light.

When Clara thought of her life before being here, there was no memory, only fear. Her past was dead and she saw no future. As she watched, a sea gull swooped low skimming the ocean's skin. It then flew high up into the blue sky to chase after the boats sailing along the coast. She stared out at the blue-green water.

Today the water was a pale blue at the horizon, giving in to a rich cobalt to a deep green where it white frothed against the rocks. Boats were surreal, seeming to sail in and out of the patches of fog that still clung to the water. Skeletal buoys waved without sound. The wind was a soft, gentle caress against her cheek. She searched her memory for a similar setting–a lake, a river, but there was only the ocean. Yet in her dreams she would often see herself sailing.

Abandoning her effort to remember, Clara wandered off the dock and onto the ragged sweep of beach. A recent storm had scattered broken shells among the rocks and sand. She thought she was like the shells–broken, displaced, lost. As she started back up the steps to the house, she saw a delivery van pull out of the driveway. Maude's dining room table and chairs must have been delivered.

Maude met her at the back door. "Come see. I'd forgotten how much I like this table."

Clara followed her into the dining room. A massive, heavily carved oak table was center stage with the same ornate carvings on the oak chairs that were spaced around it. Clara swayed and leaned against the wall.

In her mind's eyes, she saw a room with walls of stone and a lord's table set up along one wall on a small dias. Men, attired in tunics and hose and wrapped in cloaks against the damp cold, were seated in chairs' around its perimeter. A man at the head of the table pounded on its top with a pewter cup. "Hunt them down. Kill the women, let none survive."

In Clara's mind, the room faded to be replaced by another. A group of men was seated at a similar table but these men wore business suits. But Clara knew their mission was the same as those men from the past–to kill the women.

Maude touched Clara's arm. "Are you all right?"

Clara swallowed back her fear. Those men from the past were alive in the present and would kill her. She knew they would kill her. "Men. I saw men, strangers."

Maude had witnessed similar episodes and asked, "These men–do they exist in the present or are they from the past you seem to flash in on?"

"Both," Clara whispered. "Both. The man whose face I can't see. The one I'm so afraid of." She trembled as if from the cold. "He is there–then and now." She looked up at Maude. "I'm sorry. I know I'm not making any sense."

"You're making sense," Maude said. "We just haven't figured out what it all means. Come on, let's have a cup of tea. It'll warm you up." But in spite of Maude's reassurances, she was becoming more and more concerned about the visions. They didn't seem to have any basis in reality. What Maude couldn't perceive was that in actuality, they did.

Sometime later, Maude's view of the woman she now knew to be Clara Dunn Eaton Hawk was altered by the truth of who she was. Maude stood on the deck and watched as Clara dejectedly walked along the shore. Maude was afraid for her–afraid that when she learned of her past, she would be walking back into a life threatening situation. Maude sighed, she had no right to play God. No right to deny Clara her past or her future.

When Clara returned to the house, she found Maude seated by the fire. Maude glanced up and closed the file she had been reading. "We have to talk."

Clara curled into a chair. "Ready when you are."

"Do you remember my telling you that your memory loss didn't ascribe to the usual format of post traumatic amnesia?"

Clara's eyes were shadowed. "Yes, you said it was possible that I was suffering from a more complicated disorder . . . I don't recall what it was."

"Psychogenic amnesia. If this is the case than you are probably hiding from an overwhelming psychic trauma. In essence, you've disassociated yourself from the situation."

"Why? What would make me do this?"

"Suppose you were caught in a circumstance which caused you great emotional conflict and pain. One you couldn't resolve."

Clara's head ached with the effort of remaining calm. "What sort of circumstance would cause this. Something illegal?"

"Knowing you," Maude said with a smile. "I think not."

"Then why? Why do you think I'm repressing the personal segment of my life? I remember other things–how to dress, to read, how to cook, even to drive a car."

"None of which touch on the personal."

"I've tried to remember. I've done everything you've suggested. What else can I do?" Clara's voice was small and weak, filled with pain and loss. "I must have had a mother, a father," she whispered. "But I can't see their faces." She twisted the diamond ring on her left hand. "Perhaps I've a husband, someone I love."

"Think about what happens when you try to remember. Let's talk about that."

Clara frowned. "But you know."

"Humor me. Go over it again."

"Fragments. Mountains–men and women injured in battle but from a long time ago. It's almost like seeing a scene from an old movie. Men–a man I think I love. Another man who I believe wants to kill me . . . and fear."

"Two men. Go on."

"More than two men. A group of men who want to kill the women. Me, I'm one of those women, but I don't know who the others are."

"Go back to the two men. What do you see when you think of them?"

"I'm not sure. I can't see the one's face but I want him. I seem to need him. The other I'm terrified of, but he isn't from this time." Clara remembered the men at the table and the man who had insisted the women be hunted down. And of how the figures faded into men of the present time. "Or maybe he is."

"I want you to think about what happened when you were helping me unpack. Just by holding the bronze that was Max's favorite, you knew what had happened to him."

"I'm not sure where you're going with this?"

"Somewhere in the human mind is the ability to tap into an undeniable extra ordinary sense. You do this without realizing it. I can think of many other similar instances but there's no point in belaboring it."

"Are you saying I'm psychic?"

"No, I think you are far more. It's rare for those with para-normal abilities to perceive details of events to come. Even rarer is one who can perceive the past. You did this when you held the statue."

"Maude, do you think this might be some of the reason why I can't remember."

"Yes, I believe so. But I can't say in what manner. Paranormal is no more scientifically unexplainable than a disease which is considered to be incurable or the areas of the brain whose function we have no knowledge of. Because we can't explain it doesn't mean it's invalid."

Clara shrugged. "But it's meaningless. It sure isn't bringing me any closer to remembering who I am."

"You're right," Maude agreed. "I do believe this extra sensory ability is a hindrance." She leaned forward and took Clara's hand in hers. "Do you trust me?"

"Implicitly."

Maude settled back in her chair. "Clara. Your name is Clara Dunn Eaton Hawk. For several weeks now, I've known who you are."

Tears slid down Clara's cheeks. There was light in the darkness of her past. She wiped her eyes and without censor asked, "Why did you wait so long to tell me?"

"Because of the events preceding your amnesia." Maude handed her the file she had been reading.

Clara opened it and saw copies of news articles. "How did you come on this?"

"Beauty shop gossip. When I went to have my hair trimmed, I heard a woman say the Mitchell estate was so badly damaged by the explosions that one of the wings had to be bulldozed down and rebuilt. Another women said what a shame it was that all those people had died. Making conversation, I said I'd been in England and asked what had happened. She explained that there had been what was believed to be a terrorist attack at a reception for this Mitchell's niece and her husband. The husband was shot and nearly died. The wife was lost in the ocean and was believed to be dead but no body had as yet been recovered."

Clara found it difficult to speak. "Me?"

"I thought she might be you, but I couldn't be sure. I went to the library and back tracked. It's all in the file. Clara, I'm not telling you this lightly. I've spoken to colleagues. Given the longevity of your amnesia, the severity of the event. They believe if you're to remember, you need to be told the truth."

"But why did you wait?"

"I needed to do some checking. I'll explain more when you finish reading."

Clara put the file on the floor. "Please, just tell me."

"There was an explosion at Carson Mitchell's estate–a terrorist attack. He is your uncle, your mother's brother. There was a great loss of life. You disappeared into the ocean and after a time it was assumed you was dead."

As Maude talked fragmented images flashed in Clara's mind. A roar, walls collapsing, a face covered in blood, screams–a man coming toward her. "Who died," Clara begged.

"Your grandmother, Sylvia Dunn Mitchell. Your husband, Simon Hawk was shot but survived. Your Uncle Carson was badly injured but many others died–guests, security people. You were there, you saw it all. This explained the post traumatic amnesia but not the psychogenic amnesia. Not your total disassociation from your life. You gave highly confusing signals. You spoke of a past but not one in this lifetime. You were terrified of someone or something. I was genuinely afraid of what your true past held. I didn't want to send you back to a life where someone wanted you dead."

"What made you decide to tell me?"

"I spoke with a friend of my husband's who is with the Federal Bureau of Investigation. He told me the terrorist attack was retaliation for Mitchell Media's continuing investigation into worldwide terrorism."

Clara's face paled and she gave a gasping cry.

"Clara, what is it? Are you remembering anything?"

"Just flashes. Oh, god, Maude, I don't feel anything. You're talking about my family, my husband, and I'm hearing about strangers. My grandmother is dead and I don't feel anything."

Maude pointed to the file containing the news articles. "Clara, maybe it would be helpful if you read about it. There's pictures of you, your husband, your grandmother–it's possible something will strike a cord."

Clara hesitantly picked up the folder. She began to read of the celebration that had become so many people's tragedy. The folder dropped from her lap. Her eyes were blank and empty. "I'm so scared. I'm still afraid–more afraid than ever."

Maude pressed a brandy into her hand. "Clara, it'll take some time to fit all the pieces together. I think once your memory is integrated the fear will dissipate."

Clara gulped the brandy and shuddered. She extended the snifter. "I think I'd like another."

For the next several days, Clara filled her time by cooking and cleaning with a vengeance, and running for miles along the shore. Her nights were filled with dreams. Images came like shards of a broken mirror reflecting back a distortion of the truth.

Maude glanced out the window and saw Clara sitting on the deck staring out into nothingness. It was apparrant that telling Clara who she was had accomplished nothing. She was no closer to a resolution of her past than she had been before.

In the past weeks, Maude had spoken often with Stephen Cortland, a clinical psychiatrist considered to be one of the best in his field. He suggested that the best course of action might be to bring Clara together with her family. That in all likelihood, Clara's husband would be the best choice. But when Maude attempted to contact Simon Hawk, she discovered that his telephone number was unpublished. She prevailed on her friend at the bureau and he'd gotten the number for her. It was time she used it.

Maude picked up the telephone. After a single ring, the answering machine picked up. "This is Simon Hawk. Please leave a message." Followed by an abrupt beep. Maude left her name and number and explained that she had information concerning his wife, Clara, and asked that Simon return her call.

As soon as Maude hung up, she became consumed with impatience. She wanted to speak with Simon Hawk, now–right now. Time crept by with abnormal slowness. She glanced at the clock, and found that only a few minutes had passed since last she had looked. Damn the man. She stared at the phone willing it to ring.

In frustration, she sat down and brought her journal up to

date, wrote out checks for the monthly bills, and went back to staring at the telephone. Clara came into the house from her morning run. "Maude, I'll shower and run the errands. Do you have the list made out?"

"I do–library, market, drugstore." Maude thought that Clara should be gone the better part of the afternoon. If only Simon Hawk would call while she was out. "Clara, be careful on that bike."

"I think I can manage," Clara said with a faint smile. "Do you know you say that every time I leave the house?"

Maude tossed a couch pillow at her. Clara ducked and slipped into the bedroom. She took a quick shower and picked up the list. "Maude, do you want to come along?"

"No, thanks. I think I'm going to take a nice hot bath."

"Okay, I'll see you later," Clara said and was out the back door.

Maude glanced at the clock. Several hours had passed since she had left the message on Simon Hawk's answering machine. "Call," she said aloud. "Damn it, call."

Even with all Maude now knew of Clara, she was still a puzzle. There were so many unanswered questions with her paranormal abilities at the top of the list. Clara often dreamed of mountains and had several times mentioned saddle of the wind in conjunction with the dreams or visions.

Saddle of the wind. Saddle of the wind. The phrase kept running through Maude's mind. There was something about this saddle of the wind that rang a bell. Mountains, saddle of the wind. Her thoughts leap frogged–Max, caves in the mountains. He had been an amateur spelunker and had often talked of the caves explored. It was possible that he had mentioned such a place.

Maude booted up the computer and for the first time since Max's death, she entered his personal files. She scrolled to speleology. The telephone rang and she answered on the first beep. "Wakefields. No. I don't want my house sided," she snapped and ended the conversation. Damn, damn, why didn't the man call?

She returned to the computer. Under speleology were listings of caves explored. Included were detailed descriptions of each event with a analysis of the types of flora and fauna found, along with measurements and a mapping of the interior terrain. Black Hills: Wind Cave. SE N. Mexico: Calasbad. Great Smoky: Series of small uninteresting caves. She skimmed over the rest. "Ya da, ya da, ya da," she said as she scrolled the files. Somehow she didn't think what she wanted was in the states. She scrolled to the United Kingdom.

Maude stared at the screen. "Yes!" she shouted into the silence. Scotland: Grampians. Series of caves, some inter-connecting. Difficult climb to reach location. Side bar: Interesting local legend concerning a long narrow ravine enclosed by overhanging rock. Wind whistles through and anyone entering from one end can be heard at the other. Locals call it the saddle of the wind. So there we have it, she smugly thought.

The bong of the front door chimes startled her. Who, she wondered as she went to answer the door. Probably the long overdue plumber. Maude looked through the peephole. Definitely not the plumber. She pushed the intercom. "Can I help you?"

"Maude Wakefield?"

"Yes, and you are?"

"Simon Hawk."

Maude opened the door and was confronted by two of the most attractive men she had seen in a long time. One was tall, lean, and blonde. The second was tall, dark, and exotically handsome.

Simon held out his hand. "I'm Clara's husband."

Maude took his hand. "Of course you are," she said with a mischievous smile.

The second man put out his hand. "I'm Lucas Dunn, Clara's cousin. Might we come in?"

Maude stepped aside and gestured them into the foyer and on into the living room. "Please, sit down. There's a great deal of ground to cover before Clara gets back."

Simon's hands clenched into fists. "Clara is here? She's alive?"

"Yes to both questions, but there are problems."

"Go on," Simon impatiently ordered.

"Simply put, she has amnesia brought on by the trauma of

the terrorist attack at the Mitchell estate. Witnessing the explosion," she looked pointedly at Simon. "Seeing you shot was to much for her." Maude held up a hand to forestall any questions. "Let me finish. First of all, I'm an MD, PhD in Behavioral Medicine. I've been in constant contact with experts who have advised me on Clara's condition. I didn't immediately contact you because Clara was terrified of someone. A man who seemed to be from a distant past. In effect, not of this time. Her condition was made even more complicated by her paranormal abilities."

Simon and Luke glanced at each other but remained silent.

"None-the-less, her fear was very real. I needed to be certain that when she returned to her life, she would be safe."

Simon realized that Maude Wakefield has done the very best she could for Clara in what had to be incredibly difficult circumstances. "I fully understand your reasoning. What does she recall?"

"Virtually nothing. On the advice of colleagues, I've told Clara who she is. I've given her the newspaper accounts to read but her memory still isn't integrated. She gets flashes of things but for the most part, they're meaningless."

"Why hasn't she contacted me?" Simon asked.

"Confusion, fear. The fact that she still has no memory of you at all. You or anyone else from her past. Now that you're here." Maude shrugged. "Perhaps seeing you will trigger a reaction."

Luke looked out the window and saw a helmeted figure whiz down the drive and out of sight. "We'll soon see. I think she's just arrived."

Simon's stomach knotted with anticipation. Luke waited next to Maude leaving Simon standing alone in front of the fireplace. They heard footsteps come up onto the deck. The sound of water running came from the kitchen.

Clara called, "Maude, wait until you see these mums I found at the roadside stand on Slate Road. They're the last of the season but they're beautiful."

Maude's mouth was dry with apprehension. The best thing to do was to let things happen as they would. "Mums weren't on the list," she joked.

"Yes, they were. I added them," Clara said. She arranged the chrysanthemums in a lead crystal vase and brought them into the room.

Simon's voice was a harsh whisper. "Clara."

Clara lifted her head and looked directly at Simon. The vase fell from her hand and dropped onto the hardwood floor sending a cascade of water and flowers onto the Persian rug. An explosion, a man with a gun, bullets stitching a pattern of death. Her face drained of color and one hand reached toward Simon. She tumbled into his arms and into timelessness.

Maude gasped and Luke reassuringly said, "She's okay. It's the knowing."

"What in hell is the knowing?"

"A family thing. Kind of like ESP."

"Ah, that explains a great deal. I'd like to hear more about it," she said in an aside.

"No problem," Luke promised. "Looks like our trip to Scotland is postponed."

"Scotland?"

"Where we were headed when Simon got your message. Changed our flight to D.C. and here we are."

"I've some information that just may make your Scotland trip even more viable."

Simon laid Clara on the couch and held her hand. "Clara, stay with me. Don't do. Come back," he brokenly begged.

But Clara was lost in vertiginous darkness.

Drifting shapes formed. Broad ribbons of luminous color slashed through the darkness becoming a path across a formless landscape. A man, tall and broad shouldered walked toward her. Almost imperceptibly his features transformed becoming yet another man, then another. Until he became the man she loved, had always loved.

A hand touched Clara's face and she opened her eyes.

"Simon, oh Simon. I thought you were dead."

"Clara, don't ever do this to me again. I'm very much alive and so are you."

Luke drew Maude toward the couch. "So you've been hiding out here," he said gruffly. "You know you're supposed to call if you're going to be late."

Clara turned her head and saw Luke. Tears filled her eyes. "I'm sorry, Luke. So very sorry."

With tears in his eye, Luke leaned down and kissed Clara's cheek. "A joke, cuz. A feeble attempt but none-the-less a joke."

Clara looked into Simon and Luke's faces. "Maude has helped me. Without her, I truly would have lost my mind. I couldn't remember who I was. I've had amnesia."

Simon touched her cheek in a gentle caress as if to reassure himself that she was real. He took her into his arms. "No wonder you didn't call."

the knowing...

Once a philosophy and a psychic discipline which was combined with an elemental energy, all that remains is the internal force. The necessary checks and balances contained in the discipline and the philosophy have been lost in the backwash of a past fraught with violence and pain. The *knowing* is becoming more— a powerful entity without boundaries, one that can kill.

Will the women of *the knowing* control or be controlled? Look for the answer in the stand alone sequal, **Do No Harm**.

Available late 2003.

Sample pages follow

Jake Hepburn glanced through the etched glass window of The Horn and Dorset and saw that the pub was still full. He pulled open one side of the double oak door and walked up to the bar. He leaned on its edge and glanced around the room. Nothing had changed. Built in benches lined the room's perimeter. Small tables, where generations had played chess and backgammon, were spaced along their length. Paintings of the legendary Hepburn thoroughbreds lined the solid cherry paneling. At one end of the room a raucous foursome was shooting darts.

Roy Calhoun, whose family had owned the pub since the mid-eighteen hundreds, hurried from the opposite end of the bar. "Jake, good to have you home. What'll it be?"

"Guinness. So, Rory, how's life treating you? Looks like business is good."

"No complaints. Say, Jake, our regular foursome has a seven o'clock tee time tomorrow morning. Barnes can't make it. He has to fly to London. That leaves me, Dan Banning, Sloan Jameson...and you?"

"Sure. It's been a long time since I've caught up with the old crew. Is Rainey around?"

Rory laughed. "Around, he's an institution. Still earns his drinking money characterizing the tourists. He's down the other end watching the dart match."

"Buy him a pint on me and tell him I'd like to speak with him for a minute."

"Sure thing."

John Rainey came down the bar. Jake thought he looked as he always had. Closely trimmed beard, worn tweed jacket, and grey flannel slacks. Under his arm was an artist's sketch book. "Jacob Hepburn. Been a long time, laddie. What can I do for you?"

"Rainey, my Dad said you might be able to help me."

"If I can, I surely will."

"Have you ever heard of a woman who supposedly committed murder and then disappeared? She may have been English. Would have been a while ago."

Rainey took a long draw of his beer. "The English woman-was

both her name and her nationality, but I never thought to hear mention of her again. Those who might have are long gone."

"Can you tell me what happened?"

"Surely can, but it's a two-pint telling."

Jake caught Rory's eye and called, "Bring us a pitcher and keep them coming."

Jake and Rainey sat down at one of the pine tables. Rory wiped off the wet rings and set two mugs and a pitcher of beer on the table. "Enjoy."

"The English woman?"

Rainey's expression was mystified. "To this day I canna understand what happened."

"Who told you about her?"

"Told me. Nobody told me. I was there at Clouds. I saw it all."

Jake felt a trickle of excitement. "How long ago was this?"

"Summer, late twenties. I was a young buck full of himself and impressed by the fancy people in their fancy clothes."

"This place, Clouds. Where is it?"

"Up the coast on a peninsula sticking out like a little finger into the North Sea. A grand place-huge with terraces over looking the sea and glorious gardens with such flowers as would take your breath away."

"How did you come to be there?"

"Me Uncle Burke was estate manager. He'd hired me for the day to help with the serving."

"What was it that happened?"

Rainey opened his sketch book and fished a piece of charcoal out of his jacket pocket. "Let me tell it my way. Sort of backwards to get to the English woman and the rest."

"It's your telling."

Rainey's hand moved across the white paper. "Was later told that the English woman had an Irish lover she was determined to marry. Her brotherr thought differently. He'd said in front of me, Uncle Burke, and the other servants-Irish servants-that no paddy would ever live at Clouds. Didn't matter what he said. Annabel wouldn't give up Quinn. So the brother claimed Quinn stole a horse from him. Truth of it was the horse was a gift to him from herself. No matter. The brother had Quinn flogged to death."

"Was anything done about the man's death?"

"Couldn't have been. The killer was himself killed."

"How so?"

Rainey looked up from his sketch. "I'll tell you what I saw. You can decide what to believe."

"Fair enough. Go on."

"That day there was big goings on. A party for some high mucky muck in her majesty's government. There they were, the damn Brits, partying on Irish soil. The same land that had been fertilized by the life blood of the Irish Republic."

"Late twenties-things should have been improving."

"To a point but we were still infested with the British lice." Rainey drained his mug and reached for the pitcher. "Let's see, where was I?"

"The party."

"Ah, yes. The party. Was a warm day and sunny. The guests were all outside on the terrace milling around, drinking, eating with nary a care in the world. I'd just come back from fetching more bottles of wine from the cellar.

"All of a sudden there she was standing on the steps looking down. Her dress was white and there was a red stain down the front." Rainey sighed. "Later was told it was Quinn's blood. That he had died in her arms."

"The English woman?"

Rainey held up a hand. "The telling is my way."

"Sorry."

"Like I said, the front of her white dress was covered in blood. The air..it seemed to change like it was charged with energy, heavy, still. Like all the oxygen had gone. I could barely draw a breath.

"Her brother was standing in the middle of the terrace when he saw her. She said nothing just stared at him. You could see his arrogance giving way to fear. His face went white like he'd seen the devil. His eyes grew wild darting here and there like he was looking for a way to escape. He babbled something and started to back away. The veins in his throat stood out in livid ridges and blood started to trickle from his nose.

"His face...God was awful. All contorted. He kept backing away and whimpering low in his throat. I could see blood leaking from his ear. He kept shuffling away from her, his hands outstretched, begging. I knew he was begging her to let him live.

"God the blood. So much blood from his nose, his ears, his mouth. At the end he kind of stiffened and collapsed. His body curled into itself and he went still. The air changed and I could hear the cry of the gulls, people talking, their words running over each other in panic. I realized then that the whole time he'd been dying there'd been silence, not a single sound. I looked for Annabel but she was gone."

Jake took a deep swallow of beer. He felt as though a cold fist had closed over his heart. He had no way to judge whether or not the story was true. But one thing was certain-Rainey believed every word he had said.

Rainey dropped the charcoal on the table and tore the sketch from the pad. He slid it across the table to Jake. "That's just as she looked then-beautiful, dangerously beautiful. She never touched him you know. Never came anywhere near him but she brought him down. As sure as I'm sitting here, she killed him."

Jake studied the sketch. The English woman had indeed been beautiful. "She just disappeared?"

"So it was said. She ordered Clouds boarded up, furniture, everything stored away. Where she went, none could say. She was just gone."

"Who owns Clouds now?"

Rainey drained his mug and shrugged. "Far as I know no one has lived there from then to now. Whose it is, I canna say."

"Rainey, did you ever speak to my sister about this?"

Rainey seemed startled by the question. "Lily. I haven't caught a glimpse of her in years. When I've been in me cups, I may have spoken of the English woman but never to a lady. Wouldn't be seemly."

Jake pushed the sketch toward Rainey. "Please give me the directions to Clouds."

Rainey scrawled a few lines drawing a map in one corner.

"Do you think Annabel English might still be alive?"

Rainey's eyes seemed to glaze over and he stared off into space. "Could be. Annabel...she'd only be a few years older than me. I gave her one of my very first paintings-a miniature of Clouds. Wonder what became of it?"

Jake ran his hand over his face. What he had just heard of the English woman was the stuff legend was made of-frightening with an element of dangerous truth. If Rainey was to be believed, the English woman, this Annabel had never touched her brother. Yet he had died. Was it possible for her mind, the force of her will to have been the weapon? He stared at the sketch of the English woman and carefully began to roll it into a tube.

Rainey slipped a rubber band around the tube to secure it. "I keep them in me pocket for the tourists."

"Thanks for all your help. It's appreciated." Jake finished his beer and went to the bar to pay his tab. "Rory, before you talley it up add another pitcher for Rainey."

"Will do."

Jake tossed a bill on the bar. "See you in the a.m."

"Thanks, Jake. We'll whip their butts."

Jake waved a goodbye and went out into the cool night air. Moonlight sliced through the mist transforming the street into a silver ribbon. He broke into a slow jog and was soon out of the village. His breath came easily and he lengthened his stride for distance. It seemed no time at all before he was running between the granite gate posts of Hepburn Trace. Gravel crunched beneath his feet and from the stables came the soft nicker of the horses.

Jake unlocked the front door and flicked off the overhead light. Moonlight guided him through the foyer and into the library. He tossed Rainey's sketch onto the Regency table next to the door and sprawled in a chair by the fireplace where the low flames still flickered. Thoughts of the English woman, the flogging of her Irish lover which had precipitated the death of her brother brought exhaustion and a touch of nausea. A vile taste of the past.

Though the room was warm, he shuddered as if from cold. His thoughts circled from Annabel English to Lily. Why had Lily been so interested in the English woman? Was it possible that something akin to what had happened at Clouds have bearing on Lily's descent into madness? He stared into the fire until it slowly burned out. He stiffly got to his feet. It was late but he knew sleep would be a long time coming. He wearily climbed up the stairs and as he passed Lily's rooms, he wondered if the demons pursued her even as she slept.

Behind the closed door of Lily's shadowed room, a gentle breeze stirred the sheer curtains of the open window. She lay curled in the center of the four poster bed. A blue, corn flower-patterned quilt was pulled up around her shoulders. Beneath her closed eyelids, fragmented colors resembling shards of shattered stained glass pierced like blazing swords into the void to be swallowed up by the blackness. Her agony came from a manifestation of the power contained in the darkness. Its intensity drew her deeper and deeper into the abyss.

Chaos, a tumbling kaleidoscope of color and jumbled sound. Voices, a warning, eyes imploring, begging, and deep inside the white-hot core of power. A force contained but never controlled, to be kept locked in the silence. Forever trapped in the darkness.